Contracting Colonialism

Title page of *Doctrina Christiana*, the earliest known book printed in the Philippines, published by the Dominicans in 1593. Its text is in Castilian and Tagalog; prayers are rendered in both roman script and *baybayin*, the Tagalog syllabary.

Contracting Colonialism

Translation and Christian Conversion in

Tagalog Society under Early Spanish Rule

VICENTE L. RAFAEL

Duke University Press   Durham and London   1993

First paperback edition Duke University Press, 1992

© 1988 by Cornell University except preface to the paperback edition

© 1993 Duke University Press

All rights reserved

Printed in the United States of America on acid-free paper ∞

Library of Congress Cataloging-in-Publication Data appear on

the last printed page of this book.

For Bayani Severino
and Catalina Leuterio

Contents

Preface to the Paperback Edition

Grammar is politics by other means.—Donna Haraway

This book is about the uneasy relationship between translation and conversion in the Spanish colonization of the Tagalogs of the Philippines from the late sixteenth to the early eighteenth century. The coherence of this work, however, emerges in relation to the contemporary condition of postcoloniality; that is, the history peculiar to the late twentieth century of the simultaneous departures and arrivals, multiple entries, unequal migrations, border crossings, and mobile dwellings that have characterized the implosion of the "third world" into the "first." To the extent that it is written within this historical moment, this book may be regarded as a modest attempt at engaging the implications and enacting the hopes contained in recent calls for a postcolonial historiography. What is at stake in writing about early Tagalog colonial society as a site for understanding the specific articulation of a colonial discourse from a postcolonial location?

In an essay on postcolonial historiography, Dipesh Chakrabarty writes about the need to "provincialize" our understanding of Europe. Such a project would begin by

> document[ing] how—through what historical process, [Enlightenment] "reason," which was not always self-evident to everyone, has been made to look "obvious" far beyond the ground where it originated. If a language, as has been said, is but a dialect backed up by an army, the same could be said of the narratives of "modernity" that, almost universally today, point to a certain "Europe" as the primary habitus of the modern.[1]

1. Dipesh Chakrabarty, "Postcoloniality and the Artifice of History: Who Speaks for 'Indian' Pasts?," *Representations* 37 (Winter 1992): 1–26. All further references appear in the main text.
    Chakrabarty is one of the more prominent members of the Subaltern Studies group composed of scholars based in Indian, British, North American, and Australian aca-

Chakrabarty goes on to suggest that the emergence of "modernity" as such cannot be dissociated from the history of European imperialism. But equally crucial is the collaboration of "third world nationalisms" in the formation and consolidation of Europe as the presumed home of all things modern. As the imagined source and arbiter of modernity, the history of the "Occident" comes to serve as the grammar with which to speak of diverse non-European histories. Ordered by the syntax of colonial discourse, narratives of national histories in the nonWestern world cannot but reposition the "West" as the locus of their address: the guarantor, albeit a negative one, of their coherence. Hence, "Indian," "Chinese," or "Philippine" histories in all their empirical differences are discursively reduced to the terms of Western historiography as "societies" or "states" which are "developing," "democratic," "authoritarian," "socialist," and so forth. And those who write about these societies within the global imaginary of Western academic institutions—whatever their national, gender, or ethnic affiliations—are constrained to employ these categories, however critically, in order to appear reasonable and thus legitimate within and beyond their own particular contexts.

By contrast, the project of provincializing Europe entails a critique not only of the universalizing claims of modernity but also the naturalizing demands of nationality. Situated on the borders of the imperial and the national, postcolonial historiography is thus committed to a double task. On one hand, it seeks to reconstruct the network of power relations—the dialectic of coercion and complicity, violence and idealism—that binds colonizers to colonized, the nation-state to the people, and a "modern Europe" to an always yet-to-be-modernized "nonEurope." On the other hand, it is

---

demic institutions concerned with writing post-foundational and post-Orientalist histories of "India." In doing so, they have sought to employ and rethink European critical theory in ways that disrupt and unsettle essentialist categories which tend to dominate Orientalist, nationalist, Marxist, and "world historical" accounts of India. Located both within and outside of "India" and "Europe," their writings have been extremely enabling for doing postcolonial histories of other areas of the "third world." For a succinct and incisive discussion of the Subaltern Studies group, see Gyan Prakash, "Writing Post-Orientalist Histories in the Third World: Perspectives from Indian Historiography," *Comparative Studies in Society and History* 32, no. 2 (April 1990): 383–408, and the lively polemical exchanges that stemmed from this essay in Rosalin O'Hanlon and David Washbrook, "After Orientalism: Culture, Criticism, and Politics in the Third World," and Gyan Prakash, "Can the 'Subaltern' Ride? A Reply to O'Hanlon and Washbrook," both in *Comparative Studies in Society and History* 34, no. 1 (January 1992): 141–167 and 168–184 respectively. See also Ranajit Guha and Gayatri Chakravorty Spivak, ed., *Selected Subaltern Studies*, New York: Oxford University Press, 1988.

also concerned with tracking that which remains eccentric to and excessive of these binary relations, "resist[ing] and escap[ing] . . . translation across cultural and other semiotic systems, so that the world may once again be imagined as radically heterogeneous." (p. 23)

To provincialize Europe along with its formerly colonized, now nationalized others amounts not only to decentering and redrawing the geography of modernity, but also the excavation of notions of otherness in specific historical contexts. In these pages, this double project is played out through a sustained inquiry into the tight weave among practices of translation, the ideology of conquest, the rhetorical economies of conversion, confession, and reciprocity, and the contest over constructions of "natives," "Castilian," "spirits," and "death" as I draw attention to the shifting modes of authority, submission, and resistance among colonizers and colonized. Thus does this book share in the complex movement of postcolonial writings; its highly local and historically specific focus makes sense only in relation to the translocal and broadly comparative sites of its articulation. Indeed, one of the underlying (and perhaps fatal) conceits of this book is that its selective and partial history of Spanish-Tagalog encounters addresses, however haltingly, other moments and other spaces of the postcolonial terrain. And that such is possible to the extent that this book, in its concern with the intersection between signifying practices and power relations, is as much about a crucial event in Philippine history as it is about problematizing the European provenance of modernity. For in asking about the local workings of translation and conversion I also seek to understand the transformation of notions of the "local" amid the dislocations of the colonial.

Something of the tension between the local and the colonial is suggested by the frontispiece of a seventeenth-century Augustinian account of the Philippine Islands entitled, appropriately enough, *Conquistas de las islas filipinas.*[2] The dual nature of colonization, that is, its spiritual and material aspects, is represented by the neat convergence of the agents of the crown and those of the cross over a map of the archipelago. Assuming a position outside and beyond the islands, the colonizers strike their pose: a hand raising a host to heaven, a finger pointing out the seas and earth below. In doing so, they convey the rays of the Divine Sun that illuminate this scene

---

2. Fray Gaspar de San Agustin, *Conquistas de las islas filipinas, por las armas del señor Don Phelipe Segundo y Prudente; y la Espiritual, por los religiosos del orden de Nuestro Padre San Agustin . . .*, Madrid: Manuel Ruiz de Morga, 1698. Reprinted with an introduction and annotations by Manuel Merino, O.S.A., Madrid: C.S.I.C., 1975.

Frontispiece from *Conquistas de las islas filipinas.*

of conquest. However, the appearance of God's light differs remarkably from that of the archipelago. Where the former is filled with Biblical inscriptions in Latin, the latter come across as blank spaces, ready to take on the traces of the Divine Sign. In rendering visible the scene of conquest, God's light also effaces the specificity of the islands and their inhabitants.

This illustration lends to colonization the sense of having been a discursive event. It is as if *Las islas filipinas* is spoken into existence by Christian texts as these are translated by the figures of colonial authority. Yoked to evangelization and colonial administration, translation produces a field of communicative practices. Yet, the source and agents of translation appear to be outside this field, untouched by and sovereign from the signifying and political practices they have unleashed. In colonialism then, the "local" is that which is produced by a transcendent discourse: after the fact of conquest. Nonetheless, the fact of conquest must itself be located. It requires translation into an allegory of dual conquest (which in turn is translated by the text of the Augustinian account) in order to pass into posterity. Similarly, the Divine Sun, in order to be known, necessitates the mediation of signs and the incarnate form of language. As the effect of translation, the local is also the site for engendering the sense of the colonial and the cosmic. For the Spaniards, then, the colony may have been a provisional instance in the progress of Providential history. But it also inescapably entailed the provincialization of an imperialist order which, in stretching halfway across the globe, was contingent on the transaction of radically distinct languages, bodies, and material objects among colonizers and colonized. Rather than a static place, the local (as if to foreshadow the postcolonial) turns out to have shifting spatial and temporal boundaries; a nexus of asymmetrical exchanges, conflictual interests, and multiple histories joined, in this particular instance, by a vernacular of religious conversion.

It is the contentious construction and uneven appropriations of this vernacular of conversion predicated on the conversion of vernacular practices that I take up throughout this book. Rather than rehearse that history here, I want instead to briefly address the style of reading that I have brought to bear on the vernacular documents—both Castilian and Tagalog as these are positioned within the grammatical grid of God's language—that figure prominently in this study. My own situation as a postcolonial subject—that is, a first-generation Tagalog/Filipino-American male scholar writing within the shifting and contested disciplinary boundaries of the U.S. academy in the late twentieth century—in part has determined the ways in which I have chosen to understand the documents of conquest and conversion among the Spaniards and Tagalogs. At no point do I propose a theory (in the sense of a meta-language) for decoding colonial discourse. Instead, I perform a series of readings—or better still, vernacularizing practices— that enable me to posit the hybridity of colonial texts as these circulate among the colonizers and colonized. I tack between the authorizing vocabulary of contemporary critical theory and the linguistic particularity of Castilian and Tagalog sources, moving between the received and repressed narratives and artifacts of the "Philippine" past as these are mediated by the long and complex legacies of colonial rule. In doing so, I have sought to translate between a local history which remains proximate yet irreducibly foreign to me and the institutional imperatives of an American academic culture to which my work will necessarily bear an odd relation of affiliation *and* marginality.

Through a series of close readings, I attempt to work through the mutual embeddedness of the social and the textual, highlighting the contradictions between what a document says and how it says or fails to say it. I use this procedure of textual explication not to obscure the violence at the origins of colonial rule but to demonstrate how that violence—and resistances to it—reverberate on the most minute and most localized levels of social life. Far from being simply an aesthetic, my use of certain textual protocols is here meant to register the quotidian shocks of a globalizing phenomenon. My reading of vernacular texts by colonized Tagalogs in particular has been concerned not simply with recuperating the meanings of these documents, but also with reconstructing their formal properties, semantic elusiveness, and generative logic. In doing so, I draw attention to what I take to be the working of a subaltern agency brushing against the grain of Spanish expectations as it is signified by and in turn resignifies the language of colonial order.

What I would like to suggest here is that my attempt at a postcolonial reading of specific vernacularizing practices might serve to historicize, in its own circumscribed way, some of the current efforts at theorizing "difference" and "otherness." Whatever salience this book might have as a partial and uneven intervention into both the critique of colonial discourse in the "West" as well as into the nationalist historiography of the Philippines lies in its attempts at indicating the recurrence of what Chakrabarty has termed the "radically heterogenous" inhabiting the specifically local. In a sense, my project is already foreshadowed by, if not complicitous with, Spanish missionary strategies for codifying local languages and "native superstitions" by closely attending to the problematic ties between form and content, writing and speech, and meaning and affect of Tagalog and Spanish signifying practices. Yet, precisely because I write from another historical location, I find myself compelled to draw attention to the Tagalog converts' ambivalent responses to and recodings of missionary texts, characterized as they were by the evasion and reconfiguration of the grammar of a Christian-colonial discourse. Indeed, what recurs in the colonial context I examine are the ways by which translation and conversion produce the vernacular as that which simultaneously institutes *and* subverts colonial rule. Put differently, the imperialist textualization of the local not only reinvented the vernacular as a medium for consolidating the hierarchy between colonizers and colonized. Conceived as the site of interminable translations, the vernacular also effected the localization and reterritorialization of the transcendent claims of evangelization.

By reading the vernacular as the uncanny crossroads formed by and formative of the intersection of the local with the global, we can begin to understand its historical importance as a site of new social formations and shifting power relations. Deployed in the conversion of the Tagalogs, the vernacular (that is, both Castilian *and* Tagalog) served as a locus for the imposition of a colonial order which, like the notion of "reason" in other contexts, promised salvation from a backward, pagan past and assimilation into a civilized, univocal future. But to the extent that it necessarily provincialized that order, the vernacular also opened up a space for the emergence of the "popular" that would, as I argue, furnish a touchstone for different kinds of conversions and translations tangential to the colonial and, by the late nineteenth century, national order of things. Such then are the limited but, I hope, translatable and transportable claims that I seek to elaborate in the pages that follow.

Between the first and current editions of this book, I have continued to accumulate debts of gratitude from a number of people whose contributions have been far greater than I can possibly acknowledge here. In particular, John Pemberton and Mellie Ivy have taught me much in the areas of cultural studies, ethnographic politics, and Chicago blues. Steve Fagin and Lisa Lowe have been astute readers of this as well as other subsequent texts, offering many valuable comments. Others who have generously shown me different ways of understanding the arguments in this book include Oscar Campomanes, James Clifford, Vince Diaz, Nick Dirks, Jean-Paul and Eli Dumont, Johannes Fabian, Bruce Fenner, Nancy Florida, David Hanlon, Val Hartouni, Robert Horwitz, Jorge Klor de Alva, George Lipsitz, Louise

McReynolds, Resil Mojares, Roddy Reid, Michael Salman, Sonny San Juan, Michael Schudson, and Ann Stoler. I also thank Ken Wissoker for his editorial encouragement. Finally, I must acknowledge the affectionate humor and abiding patience of Carol Dahl, Yoshiko Harden, and Craig and Cristi Rasmussen which have sustained me through the years.

VICENTE L. RAFAEL

La Jolla, California

Preface (1988)

The Spanish words *conquista* (conquest), *conversión* (conversion), and *traducción* (translation) are semantically related. The Real Academia's *Diccionario de la lengua española* defines *conquista* not only as the forcible occupation of a territory but also as the act of winning someone's voluntary submission and consequently attaining his or her love and affection. *Conversión* literally means the act of changing a thing into something else; in its more common usage, it denotes the act of bringing someone over to a religion or a practice. Conversion, like conquest, can thus be a process of crossing over into the domain—territorial, emotional, religious, or cultural—of someone else and claiming it as one's own. Such a claim can entail not only the annexation of the other's possessions but, equally significant, the restructuring of his or her desires as well. Affective bonds are thus forged within a hierarchy of interests. For a conqueror consolidates his position over the people he has conquered to the degree that he persuades them to defer to his interests—converts them to the view that they serve their own interests when they serve someone else's. To be converted in this sense is to give in by giving up what one wants in favor of the wants of someone else.

Conversión, however, also has a much more prosaic meaning: the substitution of a word or proposition for another of equal significance. In this sense, it connotes translation. *Traducir* (to translate), in fact, is synonymous with *convertir* (to convert), just as it can also refer to *mudar* (to change) and *trocar* (to exchange). One who translates is said by the Real Academia to "express in one language what has been written or previously expressed in another." Translation as expression is linked as well to the explanation (*explicación*) and in-

xvii

terpretation (*interpretación*) of meaning and intention. It thus denotes events that take place within and between languages. Whereas conquest calls for the conversion of interest, translation may be seen to express and relate interests within and across linguistic boundaries.

The associations among conquest, conversion, and translation reflect as much as they are reflected by their historical configurations. Such is particularly the case with regard to the Spanish colonization of the Tagalaogs, the largest and in some ways the most prominent ethnolinguistic group in the Philippines. It is the purpose of this book to examine the emergence of Tagalog colonial society between the late sixteenth and the early eighteenth centuries from the perspective of conversion and translation. As I hope to show, colonialism in this instance was tied to evangelization. The dissemination of Christianity, however, was mediated by Spanish ideas about signification and the concomitant transfer of meaning from one language to another. The Spanish colonizers introduced into the culture of the Tagalogs more than a new kind of power relation between ruler and ruled, premised on the adherence of both to a transcendental Law; through translation they sought to establish a different practice of encoding interests, thereby reinventing the religious and political means for conceiving the link between self and society in Tagalog culture.

An appreciation of the role of translation in articulating the relationship between Christianity and colonialism provides us with a perspective from which to inquire into the nature of the Tagalogs' response to Spanish rule. How did the Tagalogs respond to the conjunction between translation and conversion? Did they go about the business of translation in a way distinctively their own? If so, how did it differ from or defer to Spanish conceptions of grammar, writing, and voice? Inasmuch as translation involves the exchange and substitution of languages and intentions, it necessarily has a social dimension. Can we understand Tagalog translation then in relation to native idioms of exchange and reciprocity which shape notions of social hierarchy? How did their concepts of reciprocity, in particular *utang na loob* and *hiya* ("debt of gratitude" and "shame"), differ from the ideas of indebtedness and hierarchy expressed in such Catholic practices as prayer and the politico-legal injunctions found in the Laws of the Indies?

The possibility that the Tagalogs' mode of translation differed from that of the Spaniards implies that native conversion could confound the missionaries' expectations. Therefore we need to ask about the conditions that both bridged and sustained the differences between Spanish and Tagalog notions of conversion. I will examine the impact of evangelization on the categories of native social life, especially in regard to masters (*maginoo-principales*) and slaves (*alipin*). I will argue that the consolidation of such changes before the economic and social transformations of the 1760s had much to do with the institution of a new vocabulary for the social comprehension of death. These considerations in turn allow us to think of conversion as coextensive with the translation of native conceptions of hierarchy and the spirit world. As we shall see, Christianity sought to refashion Tagalog society on the basis of a novel connection between death and spirits which changed the meaning of fear itself. Finally, I will suggest how questions of translation and conversion open up a path for reconsidering the emergence of nationalist consciousness at the very limits—both linguistic and historical—of colonial rule.

In examining the historical specificity of Tagalog translation and conversion, I think one has to keep in mind that for the natives, the appearance of the Spaniards seemed to be as sudden as it was arbitrary. During the early period of colonial rule (and arguably till the very end of it), the Spaniards undoubtedly seemed strange and therefore potentially terrifying to the natives. The colonizers came with preconceptions of paganism, conquest, and mission, but the colonized subjects had yet to find ways to fit "Spain" and "Christianity" into a context familiar to them. In dealing with the shock of colonization, Tagalogs sought ways to domesticate its dislocating effects. It was their interest in containing the anxiety aroused by a cluster of alien signs that motivated Tagalogs to appropriate things Spanish. Through translation and conversion, they began to see in Castilian and Christianity the possibility of marking themselves off from the novel forces confronting them. It is precisely this process of demarcation and appropriation that is the subject of this book.

When we focus on such a process, we can consider conversion not only from the Spanish point of view but, equally important, from the perspective of the Tagalogs. Indeed, one of the underlying issues I pursue in this book has to do with what conversion—propelled by the imperatives of vernacularization and ordered toward political submission—can possibly have meant to a colonized people whose language differed from that of the colonizers. Was there a sense in which conversion as translation complicated Spanish claims of control over the Tagalogs on the one hand and the Tagalogs' rapid and seemingly enthusiastic acceptance of Christianity on the other? Put more broadly, what difference did linguistic difference make in this colonial setting?

The question of linguistic difference forms a central motif in my attempt to understand early Tagalog colonial society. It is in fact the question of whether translation consolidated as much as it altered differences between ruler and ruled. In tracing the history of communication between Spaniards and Tagalogs, I seek to map the conditions that made possible both the emergence of a colonial regime and resistance to it before and during the formation of a nationalist consciousness. As we shall see, the Spaniards' efforts to translate Christian doctrine into the native vernacular transformed the vernacular and in time the consciousness of its speakers. Similarly, the Tagalogs' attempts to read and appropriate Christian-colonial discourse in their own language tended to change the meaning of that discourse and hence the very shape and feel of the colonial legacy as a whole.

In writing this book, I've incurred many debts, some of which can never be fully repaid. It is to Benedict Anderson and James T. Siegel that I owe my most important debts, intellectual and otherwise. Their enthusiasm for and criticism of this book's various stages were more valuable than I can easily convey. Indeed, the terms in which I raise many of the issues related to language, culture, and politics in the Philippine context owe their provenance to these scholars' works on Southeast Asia.

In the formative stages of this book, Dominick LaCapra offered many perspicacious observations that forced me to rethink some of the Western theoretical contexts I have sought to bring in touch with a body of non-Western material. David K. Wyatt was generous in his reading of earlier drafts, making many useful suggestions toward the reorganization of some of the arguments presented here. To Reynaldo Ileto and Renato Rosaldo I owe a special *utang na loob:* both have commented at length on the manuscript, aiding me immensely in preparing it for publication. Both in Madrid and in Manila, Doreen Fernandez was a sympathetic interlocutor, unselfishly sharing with me her time and knowledge of Philippine culture and history. William Henry Scott and John Schumacher, S.J., led me to many important sources for the early colonial period. It is because their work differs so much in style and substance from my own that I have constantly found them indispensable in formulating my ideas about the Philippines.

William Flesch accidentally suggested the title for this book and, along with Laura Quinney and Tom Reinert, helped me understand many questions regarding critical theory. John G. Ackerman and Barbara Salazar at Cornell University Press helped me to refashion my writing, patiently pointing out those spots where things seemed more obscure than necessary. I also gratefully acknowledge the comments and suggestions of Jerry Bentley, Jose Cruz, S.J., Anthony Day, Benedict Kerkvliet, Sabine MacCormack, Mary Louise Pratt, Mary Randel, Michael Shapiro, RayVi Sunico, Richard Terdiman, and O. W. Wolters. All errors of fact and interpretation in what follows are, of course, my sole responsibility.

Support for the research and writing of this book was made possible by grants from the Southeast Asia Program of Cornell University, the Social Science Research Council, the Western Societies Program at Cornell, and the American Council of Learned Societies. I am grateful also for the help afforded me by Carolina Afan of the National Library in Manila and the Institute of Philippine Culture at the Ateneo de Manila University. The Center for Asian and Pacific Studies and the Philippine Studies Program at the University of Hawaii at Manoa provided me with travel funds and occasional forums to discuss parts of this work. A generous fellowship from the Andrew W. Mellon Foundation allowed me to spend a year as a Visiting Fellow at the Stanford Humanities Center, where the final revisions for this book were completed. Beyond these institutional supports, I am also happy to acknowledge here the very personal debts I owe to Carol Dahl and to Bayani, Catalina, Jose, Ut, David, and Enrique Rafael. It is because their contributions were decidedly nonacademic that they proved to be in every way crucial.

Chapter 1 and parts of Chapter 2 have previously appeared in *Notebooks in Cultural Analysis,* vol. 3, edited by Norman F. Cantor and Nathalia King (Durham: Duke University Press, 1986). Parts of Chapters 3 and 4 have been published in *Comparative Studies in Society and History* 29 (April 1987). I thank the respective publishers for permission to use these sections.

VICENTE L. RAFAEL

Stanford, California

Contracting Colonialism

From this moment forward, all my writings are fishhooks: perhaps I know how to fish as well as anyone? — If nothing was caught, I am not to blame. There was no fish.

—Friedrich Nietzsche

Translation intends language as a whole. . . . It is midway between poetry and doctrine. Its products are less sharply defined, but it leaves no less of a mark on history.

—Walter Benjamin

Fishing Out the Past

Halfway through his novel *Noli me tangere* (1886; variously translated as "The Lost Eden" and "The Social Cancer") the Filipino nationalist Jose Rizal gives us a hilarious description of one kind of Tagalog response to Spanish clerical authority. It occurs in the midst of a long-winded and bombastic sermon—"a kind that everyone always gives"—delivered by Father Damaso, the former parish priest of the town of San Diego. He begins by addressing the congregation with a biblical quotation in Latin and proceeds first in Spanish, then in the vernacular, Tagalog. If the comedy of this scene is to be appreciated, the tale must be quoted at length. Father Damaso begins the Spanish portion of his sermon thus:

Radiant and resplendent is the altar, and spacious the portals of this church; but between them is the air that will transport the holy and divine message that will spring forth from my lips. Listen then, with the ears of the soul and the heart, so that the words of Our Lord may not fall on stony ground and be eaten by the birds of Hell, but rather that you may sprout and thrive like holy seed in the field of our Venerable and Seraphic Father San Francisco. Ye great sinners, captives of those Moro pirates of the spirit who prowl the seas of eternal life in powerful vessels of the flesh and the world, . . . behold with reverent remorse one who rescues souls from the devil's thrall, an intrepid Gideon, a valiant David, . . . the Constable of Heaven, braver than all the constabulary [*guardia civil*] put together . . . one who, with only a wooden cross for a gun, dauntlessly puts to rout the eternal bandits [*tulisan*] of darkness and all the hordes of Lucifer, and would have annihilated them forever had these spirits been immortal! This marvel of Divine Creation, this unimaginable prodigy, is the blessed San Diego de Alcalá, who . . . is

1

but a soldier in the most powerful army that Our Seraphic Father San Francisco commands from Heaven and to which I have the honor to belong as corporal or sergeant, by the Grace of God.

In listening to this veritable flood of Spanish words, however,

the unlettered natives . . . fished nothing out of this section except [*no pescaron del párrafo otra cosa que*] the words *guardia civil, tulisan, San Diego,* and *San Francisco;* they observed the sour face of the lieutenant, the bellicose gesture of the preacher, and deduced that the latter was upbraiding the former for not pursuing the bandits. San Diego and San Francisco would, however, carry the matter out themselves, and very well indeed, as could be seen in a painting existing in a convent in Manila which showed San Francisco armed only with his cincture fending off the Chinese invasion during the first years of discovery. The devotees were then pleased, they thanked God for His assistance, not doubting that once the bandits had disappeared, San Francisco would destroy as well the *guardias civiles.* They redoubled the attention with which they followed Father Damaso as he continued.[1]

The laughter in this scene, as in similar passages in the novel, arises as we witness the congregation skid from word to word without connecting what they hear to the priest's actual message. Instead, they "fish out" discrete words from the stream of the sermon, arbitrarily attaching them to their imaginings. Curiously enough, the drift away from the content of the sermon only pulls them back with "redoubled attention" to Father Damaso's speech. It appears that the natives are compelled to submit to the priest's authority despite, indeed because of, the fact that his sermon is *almost* incomprehensible.

The humor here is undoubtedly tendentious. Rizal's point was that both the Spanish priests and the native converts had made a travesty of the Catholic faith after more than three centuries of colonial rule. Resentful of clerical authority and influenced by Enlightenment ideals, the native writer identified with a politically expectant bourgeoisie and sought to parody the more blatantly inept manifestations of a priest-ridden society.

But like all of Rizal's writings, this scene is far more instructive

---

1. Jose Rizal, *Noli me tangere* (Quezon City: R. Martinez, 1958), p. 170 (my translation). This is a facsimile of the first edition, published in Berlin in 1886.

than its manifest political intent may lead us to believe. On one level, it can certainly be read as an instance of the failure of authority to legitimize its claim to power in a stultifying colonial regime. But on another level, it suggests a distinctive Tagalog strategy of decontextualizing the means by which colonial authority represents itself. Such a strategy short-circuits the linkages among the priest's message, the language in which it is put, and the intended effect of both on the congregation. The priest's words rouse in the Tagalog listeners other thoughts that have only the most tenuous connections to what he is actually saying—not surprisingly, inasmuch as Father Damaso speaks in Latin and Castilian, languages that remained largely incomprehensible to the great majority of the natives throughout the centuries of Spanish rule. Their response, however, is not simply a matter of boredom, indifference, or rejection. In fact, they anxiously attend to Damaso's voice, hoping to catch some of the words that are thrown their way. It is as if they saw other possibilities in those words, possibilities that served to mitigate the interminable verbal assaults being hurled from the pulpit. To the extent that such random possibilities occur, the native listeners manage to find another place from which to confront colonial authority—one that appears to be tangential to the position of subordination ascribed to them by both Father Damaso and Rizal.

Scenes of this sort may appear to be incidental to the primary political intent of the novel to unravel the oppressive conditions wrought by the Spanish domination of Philippine society.[2] Yet the process of listening-as-fishing is suggestive of the conditions that permit subjugation and submission to exist in the first place. The passage unfolds in such a way that the scene of fishing for meaning has the feel of a typical and commonplace occurrence in colonial society. For this reason, it points to some of the more subtle workings of the most important dimension of Spanish colonization: that of religious conversion.

Historians have readily acknowledged the crucial significance of conversion in the history of lowland Philippine communities. Nonetheless, surprisingly little attention has been paid to the processes and dynamics of this phenomenon in postwar historiography. Such is

2. See Rizal's prologue in *Noli me tangere*, addressed to "Mi Patria," to get a sense of this intent.

particularly the case for the early colonial period, which conventionally spans the late sixteenth to the early eighteenth century, that is, the period of the initial spread and consolidation of Spanish rule before the economic and social changes of the 1760s. The overwhelming majority of sources available from this period in Philippine history were written by the colonizers rather than the colonized. It was in the interest of the colonizers, located at the farthest remove from the metropole, to dominate the recording and interpretation of events. The Spaniards brought in the printing presses, and through the colonial policy of censorship they monopolized and regulated the production and reproduction of devotional books, historical accounts, fiscal and legal records, and the like. Relying wholly on these tendentious documents, the handful of studies dealing with the early colonial period have tended to situate Philippine history in terms either of the "Christianization" of the subject populace or of the "Hispanization" of native cultures. In this regard, the two most influential and oft-cited works are *The Jesuits in the Philippines, 1581–1768,* by the Filipino Jesuit historian Horacio de la Costa, and *The Hispanization of the Philippines: Spanish Aims and Filipino Responses, 1565–1700,* by the American scholar John Leddy Phelan.[3]

Father de la Costa, a Tagalog intellectual whose educational training was very similar to Rizal's, was concerned primarily with producing a comprehensive narrative of the Jesuits' acitivities in the archipelago from their arrival to their temporary expulsion from the islands. The result is a predominantly sympathetic, often anectodal, and richly documented portrayal not only of Jesuit evangelical labors but of Spanish missionary activities as a whole. The fact that evangelization figured in nearly all aspects of Spanish colonization gives De la Costa's work enduring historiographical value.

Engaging as this wide-ranging narrative of Jesuit activities is, it is nonetheless constrained by the author's conscious assumption of the providential structure of history. For De la Costa, the story of the Jesuits in the Philippines was and continues to be part of the larger epic of Christianization to which his own account—as genial in tone as it is scrupulous in its scholarship—is unquestionably committed. What one misses and perhaps should not expect is a certain critical distance from the fundamental goals of evangelization. For underly-

3. Cambridge: Harvard University Press, 1961; Madison: University of Wisconsin Press, 1959.

ing his work is a deep admiration for the Spanish fathers and an abiding gratitude for what he regards as the missionaries' ultimately benevolent legacy to the Philippines.

Phelan, on the other hand, was primarily a Latin American specialist. His interest in the Philippines—a country he never visited and whose languages he did not know—was part of a larger ethnohistorical concern with the process of Hispanizaton. More succinct in its coverage than De la Costa's rambling, leisurely account, Phelan's book contains a series of compact observations not only about evangelization but about Spanish colonial rule in general. A comparativist thread runs through his book as he evaluates the differing impacts of colonial rule on Mexico and on the Philippines. He concludes that the Philippines, unlike Mexico, were subjected to "indirect" rather than "direct" Hispanization. In retrospect, Phelan sees this indirect impact as beneficial to the Philippine natives in that it resulted in Hispanization that was less thoroughgoing "but better digested." Spain, despite its imperialist motives, deserves credit for "having [given] the Filipinos something in return," namely, "law and order" among the diverse ethnolinguistic groups in the country, "cultural unity" courtesy of the Christian faith, and "Western civilization," no small gift to a region that at the time of his writing (1959) was "dominated by revolutionary and anti-Western nationalism." Concomitantly, he commends the natives' "capacity . . . for creative social adjustment" to the colonial regime. He cites as evidence the remarkable paucity of local revolts among the subject peoples of the lowlands. He sees Spanish intentions and native responses as having led to the historical "synthesis" of the two cultures, most pronounced in the emergence of the religious syncretism characteristic of "folk Catholicism."[4]

Though differing in approach and emphasis, De la Costa and Phelan have two things in common. First, both take the structure of Christianity for granted as an unproblematic given of colonial rule. And once taken for granted, it is seen ultimately to have exercised a mitigating effect on Spanish imperialism and a civilizing influence on native culture. What is wanting is a critique of colonialism that would also account for the curious place of Christianity in early colonial society. As we shall see, Christianity set the rules of the colonial enterprise while maintaining a position above those rules. It also

4. Phelan, *Hispanization of the Philippines*, pp. 157, 161, viii.

sought to define the boundaries of native culture while at the same time claiming an attachment to an origin outside of those boundaries. This structural ambiguity of Christianity and its concomitant political implications are attenuated when one speaks of "folk Catholicism" and "religious syncretism" in the context of colonial society. The appeal of and to Christianity on the part of Spaniards and native converts alike had to do precisely with the fact that fragments of it remained irreducibly foreign to both. Such fragments, as in the Rizal passage quoted above, served to signal an "outside" that lent itself to being located, appropriated, and valorized in different ways by the rulers and the ruled.

The second thing that joins Phelan's and De la Costa's works is related to the first. Both mention but quickly skirt the most apparent aspect of evangelization: its vernacular transmission. In the same way that they bypass the ambiguity of Christianity, they avoid the question of the linguistic determination of conversion. Both authors rely exclusively on Spanish-language source materials at the expense of those written in the vernacular. In doing so, they accord to Spanish sources a measure of veracity that they implicitly deny to documents in the vernacular when they set about reconstructing colonial history. The unproblematic treatment of the structure and logic of Christianity coupled with the exclusion of native-language source materials, whether written by Spaniards or by Tagalogs, has established a perspective that sees external influences as exercising the primary and privileged role in shaping developments within native societies. This view passes over questions of how the primacy of Christianity and of the Spanish language is constituted and how their privileged position is thought of and quite possibly subverted in the process of being instituted in native colonial society. What emerges instead is a picture of the inevitably evolutionary progression of Philippine history under Spanish rule. Seen retrospectively, local histories are read in terms of a language and a history alien to them, sublated in what is already known about the global spread of Christianity in one case and in that of the Spanish empire in the other. Anchored to the reductive categories "Christianization" and "Hispanization," these works end up unwittingly rehearsing the Spanish logic behind conversion and conquest.

Such categories, however, are unable to account for the historical basis of "fishing" scenes such as the one in Rizal's *Noli me tangere*.

The penchant for hooking onto discrete words in the friar's sermon results in some kind of native submission. But it is a submission purchased at the expense of marginalizing the meaning and intent behind the discourse of authority. What is depicted here is therefore a social order premised not on consensus between ruler and ruled but on the fragmentation and hermeneutic displacement of the very basis of consensus: language. This mode of linguistic displacement takes on an added import given the imperative of evangelization—the dissemination of God's Word—which in significant ways determined the imposition of colonial rule.

Religious conversion was crucial to the consolidation of Spanish power in the Philippines. But as Reynaldo Ileto has convincingly shown, Catholicism not only exercised a profound impact on the patterning of notions of authority and submission in colonial society; it also furnished the natives with a language for conceptualizing the limits of colonial and class domination. The idiom of religious conversion was crucial, then, for this reason: it shaped the terms of native surrender just as it lent itself to the articulation of popular resistance to a colonizing power.[5] Conceived dialectically, conversion requires one's submission to and incorporation of the language and logic of Christianity as the condition of possibility for defining and subsequently overcoming one's prior state of subordination, whether to a pagan past, a colonial overlord, or the local elite.

Yet scenes such as the one in the church at San Diego allude to the persistence of a different kind of conversion, predicated on a random rather than sustained confrontation between the interests of the rulers and the ruled. As we have seen, the priest's message was not internalized. It was not given a place in the listeners' minds in relation to which all their other past and future thoughts could take shape. Instead, the native listeners moved to appropriate fragments of the

5. See, for example, the seminal book of Reynaldo C. Ileto, *Pasyon and Revolution: Popular Movements in the Philippines, 1840–1910* (Quezon City: Ateneo de Manila University Press, 1979). Indeed, much of the initial impetus for this study came from Ileto's work. See also the fascinating though more conventional book by David R. Sturtevant, *Popular Uprisings in the Philippines, 1840–1940* (Ithaca: Cornell University Press, 1976), of which more will be said below. In this connection, it is also well worth recalling that the genesis of Philippine nationalism is considered to have owed a great deal to the struggles of the mestizo and *indio* secular priests to attain equal status with the Spanish regular priests, culminating in the martyrdom of Fathers Gómez, Burgos, and Zamora in 1872.

priest's discourse and so to deflect the force of his intentions. They were stirred, but in ways that led to neither active agreement with nor outright rejection of the priest and his language. Indeed, this scene is marked by a near-chaotic exchange of signs which makes it impossible to see the Tagalog position as either clearly opposed to or unequivocally collaborative with the colonial order as represented by the priest. Such moments point less to the apolitical or even protopolitical aspect of native response to Spanish rule than to the possibility of an alternative history of submission existing in a residual relation to the Christian, colonialist, nationalist, and humanist conceptions of the past.

To specify the workings of this other historical possibility, let us turn to an exchange that occurred some eighty years after the publication of Rizal's novel. In 1966 the American historian David Sturtevant, with the aid of the Filipino writer F. Sionil Jose, interviewed Pedro Calosa, the leader of the 1931 peasant uprising in Tayug, Pangasinan, a province north of Manila. Calosa's replies (in Ilocano, a Philippine language related to Tagalog, and translated by Jose into English) to Sturtevant's questions (in English, translated into Ilocano also by Jose) are instructive in the view they afford of a way of looking at the past remarkably at variance with that of his Western interlocutor.

Sturtevant wants to set the historical record straight, to verify the circumstances and events of the peasant uprisings in the late nineteenth and early twentieth centuries. Calosa's flat responses tend to skim over the details surrounding the revolt:

> Sturtevant: How did you organize the people? Did you have secret handshakes, code words, blood pacts, and *anting-anting* [amulets]?
> Calosa: Yes, we had all those things, but we need not discuss them. You already know all about them or you wouldn't ask the question.
>
>   · · ·
>
> Sturtevant: Speaking of Tangulan [a peasant organization in the 1920s], what did you think of their leader, Patricio Dionisio?
> Calosa: Don't ask me that. You have talked to Dionisio, you already know the answer.
>
>   · · ·
>
> Sturtevant: On the night of the uprising, what happened?
> Calosa: You know the story. The people gathered outside San Nicolas, thirty to forty of them in the beginning. They took over the Pantran-

co buses and rode into town. That was the night the constables ran
away from our women.

But it is very difficult for me to talk of this. You already know all
about it anyway. I cannot tell you the minor details because I wasn't
there. I was in my house during the attack on Tayug.[6]

Sturtevant's queries seek to infuse a sense of personal depth into the
government reports, newspaper stories, and court depositions that
make up the main sources of his account of the uprising. But Calosa's
narrative moves in a different direction. He seems uninterested in
recounting his own role and responsibility in the uprising, nor does he
seem to care about elaborating on the aims, ideals, successes, and
failures of the peasant society he led. Rather than draw lessons from
the past, he prefers to dwell on moments marked by haunting:

Sturtevant: Was Felipe Salvador's [another peasant leader Calosa had
met as a child] Santa Iglesia [movement] the same as Guardia de
Honor?[7]
Calosa: The Santa Iglesia and the Guardia de Honor were the same. . . .
Salvador tried to destroy the sources of hate. . . . It is true, he was
captured by the constabulary and hanged. But he did not die. His
personality lived on and took different forms. I knew him in Honolu-
lu. In Hawaii he was called Felipe Santiago. When I was in prison he
was a crazy man in the next cell. I talked with him and he told me
many things. He *was* Felipe Salvador. You understand!

. . .

Sturtevant: When did you come home [from Hawaii]? When and why
did you form your society?
Calosa: I was deported from Hawaii after I got out of prison [for
organizing a general strike among plantation workers]. I came home
late in 1927. Conditions were still bad. The personalities of Rizal,
[Andres] Bonifacio, and Felipe Salvador appeared before me. They
told me to form an association to end the suffering of the poor. I
know Rizal's personality well. When I was in chains in Corregidor

6. Appendix B, "An Interview with Pedro Calosa," in Sturtevant, *Popular Uprisings,* pp. 274–275.
7. The Guardia de Honor was a peasant organization that had its beginnings in
1872 as a confraternity (i.e., a lay religious organization) in Manila. By the 1880s it
had begun to attract a massive following among both rural and urban people and was
hostile both to Spanish clerical authorities and, in the 1890s, to the revolutionary
government of Emilio Aguinaldo. In December 1898 the Guardia de Honor led an
uprising in Tarlac, momentarily seizing control of the town from Aguinaldo's forces.

after the uprising—it was in July of 1934—his personality told me "I will come again." He did not say when. He helped me escape.

Sturtevant: Escape?

Calosa: Not that way. My body stayed, but my personality escaped. I set it to haunt three people: Manuel Quezon [the president of the Commonwealth], Aurora Quezon [the president's wife], and the American secretary of war.

Sturtevant: Getting back to your association, what did you call it? How large did it become?   [Pp. 272, 273]

Calosa's recollections of being haunted by and haunting others disorient Sturtevant's efforts to arrive at an empirical confirmation of events in the past through their retelling by one of the major participants. Calosa's mention of escaping from prison raises Sturtevant's expectation of becoming privy to a significant detail that may have been omitted from the official accounts of the events in question. Calosa, as if reading Sturtevant's mind, insists that the escape was of a different kind, involving the haunting of the Quezons and the American secretary of war. Sturtevant, perhaps sensing that he has been shut out of Calosa's version of the past, abruptly changes the drift of the interview, eager to get back to the realm of familiar facts. Yet his efforts are repeatedly met by more tales of haunting:

Sturtevant: Did you get to know any Sakdals [members of yet another peasant organization in the 1930s] in Bilibid [prison]?

Calosa: I was not in Bilibid very long. They transferred me to Corregidor and kept me in chains. That is when I haunted Quezon and the secretary of war.   [P. 275]

Questions about the past initiate in Calosa's mind a movement akin to the fishing expedition of the native devotees who listened to Father Damaso's sermon. The affectless tone of his narrative makes it appear that memory entails a process of floating over a sea of randomly connected details. The elements that become highly charged in his account are precisely those haunted moments when he was fished out, as it were, by personalities who drifted out from the past. Such moments allow him to imagine haunting—or hooking—others in the present.

Peculiar to the narrative of haunting is the assumption that figures of the past—Rizal, Bonifacio, and Salvador in Calosa's case—are not really dead. Or more precisely, that the death of those people does not preclude the ever-present possibility of communicating with them directly. The death of others, therefore, does not lead to the sublation of one's memories of them while they were still alive, that is, their conservation in a realm of historical consciousness that sees the past as distinct from the present. Rather, to be haunted by the personalities of the dead is to be struck by their sudden appearance from out of a tangle of thoughts in one's mind and to hallucinate their unexpected presence. Such meetings with the dead are like those occasional encounters with the words of the Spanish priest: out of a barrage of unreadable signs, the churchgoers are struck by recognizable words that they have heard before; and hanging on to those words, they proceed to spin out discrete narratives that bear no relation to the logic and intent of the priest's discourse. Calosa's stories of haunting circumvent Sturtevant's efforts to plumb his memories of historical events. His memories of the past are not of sustained struggles and confrontations. Thus his narrative does not move toward a conceptual summation and generalization of his encounters with social institutions, political organizations, and conditions of oppression. The past appears metonymically as a series of names, dates, and events interspersed by moments of visiting and being visited by the spirits of historical personages. This process of association instigated by the momentary intrusion of something or someone that has been seen or heard of before is similarly at work in the submission of the native converts to clerical authority in Rizal's novel. Indeed, just as the priest's sermon comes across as "a kind that everyone always gives," the various peasant movements that Sturtevant inquires about—"the Rizalistas, the Divine Crusaders of Christ, the Watawat, are [they] like the old ones?"—Calosa regards as "all the same banana" (p. 276). That is, they are fragments of local histories that since Spanish colonial times have recurred sporadically in the archipelago.[8]

8. For the most perspicacious analysis of these movements, see Ileto's essays "Tagalog Poetry and the Image of the Past during the War against Spain," in *Perceptions of the Past in Southeast Asia*, ed. Anthony Reid and David Marr (Singapore: Heinemann, 1979), pp. 379–400; "Rizal and the Underside of Philippine History," in *Moral Order and the Question of Change: Essays on Southeast Asia*, ed. David K. Wyatt and Alexander Woodside (New Haven: Yale University Southeast Asian Studies, 1982), pp. 274–337; "Orators and the Crowd: Philippine Independence Politics, 1910–1940," in *Reappraising an Empire: New Perspectives on Philippine-American History*, ed. Peter W. Stanley (Cambridge: Harvard University Press, 1984), pp. 85–114; and his book *Pasyon and Revolution*.

Here it is necessary to clarify what I mean by "local history." Listening-as-fishing and remembering-as-haunting both entail the appropriation of what comes before oneself (in both temporal and spatial senses). They are ways, therefore, of localizing what is outside of one. Calosa's recollections of haunting serve to place events in the past in relation to spirits who are free to cross the boundary that separates the living from the dead. Similarly, the people who fish in church resituate bits of what they hear in relation to thoughts that hover over the priest's words. Calosa sees in past events the workings of something—ghosts, spirits of dead heroes—that is neither present nor absent. The native converts read into Father Damaso's sermon references—to bandits, to Chinese invaders—that are not there but that are nonetheless evoked by fragments of his discourse. In each case, what triggers interest is the sudden appearance of things that slide away from their context and so are susceptible to recontextualization. It is this double process of identifying something that seems to have no recognizable place—something alien and foreign, which comes from outside—in conjunction with the attempt to construct a context for it that informs Tagalog, and possibly other, local histories. Thus is it also, as I shall argue, a feature of Tagalog translation and conversion.[9]

The link between processes of localization and translation in Tagalog history can perhaps be clarified by reference to some of the more recent assumptions about early Southeast Asian history. Much of what we know about early Tagalog society shortly before and during the early period of colonization comes from foreign, overwhelmingly Spanish missionary sources. I shall be exploring the substance and perspective of these writings. It should be noted at the outset, however, that the persuasiveness of my inferences regarding the dynamics of pre- and postconquest Tagalog society derives in part from a view of that society as part of a larger Southeast Asian region before the intrusion of the West. The assumption here is that Tagalog society not only participated to a lesser or greater degree in the region's maritime commerce but, even more important, shared in certain cultural practices prevalent throughout Southeast Asia.

---

9. The choice of studying the Tagalogs rather than other linguistic groups in the archipelago was primarily pragmatic. A great deal of the available documentation for the early colonial period pertains to the Tagalogs; and having been born and raised in the overwhelmingly Tagalog city of Manila, I am more familiar with Tagalog than with any other indigenous Philippine language.

O. W. Wolters has called attention to the cultural commonalities in the region which predated the transmission of Hindu-Buddhist, Islamic, and Western influences and persisted well into the colonial and postcolonial periods.[10] These practices should not, however, be seen as core concepts eternally untouched by external pressures or as immutable traits that lend permanence to an obscured though ultimately knowable Southeast Asian identity. As Wolters suggests, they should rather be thought of as the means by which the myriad local cultures set themselves off yet bound themselves to what came from the outside. The historical particularity of these local cultures can thus be articulated with reference to their ways of differing from outside forces while deferring to them.

What were some of these cultural practices that Tagalog society had in common with most Southeast Asian polities which are pertinent to our concerns? Wolters sums them up as follows: "Cognatic kinship, an indifference towards lineage descent, and a preoccupation with the present that came from the need to identify in one's own generation those with abnormal spiritual qualities are, in my opinion, three widely represented cultural features in many parts of early Southeast Asia."[11]

In traditional Southeast Asia, kinship—determining the construction of descent and genealogy—was crucial in the development of authority and hierarchy. Cognatic kinship involving the recognition of bilateral descent resulted in, among other things, the "downgrading of the importance of lineage based on claims to status through descent from a particular male or female." Thus kinship networks in the region have been characteristically arbitrary, tending to extend far beyond the nuclear family. In addition, the marginalization of lineage descent made genealogy shallow. Wolters points out that ancient Cambodian genealogies, for example, "were important not to justify a ruler's legitimacy but to distinguish those among his contemporaries—probably distant kinsfolk identifiable through their forebears—whom he could regard as his supporters." Similarly, in Bali and in the Philippine archipelago, "the achievement of founding a line of descent is emphasized rather than that of perpetuating an old one."[12]

10. O. W. Wolters, *History, Culture, and Region in Southeast Asian Perspective* (Singapore: Institute of Southeast Asian Studies, 1982).
11. Ibid., p. 9.
12. Ibid., pp. 4–5, 20n, 6n.

Genealogy thus acted as a provisional, revisable marker rather than as an unassailable organizing principle of authority. It was a means of differentiating and reckoning kinship alliances and thereby accentuating the ruler's current status vis-à-vis those he ruled, not an immutable basis for the establishment of dynastic states and feudal prerogatives. There was far less interest in maintaining old and distant ties that went back in time than in cultivating new kinship networks that would spread out in space. This practice has had an important effect in structuring leadership in traditional societies where wealth was measured on the basis not of private property but of ever-shifting popular support.

In effect, anyone who displayed an inordinate ability to attract and mobilize a network of loyal followers for ritual, agricultural, commercial, or military purposes could claim to be what Wolters calls a "man of prowess." As such, he gained the status of the community's "Ancestor," displacing or incorporating previous ancestors into his lineage. These leaders were able to attract followers and extend their networks of dependents because others perceived them to have a surplus of spiritual energy, as evidenced by their ability to promote a series of beneficial reciprocal exchanges between the earth and the cosmos—the known and unknown realms of society—as well as among that society's various members. Conversely, the breakdown of such exchanges, leading to chaos and the disruption of social life, was attributed to the ebbing of the ruler's spiritual energy, and the people then attached themselves to a new authority figure. Power and reciprocity were thus seen to originate in discrete and substitutable centers of authority.[13]

That such a pattern should persist is all the more understandable given the absence of a tradition of either a Western- or Chinese-style state apparatus in Southeast Asia. Early Southeast Asian communities never had impersonal bureaucratic machineries to regulate intra- and

---

13. In this connection see the highly influential essay of Benedict Anderson, "The Idea of Power in Javanese Culture," in *Culture and Politics in Indonesia,* ed. Claire Holt, Benedict Anderson, and James T. Siegel (Ithaca: Cornell University Press, 1972), pp. 1–69. For Sumatra, see the important works of James T. Siegel, *Rope of God* (Berkeley: University of California Press, 1968) and *Shadow and Sound: The Historical Thought of a Sumatran People* (Chicago: University of Chicago Press, 1979); and for Java, see Siegel, *Solo in the New Order: Language and Hierarchy in an Indonesian City* (Princeton: Princeton University Press, 1986).

interregional affairs. In their place was a multiplicity of competing centers whose rulers, as Wolters points out, sought less to colonize their rivals' realms than to "bring [them] under his personal influence and accommodate them within a network of loyalties to himself." Traditional Southeast Asian polities and politics, therefore, involved the constant redrawing of kinship ties, the reinvention of genealogies, and the "endless shifting" of geographical boundaries and centers of authority.[14]

In the absence of centralized state bureaucracies, authority and social hierarchy devolved upon the projection and recognition of the *potential* for engaging in dyadic, reciprocal exchanges among those within and outside of the kinship network. And as politics in the region was not centralized, the representation of this potential varied from society to society. Such terms as "power," "spiritual energy," and "men of prowess" all had highly idiomatic inflections. It follows that the projection and recognition of authority were always a local matter, their expression inextricably bound to the signifying convention specific to a community or a group of communities.

As Wolters stresses, the history of early Southeast Asia can thus best be appreciated as a series of local histories, a plurality of subregional developments whose outlines do not necessarily form a whole. Change within these subregions can then be understood in terms of the vernacularization, as it were, of foreign influences in local contexts. This notion of local history as entailing a history of vernacularization resonates with the problem of translation I spoke of in the Preface. It enables us to consider the history of a native society in terms other than those set by the reified and reifying categories of "Christianization" and "Hispanization." The writing of local history can focus instead on the question of *localization;* that is, on the particular ways by which the boundaries that differentiate the inside

---

14. Wolters, *History, Culture, and Region*, pp. 17, 24. See also Karl Hutterer, "Prehistoric Trade and the Evolution of Philippine Societies: A Reconsideration," in *Economic Exchange and Social Interaction in Southeast Asia: Perspectives from Prehistory, History, and Ethnography,* ed. Hutterer (Ann Arbor: Michigan Papers on South and Southeast Asia, 1977), p. 191. Wolters concurs with Hutterer that "there is no evidence whatsoever for the formation [in prehispanic Philippine societies] of bureaucratic structures that would have interjected between the chief and the daily affairs of politics, commerce and religion as is usually found in state societies" (p. 13n).

from the outside of native societies are historically drawn, expanded, contracted, or obscured. There is a sense, then, by which localization can be conceived of as coterminous with the translation of that which appears as heterogenous to a particular society: the process at once linguistic, social, and political which demarcates and reformulates what is "new" and out of place in relation to that which is already known and accepted.

Tagalog history comes across as "local" to the extent that it exists in relation to forces and events outside of it. We have no record of "Tagalog" as a distinct category before the coming of the Spaniards. In the first place, as William Henry Scott has shown, no indigenous accounts antedating the Spanish conquest are available. Chinese accounts dating back to the Sung dynasty refer to traders from parts of the archipelago, but designate them all as "barbarians." The only other prehispanic European reference to Philippine natives—in Tome Pires's early-sixteenth-century *Summa oriental*—mentions natives of the island of Luzon who traded in the ports of Malacca and Canton.[15] It is not until the Spanish conquest that distinct ethnolinguistic groups are designated, most of them in terms that are still in current use. It is as if "Tagalog," along with "Ilocano," "Visayan," and so forth, did not exist as historical and linguistic categories before Spanish writers classified and categorized them as such. Thus one cannot write about Tagalog *local* history without taking into account the presence of alien colonizers who recorded and so lent documentary density to the reality of "Tagalog" as a distinct ethnolinguistic group among numerous others in the archipelago. People who spoke Tagalog certainly existed before the Spaniards took note of them; yet our ability to speak of them as a group qualitatively distinct from other groups is directly dependent on their having been previously objectified—through the translation of their language, the descriptions of their customs and politics, and the recording of their responses to colonial authority—in Spanish accounts. As we invariably approach Philippine local histories through the grid of foreign sources, we must perforce ask about the history and structure of that grid if we are to understand its success or failure as a vehicle to convey its object, in

15. "Philippine archeology, two medieval Chinese accounts and a comparison of Philippine languages are at present the only valid prehispanic source materials available for the study of Philippine history" (William Henry Scott, *Prehispanic Source Materials for the Study of Philippine History*, rev. ed. [Quezon City: New Day, 1984], p. 139). Scott discusses early Chinese accounts and that of Pires on pp. 63–78 and 83–84, respectively.

this case the Tagalogs. Hence the need to situate Tagalog history not only within the context of early Southeast Asian polities and politics but in relation to the discursive grid and geographical spread of Spanish imperialism by the late sixteenth century.

Since the Spaniards drove the last Moors from Granada, religious conversion as the ultimate goal of conquest was never seriously questioned by either conquistadores or missionaries. Both believed that the diverse inhabitants of the world were fated to the universal claims of Catholicism. Yet all attempts to realize this fatedness hinged on the secular intervention of a colonial state apparatus. Colonial hegemony, however, could be legitimized and regulated only as a function of the crown's Christianizing mission. Thus a fundamental tautology shaped the trajectory of Spanish imperialism. Catholicism not only provided Spain's colonial enterprise with its ideological frame; it also embedded the structure of colonial rule within the practice of religious conversion. Indeed, it was precisely the stated priority of conversion that provided the perspective from which to criticize or affirm colonial rule.[16]

The points of connection between conversion and colonization are obvious enough on the institutional level of Spanish rule. The persistence of the *patronato real* (the royal patronage of the church in the Indies), the preponderant influence of the religious orders in shaping colonial policy and practice, and the role of the Spanish priest in soliciting the native's adherence to the laws of king and God exemplify the institutional character of this link.[17] Still, we must ask: What predicated these connections between Catholicism and colonialism? Why was conversion to one necessarily a form of submission to the other? How exactly was this relationship articulated, especially as it obtained in the Philippines?

The Portuguese adventurer Ferdinand Magellan, under the employ

---

16. In this connection, see Fernando de Armas Medina, *Cristianización del Perú, 1532–1600* (Seville: Escuela de Estudios Hispano-Americanos, 1953), pp. 1–50; and Robert Ricard, *The Spiritual Conquest of Mexico*, trans. Lesley Byrd Simpson (Berkeley: University of California Press, 1966), pp. 1–132. For a more recent and intriguing discussion of the writings of Columbus and Bartolomé de Las Casas regarding the "fatedness" of all peoples to Christianity, see Tzvetan Todorov, *The Conquest of America: The Question of the Other*, trans. Richard Howard (New York: Harper Colophon, 1984), esp. pp. 43–50 and 161–163. My own discussion of the link between colonization and conversion is found below in chap. 5.

17. See Horacio de la Costa, S. J., "Episcopal Jurisdiction in the Philippines during the Spanish Regime," in *Studies in Philippine Church History*, ed. Gerald Anderson (Ithaca: Cornell University Press, 1969), pp. 44–64.

of the Spanish crown, brought the Philippine archipelago to the king's attention in 1521. In the decades that followed, a series of ill-fated Spanish expeditions were sent out to Las Islas Filipinas, as the islands were eventually named in 1541, in honor of the heir apparent to the Hapsburg throne, Philip II. The first permanent Spanish settlement was not established until 1565, under the aegis of Miguel López de Legazpe, in Cebu. In 1571 the colonial capital was moved to Manila and by the turn of the sixteenth century most of its surrounding areas had been brought under Spanish jurisdiction, thanks largely to the efforts of missionaries in baptizing souls and persuading natives to build churches, pay tribute, and fight Spanish wars.[18]

Colonized nearly half a century after the conquest of the New World, the Philippines were chronologically and spatially at the tail end of the Spanish empire. Geographical distance and the relative absence of precious metals in the country dissuaded Spaniards from settling there in great numbers. The few who did so lived mainly in Manila, within the fortified walls of the old city, Intramuros. Until the early nineteenth century, Spanish fortunes depended largely on the highly erratic Manila–Acapulco trade, annual subsidies from the Mexican viceroy, and fixed tributes and labor services extracted from the natives (about which more will be said later).

In considerable contrast to conditions in the New World, the relatively small number of Spaniards in the Philippines ruled out large-scale miscegenation and the early emergence of a politically contentious mestizo class, along with the eventual marginalization of the local languages in favor of Castilian. It also precluded the drastic economic and ecological changes that accompanied the establishment of mining industries and enormous landed estates in the Americas. The Philippines thus escaped the demographic disasters stemming from the spread of new diseases, severe working conditions, and wars which befell the Amerindians in the sixteenth century. Finally, the relative paucity of Spanish settlers in the archipelago prevented the colonizers from relying on sheer coercion and required them to depend on evangelization to establish and validate their power. Thus the Spanish priest came to occupy a role of considerable importance

18. The most helpful and concise narratives of the Spanish conquest of the Philippines can be found in two books by Nicholas Cushner, *Spain in the Philippines: From Conquest to Revolution* (Quezon City: Ateneo de Manila University Press, 1971) and *The Isles of the West: Early Spanish Voyages to the Philippines, 1521–1564* (Quezon City: Ateneo de Manila University Press, 1966).

in the spread and consolidation of colonial rule. For the vast majority of the natives throughout most of the three centuries of Spanish rule, the Spanish cleric (natives were not ordained into the priesthood in any significant numbers until the late eighteenth century) came to represent their most tangible link to the Spanish *imperio*.[19] But as I mentioned earlier, if the Catholic church was to take root among the heathen, its message had to be rendered in terms that were familiar and minimally comprehensible to them. The result was the standard missionary practice of preaching the Gospel in the native tongues of the subject peoples.

The methods for converting the *indios* in the Philippines were determined in large part by Spanish experiences among the Indians of the New World. By the time the Spaniards had established themselves in the archipelago, debates about the proper procedures for dealing with pagan practices, native lands and leaders, and local cultures had been more or less resolved among theologians and jurists in Spain. Such was the case as well with questions pertaining to the use of local languages in the propagation of the Christian faith. Hence by 1582 the Manila Ecclesiastical Junta elevated the practice of translation to the level of official policy.[20] In 1603 the king issued a decree requiring every missionary in the Philippines to have the "necessary competency, and know the language of the *indios* whom he should instruct."[21] "Nothing can be done in the ministry," a Franciscan wrote in the seventeenth century, "if the religious do not learn the language of the natives."[22]

19. For a comparison of the Spanish impact on the Philippines and on the New World, see Phelan, *Hispanization of the Philippines,* chap. 8. Also instructive are the essays found in *The Inca and Aztec States, 1400–1800: Anthropology and History,* ed. George A. Collier, Renato I. Rosaldo, and John D. Wirth (New York: Academic Press, 1982), esp. Rosaldo's "Afterword," pp. 459–464. As my chap. 5 will make clear, precolonial Philippine societies differed greatly from those found in Mesoamerica in the sixteenth century. Philippine societies were highly decentralized. Unlike the Aztecs and Incas, the Tagalogs at the point of Spanish contact had no massive urban complexes, elaborate supravillage organizations, far-flung tributary relationships, or institutions of divine kingship.

20. This process is discussed in John Schumacher, S.J., "The Manila Synodal Tradition: A Brief History," *Philippine Studies* 27 (1979): 309; also Costa, *Jesuits in the Philippines,* p. 35.

21. In *The Philippine Islands, 1493–1898,* ed. Emma Blair and James Robertson, 55 vols. (Cleveland: Arthur H. Clark, 1904), 20:250–252.

22. Quoted in John Schumacher, S.J., *Readings in Philippine Church History* (Quezon City: Loyola School of Theology, 1979), p. 74.

The vernacular, however, posed problems in the Philippines which the missionaries in the New World did not have to face. It is well known that many of the diverse Indian populations of Mesoamerica and the Andes had come under the sway of the Aztecs and the Incas, respectively, before the Spanish conquest. As a result, the Aztecs' language, Nahuatl, and the Incas' language, Quechua, had become so widespread by the sixteenth century that they could serve as lingua francas for the administration of the Indian populace in postconquest New Spain and Peru. Indeed, Spanish missionaries often found it more expedient to convert other native groups in these languages than to learn a variety of native tongues, so that Indians who spoke other languages came to learn Nahuatl and Quechua from the Spaniards themselves. After years of Spanish proselytizing in these Indian lingua francas, numerous other Indian languages lost currency and eventually died. At the same time, the generalization of Nahuatl and Quechua reinforced the division between the language and culture of the Spanish rulers and those of their Indian subjects.[23]

Again conditions were far different in the Philippines. Because of the absence there of supravillage organizations, not to speak of empires, the archipelago had no common language that the Spaniards could adopt in its dealings with various native societies. For this reason, Philippine vernaculars withstood the Spanish conquest. Indeed, in the absence of a lingua franca, these local languages proved indispensable in the conversion of the local populace, and the missionaries codified them in grammar books (*artes*) and dictionaries (*vocabularios*) from the late sixteenth century on. Appended to many of these linguistic studies were confession manuals for the benefit of the missionaries who ministered to the spiritual needs of the native converts.

The translation of the Christian doctrine into the native vernaculars did not, however, leave the local languages unchanged. Such highly charged terms as *Dios, Espíritu Santo,* and *Jesucristo,* for which the Spaniards found no adequate equivalents in the local languages, were retained in their untranslated forms to punctuate the

23. See John Howland Rowe, "Inca Policies and Institutions Relating to the Cultural Unification of Empire," and Frances Karttunen, "Nahuatl Literacy," both in *Inca and Aztec States,* ed. Collier et al., pp. 95–96 and 408–410, respectively. I thank Renato Rosaldo and Sabine MacCormack for patiently answering my questions about Nahuatl and Quechua during the Spanish colonial period.

flow of Christian discourse in the vernacular. In the interest of conversion, translation prescribed just as it proscribed the language with which the natives were to receive and return God's Word. We will have occasion to examine this double process at work in our reading of the more influential Tagalog grammars and dictionaries compiled by the missionaries in conjunction with some of the standard clerical guides and devotional manuals published and republished in translation throughout the centuries of colonial rule. These texts in and about the native languages point to the crucial role of linguistic transfers in consolidating Spanish power on the one hand and soliciting native responses on the other. By foregrounding Spanish and Tagalog ideas about language and signification, I suggest how translation defined to an important degree the limits and possibilities of conversion.

Translation, by making conceivable the transfer of meaning and intention between colonizer and colonized, laid the basis for articulating the general outlines of subjugation prescribed by conversion; but it also resulted in the ineluctable separation between the original message of Christianity (which was itself about the proper nature of origins as such) and its rhetorical formulation in the vernacular. For in setting languages in motion, translation tended to cast intentions adrift, now laying, now subverting the ideological grounds of colonial hegemony. The necessity of employing the native vernaculars in spreading the Word of God constrained the universalizing assumptions and totalizing impulses of a colonial-Christian order. It is this contradiction precipitated by translation that we see played out in the history of Tagalog conversion. Premised on a different sense of what it meant to submit to and negotiate with authority, Tagalog conversion alternately supported and deflected the exercise of Spanish power to the extent that that power was formulated in a language other than that of its original agents.

From the perspective of colonizers imbued with a sense of mission, translation and conversion appeared to be necessarily related, setting and sustaining the conditions for a history of conquest and salvation. For just as the workings of conversion betray the basis for Spanish notions of authority and submission, the operations of translation encode Spanish ideas about the representation of power. But by looking at the translation—or, more appropriately, vernacularization—of conversion in Tagalog culture, we can also discern alternative native responses to the dominant and dominating interpretation of the past.

It is precisely this latter possibility that underlines the problematic nature of translation in a colonial context. Considered as both an aesthetic and a politic of communication, translation not only discloses the ideological structure of colonial rule; it also illuminates those residual but recurrent aspects of Tagalog history—the history, for example, of "fishing" and "haunting"—which set it apart from the received notions of cultural syncretism and historical synthesis.

CHAPTER 1

The Politics of Translation

Language and Empire

When we try to understand the relationship between language and colonial politics, it helps to recall that the beginnings of the Spanish empire in the last decade of the fifteenth century coincided with the first attempt to install Castilian as the dominant language of the emergent Spanish state. In 1492, the Spanish humanist Antonio de Nebrija published his *Gramática de la lengua castellana* in Salamanca.[1] Dedicating his work to Queen Isabella, Nebrija claimed that "language is the perfect instrument of empire."[2] Surveying the record of antiquity, Nebrija writes in his *Prólogo* that "one thing I discovered and concluded with certainty is that language was always the companion of empire; therefore it follows that together they begin, grow, and flourish, and ·together they fall" (p. 3).

The history of classical antiquity, particularly that of the Roman Empire, provides Nebrija with the basis for asserting the crucial role of the Castilian vernacular in the establishment of Castilian hegemony over the Iberian Peninsula. In the tradition of Spanish Renaissance humanism, he assumes a natural connection between language and politics: the assertion of one is accompanied by the

1. Edited with an introduction by Ig. González-Llubera (London: Oxford University Press, 1926). All quotations from Nebrija are from this edition.
2. Cited in J. H. Elliot, *Imperial Spain: 1469–1716* (New York: New American Library, 1963), p. 125. See also Henry Kamen. *Spain, 1469–1714: A Society in Conflict* (London: Longman, 1983), pp. 57–58.

spread of the other.[3] The ability of Castilian to play such a role was due to its genealogy. Nebrija and the Spanish philologists who followed in his wake held to the belief that the vernacular was derived from Latin—but Latin of a corrupted sort rather than that of classical authors. In order to legitimize the Castilian vernacular and make it into a suitable language of the state, it was necessary to order it, to harmonize its parts, to standardize its orthography: in short, to endow it with a grammar. It would thus come to possess a value analogous to its "proper" precursor, classical Latin, whose immutability rested on the fact that its form had been fixed by grammatical laws.[4] Castilian, therefore, had not only to represent the power of those who spoke it but also to reflect its structural origin. The spread of the vernacular, aided significantly by the rise of print capitalism in Spain,[5] made it imperative to reformulate the status of Castilian in relation to the language it was usurping. By establishing the vernacular on the foundations—grammatical as well as mythological— of classical Latin, such Spanish philologists as Nebrija could put forth this linguistic transgression as a natural succession of languages and empires. The reconstruction of Castilian on the basis of Latin grammatical theory and the use of the rules of classical rhetoric in its literary productions made it possible to negate the past while simultaneously preserving its authority. Indeed, Nebrija asserts that the proper learning of Castilian led not to a forgetting of Latin but to its more efficient appropriation, "because after one has learned Castilian grammar well—which is not very difficult because it is the language that one already knows—when one goes on to Latin, it will no longer be obscure, so that one can learn it more rapidly" (pp. 7–8).

This view of a dialectical relationship between Latin and Castilian was by no means limited to Spanish intellectuals in the employ of the crown. Sixteenth-century theologians would echo similar notions when they defended their use of the vernacular in writing devotional

3. Benedict Anderson, *Imagined Communities: Reflections on the Origin and Spread of Nationalism* (London: New Left Books, 1983), contains an illuminating discussion on the political implications of the spread of the vernacular in the formation of modern states.

4. See Nebrija, *Gramática*, p. 5; also Juan Alcina Franch and José Manuel Blecua, *Gramática española* (Barcelona: Ariel, 1975), pp. 71–72.

5. Lucien Febvre and Henri-Jean Martin, *The Coming of the Book: The Impact of Printing, 1450–1800*, trans. David Gerard, Geoffrey Nowell-Smith, and David Wootton (London: New Left Books, 1976), provides historical details; see also Anderson, *Imagined Communities*, chaps. 4–6.

literature and in translating sections of the sacred text. The Augustinian priest Luis de León, for instance, defended his use of the vernacular against charges of heresy leveled against him by the Inquisition by referring to classical models.[6] He points to the works of Plato and Cicero as well as to those of the Church Fathers, claiming the legitimacy of his task as a translator on the basis of those models of antiquity who wrote in their own language. He argues that the suitability of the vernacular for expressing the Divine Will has to do with the way its prosody can be made to coincide with the rhetorical norms of classical texts. Furthermore, "words are weighty not because they are in Latin but because they are said with the gravity that is appropriate to them, whether they be in Castilian or French." And what gives language its gravity is ultimately the message it conveys, the very same message that can be deciphered from classical texts. Father de León's comparison of the vernacular languages with the "milk that children drink from their mother's breast" can thus be read as a strategic way of establishing the continuity not only of Castilian with the sacred languages but of the translator with his precursors.[7] Language as nourishing milk enables the faithful son to express the truth of the Father.

It is not difficult to see how the political frame that Nebrija constructs around Castilian joins up with the theological context that Luis de León applies to the translation of doctrinal texts into the vernacular. Both presuppose the nonarbitrariness of classical languages, particularly Latin, by virtue of the authority of their original speakers and writers. It followed that the assumed universality and stability of Latin's grammatical and rhetorical structure would provide the ground from which the vernacular could be deployed for politico-theological ends. From this perspective, the task of translation can be viewed less as a decanonization of Latin than as an act of homage to a language that, like its original speakers, is dead. The turn to the vernacular is thus mythologized as a return—one might even say conversion—to Latin insofar as the language of antiquity con-

6. Father Luis de León (1527–1591) was a noted theologian at Salamanca, a major figure in the Golden Age of Spanish vernacular literature, a teacher of the Spanish mystic Saint John of the Cross, and a defender of the works of Saint Teresa of Ávila. He was imprisoned by the Inquisition between 1572 and 1576. My discussion of León is based on the essay and excerpts from his works in Carlos Noreña, *Studies in Spanish Renaissance Thought* (The Hague: Martinus Nijhoff, 1975), pp. 150–209.
7. Ibid., p. 194.

tinued to exemplify the means to convey the gravity of the same truth. Latin was invested with the sense of providing the structural model for the reordering and translation of all other vernaculars in the world. In this sense, the humanist appropriation of Latin paved the way for the reinvention of the vernacular. One's own native tongue—in this case Castilian—was to be spoken and written in terms of another language. To speak Castilian now was to acknowledge and thus to defer to the grammatical and rhetorical context of Latin. That Castilian could and did become the "language of empire" was due to its translatability into other languages; and this notion of translatability in turn hinged on the possibility of subordinating the speaker's first language to the structural norms of a second.[8]

Dominating the Vernacular

The Spanish missionaries who ventured out to claim native souls in the Philippines were very much the recipients of the ideas about language outlined above. Confronted by the task of "dominating" the languages of the natives,[9] they wrote and read grammar books and dictionaries that would provide them with the means of communicating the authority of God and king. These works dealt with most of the major language groups in the archipelago. But the most widely studied was Tagalog, the language spoken in the most thickly populated and fertile regions of southwestern Luzon, including the areas adjacent to the colonial capital of Manila.

Where Tagalog *artes* are concerned, the most highly esteemed name was that of the Dominican priest Francisco Blancas de San José. With the aid of the Tagalog printer Tomas Pinpin, Blancas published his massive *Arte y reglas de la lengua tagala* in 1610. It went through two more editions, in 1752 and 1832, and was consistently held up by the missionary writers as well as by Filipino intellectuals of the succeeding centuries as the most comprehensive codification of the

8. For an indication of the prevalence and application of Nebrija's notion of translation among Spanish missionaries in the New World, see Sabine MacCormack, "'The Heart Has Its Reasons': Predicaments of Missionary Christianity in Early Colonial Peru," *Hispanic American Historical Review* 65 (1985): 446–448, and Ricard, *Spiritual Conquest of Mexico*, pp. 39–60.

9. Spaniards then, as now, always referred to learning a foreign language as a matter of "dominating" it.

Tagalog language.[10] As an exemplary *arte*, Blancas's work reveals some of the more dominant tendencies that were to be reflected and refracted in the books of other missionary writers on language.

One is immediately struck by the book's use of Latin and Castilian as the principal points of reference in the reconstruction of Tagalog grammar. The linguistic machinery of Tagalog is divided and classified into *nombres, verbos, adjetivos, voces (pasiva/activa)*, and so on. And its grammatical permutations and transformations were labeled as *acusativos, ablativos, imperativos, pretéritos, presentes, futuros*, and so on. Thus the Spanish missionary names and constitutes Tagalog as a linguistic system whose coherence comes through the grammatical grid of Latin. Perhaps this was inevitable, inasmuch as Blancas's *arte*, like the others that followed it, was written specifically for the benefit of Spanish missionaries.

Curiously, Blancas uses no Tagalog terms to designate Tagalog grammar. The impression one gets from this and other *artes* is that grammar did not exist for the Tagalogs before the missionaries began to write about their language. In order to transform Tagalog into an effective instrument for the translation of Christian doctrine and the conversion of the Tagalog natives, the missionary writer, it seems, had first to determine its parts. To do so he turned to external apparatuses: Latin grammar and Castilian discourse. Latin and Castilian act on Tagalog, transforming it into a useful tool for translation and conversion. Just as one learned Castilian by referring to Latin, one learned Tagalog only if it had been codified in terms other than its own. What might seem like a paradoxical procedure derives from what we have seen with regard to sixteenth-century Spanish notions of translation, whereby vernaculars were decoded in terms of a master language and placed in a hierarchical relationship to one another.

For the Spanish missionaries, translation thus presupposed the existence of a hierarchy of languages. This supposition, in turn, hinged on construing the fact of linguistic diversity as a sign to be read in terms of a source and a receiver. The identity of both was believed ultimately to be God the Father. All languages in the world were seen to exist in a relationship of dependency on God's Word, Christ. It was

---

10. The three editions are not wholly identical in content, particularly where the prefatory remarks and dedications are concerned. In my discussion of the text, I quote from both the 1610 edition (Bataan: por Tomas Pinpin) and the 1832 edition (Manila: D. Jose Maria Dayot por Tomas Olivas).

Christ who, in instituting the church in the world, established for it a set of signs that have for their ultimate referent the Divine Sign. And it is the privileged Sign-Son who in turn brings with it the intention of the Father. The circulation of signs in the world was therefore believed to be derived from and destined toward this divine commerce between Father and Son. The translation of languages was carried out not to erase linguistic difference but to acknowledge its existence within the framework of divine commerce. The translatability of a language was precisely an indication of its participation in the transfer and spread of God's Word. Hence we read in the opening pages of Blancas's *arte* a "prayer with which to ask our Lord God for help in order to obtain the language necessary for the dignified preaching of his doctrine."

Until the first half of the twentieth century, Latin continued to be the privileged and universal language of the Catholic church. Reacting against the vernacularizing tendencies of the Protestant Reformation, the Council of Trent explicitly authorized Latin as the only legitimate medium for the Bible. In Spain, while devotional literature and biblical studies were carried out in the vernacular, the Bible remained in Latin until the end of the eighteenth century.[11] Despite the spread of Castilian in Spain, Latin was thought to stand in such close relation to God's own language that it still functioned as the special medium for framing God's laws and for conducting the liturgy of the church. The special status accorded to Latin was inextricably bound to the nature of the message it bore within itself. That Tagalog should be organized around the matrix of Latin is a function of the Spanish belief in the proximity of Latin to the spirit of God's Word, a proximity that lent Latin its authority to preside over the vernacular languages.

But as I pointed out earlier, the reconstruction of Tagalog in terms of Latin was done in the Castilian language. Here Castilian stands as the mediating term—one that is genetically and historically related to Latin—in the linguistic transaction between Latin and Tagalog. In linking the two, Castilian served as the narrative screen in the labor of translation. Within the context of colonization, whereby Latin guaranteed the transfer of God's Word, Castilian played the key role of a privileged passage from Latin to Tagalog. Thus Castilian tied transla-

11. See J. M. Sola-Sole, "The Bible in Spain," in *New Catholic Encyclopedia* (New York: McGraw-Hill, 1967), 2:483–484.

tion to a double movement: on the one hand, that of articulating the linguistic machinery of Tagalog with reference to Latin grammar; on the other hand, that of converting (for this is the other meaning of *traducir* in Spanish: *convertir*) Tagalog signifiers, tying them to Castilian signifieds. The writers of *artes* and *vocabularios* were then charged with the task of simultaneously retaining the syntax and sound of Tagalog while creating a space behind the words within which to lodge referents and meanings other than those that had previously existed.

But as I noted in the Introduction, certain key terms retained their Latin or Castilian forms—*Dios, Virgen, Espíritu Santo, Cruz, Doctrina Cristiana,* and the like. In order to maintain the "purity" of the concepts that these words conveyed, the missionaries left them untranslated, convinced that they had no exact equivalents in Tagalog.[12] That this notion of untranslatability should stand guard over the movement of translation is once again indicative of the belief in the intrinsic supriority of some languages—in this case Latin and Castilian—over others in the communication of God's Word. The untranslatability of a word meant that it was adequate to the expression of a certain concept. To use the signifier *Dios* rather than the Tagalog *bathala* presupposed the perfect fit between the Spanish word and its Christian referent in a way that would be unlikely to occur were the Tagalog word used instead. The coupling of translation with the notion of untranslatability was intended to position Tagalog as a derivative of Latin and Castilian and therefore an instance in the divine production of signs. Just as conversion and colonization were meant to reclaim the "fallen souls" of the natives and

12. This practice grew partly out of the recommendations of the Council of Trent and partly from the practices of second-generation Spanish missionaries in Mexico and Peru in the late sixteenth century. The impulse behind this practice, as behind many other facets of the Counterreformation, was the wish to standardize the discourse of Catholicism in the face of Protestant threats and the persistence of local practices, especially in the New World (but within European towns and villages as well). Ecclesiastical officials and missionaries were concerned about the danger of conflating "pagan" religious beliefs and practices with Catholic ones. In the Andes, for example, the earlier practice of substituting Quechua words for Christian terminology was severely restricted, traditional culture violently repressed, and even the use of the quipu prohibited and branded as superstitious. See MacCormack, "'The Heart Has Its Reasons,'" pp. 450–458, and "From the Sun of the Incas to the Virgin of Copacabana," *Representations* 8 (Fall 1984): 50. For a discussion of the effects of the reforms of the Council of Trent in Spain, see Kamen, *Spain, 1469–1714,* pp. 181–190.

subject them to the authority of God and the administration of the king, translation was believed to be instrumental in construing the local language as yet another sign to be brought back—"reduced," as Spaniards were wont to say—to its proper Source and Destination: God the Father.

The investment in the figure of the Father as the authorizer of translation and conversion and in that of the Spanish father as the administrator of these tasks as God's chosen representative on earth can be gleaned from the *prólogos* and dedications of missionary works on language. In the prayer that begins Father Blancas's *arte* we read a remarkable condensation of these ideas:

All-knowing God whose wisdom shines forth in all your works and in the multitude of languages that are all so harmonious in their variety and in their marvelous difference of pronunciation proper to each one; Lord God, jealous lover of souls, to rid them of the errors of idolatry and bring them to the knowledge of their true creator and father, fill the hearts of your ignorant and repentant men with your celestial wisdom and give them the gift of tongues with which they may speak about everything they do not know; because with such a gift, they may communicate your celestial doctrine to all and with it your love and grace as well as your glory; I implore you, my Lord, with all the humility of which I am capable, to help this poor, ignorant minister of yours and give him what is needed to help these other poor souls so that they may know and love you. You have so resolved that through the ear may enter the good doctrine that will save us all. And how will it enter their ears if there is no master who tells and teaches it to them? And how will it be said and taught by him who does not know the language to declare it in? I do not ask you, my God, for the gift of tongues that you have given to the Apostles and other saints, as I do not deserve so great a gift. It is true that if you were to look at my merits, you would give me none of the things I ask for. For I merit nothing. But Lord, look at the chosen and predestined that you have in this land, and for the love you bear them, I ask you this: since it is the means by which you wish to communicate with them, and for the honor and the reverence that is owed you, give me the means by which I can carry it out competently and honorably. Look at the poverty of your listeners' abilities and weakness of their hearts; and enrich him who speaks to them with the spirit and efficacy that is granted to those who are alive and awake with the clear and harmonious and well-ordered words that they declare to those who are ignorant of them. Give me, Lord, energy and enthusiasm so that without impatience I may learn the language of which the souls of those around me are in need . . . that with your favor, I may be able to work in this language with much care . . . without acquiring distaste for its tedium . . . for it has been so ordained that the most important thing is the salvation of our souls for the sake of your honor. What does it cost you, Lord, wealthy in all things, to give me this? What difficulty would it be to you, Omnipotent God? . . . I ask of you a fiery language to embrace my breast, that your listeners may be inflamed by your love: and so that they and I may love you: and in loving, deserve you in this life and in the other where we will reach and see you. Amen. [*Arte,* 1610, pp. 5–6]

In this passage translation is closely associated with two other phenomena: the economy of gift giving and the ritual recognition of indebtedness. Father Blancas addresses his appeal to the "true creator and father" whose wisdom is read into the diversity of the world's languages. Amid a Babel of tongues a single authority is acknowledged, one who listens and has the power to dispense the gift of tongues to the priest as He once did to His apostles. A key feature of this appeal is the rhetoric of humility. Father Blancas repeatedly refers to himself as poor, ignorant, and undeserving of the gift he is seeking. It is precisely by denying his own merit that Blancas is able to ascribe to himself a place in the circuit of exchange between God and man, as the recipient of a gift. He proclaims that he deserves nothing because he is nothing. As one who lacks, then, the writer can ask for a gift—in this case, the gift of language with which to speak the truth of the Father.

The transaction (*diligencia*) between the writer and God involves the transfer of a gift that takes the specific form of speech. Speech filled with the "celestial doctrine" of God is received by the priest and retransmitted orally. The ear is conceived as the privileged zone of exchange between God and His people, His message mediated by the mouth of the priest. The humble minister who hears God's words now assumes the position of a master teacher as he negotiates these words into his listeners' ears. Speaking in a tongue that transparently conveys God's doctrines and love, he makes the celestial gift heard. And it is in hearing that human beings come to recognize themselves as creatures in debt to their creator. Indeed, the act of listening to God's words as spoken by the priest is thought to constitute an act of returning to God what one has received from Him in the form of honor and love. In this sense, to listen to the priest voicing God's gift is to realize oneself as subjected to, as well as a subject in, a network of obligations. The receipt and payment of this gift of speech are then mediated by the figure of the Spanish father in prayerful commerce with the divine Father.

Hence for the missionary, translation demands the conversion of language into a gift that comes from God. He reads into the vernacular the sign of celestial beneficence. The vernacular is thus ascribed a value not in relation to its community of native speakers but insofar as it is made to bear the marks of God's grace. Thus when a missionary speaks Tagalog, he is regarded much less as one who has an innate ability to learn a foreign language than as one who has been endowed with a gift from above. Translation is thus conjoined with indebtedness. One's ability to communicate in another language is due to one's recognition of intentions apart from one's own. In Father Blancas's case, those intentions have an indisputable origin. In setting translation within the context of indebtedness, he defers to that origin. In return for his humble gesture, he receives the gift of language. This gift demands a return: he is compelled to disseminate it among those who are otherwise incapable of acquiring it, that is, among native speakers ignorant of the divine Word already inscribed in their "own" language. It is the act of oral dissemination that simultaneously signifies the priest's repayment of his debt to God and his listeners' assumptions of their own debts and obligations to the Spanish father and the divine Father. Within the context of conversion, speaking and listening to God's words are distinct but continuous acts that constitute the believers' participation in the divine commerce. They are offerings that the faithful give up in response to the gift of language they receive.

To the extent that translation is a matter of seeing the vernacular as a gift from God, the task of translation takes on a ritual aspect. We get a sense of this notion in Blancas's plea for a "fiery language" so that, like the Apostles on Pentecost, he may preach the Gospel in an unknown tongue. The Pentecostal flame bestowed by the Holy Spirit provides the writer with the model for a kind of "pure language," one that acts directly on the bodies of priest and converts. This idealized language that Blancas sees burning within the diverse sounds of other languages is the image of God's Word signaling the promise of salvation. Visualized as an eternal flame, this Word lies at the other side of

all other words in all other languages. It is that from which all translations spring and to which they ought properly to return. To preach
the Word in the vernacular is to realize this vision, and thereby to
memorialize Christ's promise to his apostles.

Blancas writes later in his *Prólogo,* addressing this time his missionary readers: ". . . our Redeemer and Master Jesus Christ made the
promise that St. Mark refers to in his last chapter, giving his word
that those who believe in him and receive his doctrine will speak in
different languages . . . thus is such a gift promised and given not to
everyone but only to those who are judged to be worthy by the Holy
Spirit to communicate [His message] for the good of the church"
(p. 7).

The preaching of the Gospel in a foreign tongue is construed as a
way of participating in the ritual of recalling the promise of salvation.
Translation commemorates the perfect Word of the Father. Just as
Christ died and rose again so that God's children might realize their
indebtedness to Him, the missionary-translator resurrects, as it were,
the vernacular in order to spread the meaning of the Sacred Sign. He
situates native speech within a different context as part of a set of
codes ordered hierarchically in relation to the Father's Word. By
asking for a "fiery language" that "your listeners may be inflamed by
your love," Father Blancas seeks to render Tagalog wholly subordinate to the language and intentions of an Absolute Other. Rendered
transparent to the message of God and the missionary, the vernacular
can then be appropriated for purposes separate from those of its
native speakers.

The possibility of resituating the vernacular within a hierarchy of
languages hinges on establishing a continuity between translation and
the ritual commemoration of the central tenet of Christianity: the
death and resurrection of Christ. Such is conceivable if one thinks of
rituals, first of all, as forms of linguistic events. An essential feature of
a ritual is that, like language, it is reiterable. But unlike other forms of
speech, rituals are believed by their practitioners not only to reflect an
event that has already occurred but to cause that event to happen
again. In the Catholic mass, for example, the death and resurrection
of Christ is not merely recounted but reenacted as well. The mode of
this repetition, however, is symbolic. Liturgy may be said to translate
a prior occurrence into its repeatable form, that is, into a set of codes
that may be adopted by a potentially indeterminate number of speak-

ers and actors. In this case, ritual brings forth not the reality of salvation (for if everyone were already saved, the need for ritual and its repetition would vanish) but the *promise* of salvation. Ritual speaks therefore of something that is yet to come. It thus points to an absence in relation to which the repetition of discourse takes on meaning. Without this absence, there would be no ritual, and without the imperative to repeat the promise of salvation, translation would cease to have a value akin to that of ritual.

For Blancas, then, the value of translation lies in its capacity to mime the ritual process of marking out the place and time in which all sense of indebtedness and all forms of speech originate and to which they finally return. Rituals are meant to retrace symbolically the path of this return and thereby repeat the promise of salvation: the hope that the Son's followers will be reunited with their Father in heaven. Similarly, translation is regarded as a way of making known the origin and destination of all languages with reference to the sacred Sign. In recalling the gift of tongues bestowed by Christ on his apostles, the translator reiterates his task of invoking the wish to join together the diverse vernaculars of the world in the service of the Word. This task, in turn, necessitates the continued rearticulation of prayers and sermons, grammar books and translations. In this way, translation participates in the paradoxical movement of the Christian Sign. Like ritual, it is meant to signify a sacred absence, that is, a realm that, because it is above and beyond all forms of representation, stands as the ultimate limit and sanction of everything that can be said.

For translation to lead to conversion, it must therefore be based on the promise of salvation, here read as the total and totalizing realization of the Source and Destination of all signs. But as salvation is a promise yet to be fulfilled, it must be ritualized, repeatedly voiced and submitted again and again to the figures of speech. Hence, just as the significance of Christ's death and resurrection can be communicated only if it is ritually repeated and thus its reality deferred, translation leads to conversion at the same time that it promotes the promise of a fully transparent language ruling over linguistic diversity. And the power of that promise qua promise is based precisely on its ability to point to another place and another time that frames as it regulates the multiplication of translations and the repetitions of rituals inherent in conversion.

Translation is designated as a passage to conversion; conversion, in turn, underwrites the indefinite running on of translations. It is perhaps for this reason that *artes* and *vocabularios* continued to be written and republished in the Philippines until the last decades of Spanish rule. In converting the Tagalog language to the terms of Latin grammar, on the one hand, and Spanish-Catholic concepts into Tagalog words, on the other, the missionaries ensured the position of Castilian as an indispensable mediator of linguistic transfers analogous to the Spanish priest as the exalted broker in the transactions between God and his converts. The conjunction of translation and ritual situated the Spanish priest and the Castilian language as the privileged conduits in the reiteration of the promise of salvation. That is, their positions of authority derived from their ability repeatedly to demarcate the boundary in relation to which language and religion could be constituted.

The repetition of rituals and translations is a key to understanding their efficaciousness. That they can be reiterated indefinitely gives rise to the prospect of establishing a colonial-Christian order on a global scale coterminous with the hierarchical rearrangement of languages. However, the repetitiousness inherent in translation could also lead to other possibilities, outside of the socioreligious and linguistic contexts assumed by the missionaries. In Blancas's *arte*, these possibilities are reflected in a kind of boredom that at times intrudes into the task of translation. In his *Prólogo*, for example, he appeals to God to give him "energy and enthusiasm so that without impatience [*sin enfado*] I may learn the language of which the souls around me are in need . . . that . . . I may be able to work in this language with much care . . . without acquiring distaste for its tedium."

The tedium of the labor involved in learning the local language has to do with the need to detail its separate parts. Blancas likens the workings of Tagalog to a machine for generating words needed to convey God's message. This image of language as machine stands in stark contrast to the previous notion of language as gift of the Holy Spirit. As a gift from above, language lent itself to the exchange of love and obligations—an exchange that the practice of translation reenacted. But translation could proceed only if one had taken into account the mechanical operation of language. To this end its parts had to be enumerated and their relationship analyzed. Taken separately, the parts of the vernacular do not add up to a whole that calls to mind a referent outside of and governing its production. Instead, each part is seen merely to refer to another: noun to verb, subject to predicate, the passive to the active, and so forth. The identity of each component is thus determined simply by the way it contrasts with other elements in the language rather than by any single speaker. In other words, the mechanical constitution of language raises the possibility of another kind of repetition whereby what is reiterated is not the promise of a message but only the persistence of a differential system whose elements exist independent of any source, receiver, or preconceived content. Thus translation reveals the impersonal workings of language: the sense that language comes before the formation of a community of hearers and speakers, not to speak of priests and converts. It can therefore exist apart from religion. Words can refer only to other words, grammar can operate outside of the rules of rhetoric and meaning, and language can thus deviate rather than flow from social order. The mechanical operation of language, once sensed, tended to attenuate the link in the missionary's mind between ritual and translation. Tedium then arose in response to the prospect of translation occurring outside of the discourse of salvation rather than in coordination with it. In such a situation, the translator may end up simply talking to himself, with neither God nor other Christians to connect with.

In Blancas's text, translation manifests the mechanical side of language most perniciously perhaps, in its examples. To illustrate the grammar and syntax of Tagalog, Blancas is compelled to juxtapose prosaic with sacred words: "*ang aquing bahay:* my house: *ang bahay co:* the same thing: and if one were to say it in reverse, it would sound bad: *ating Panginoon:* Our Lord: *Panginoon natin:* the same thing" (*Arte,* 1832, p. 31; words rendered in English appear as Castilian in the original). Syntactical considerations result in the somewhat unholy alliance of Referent with text in this example. The writing of an *arte* originally motivated by a desire to render glory to God effects instead His transfiguration into a signifier in a chain of other signifiers, such as *bahay* and *casa.* In another example—"when our Lord Jesus Christ was preaching he was accustomed to &c: *cun nangangaral ang ating Panginoon Jesu-Cristo &c*" (p. 60)—"Jesu-Cristo" is wheeled in to illustrate the preterite form rather than to invoke the teachings of the Father. Indeed, the "untranslatable" name of Christ is rather unceremoniously cut off by the typographical device "&c."

Here tedium arises from the sense of being caught up in the conversion of the metaphor of language as gift into the interminable metonymy of semiotic substitution. Where grammar and syntax were concerned, the Christian doctrine tended to be pulled into the labyrinth of the doctrine of verbs and their tenses. Such a contradictory movement in the writing of an *arte* is due not only to the irreducible difference of the native vernacular but to the internal divisiveness of the very notion of an arte as well.

Arte is derived from the Latin *ars,* "skill in joining something, combining it, working it, etc." It also pertains to "artistic and scientific action" and to "skill applied to morals so far as it is made known by external action." Eventually it also came to "designate grammatical analysis . . . as a title of books in which such theories are discussed."[13] Books combining grammar and morals—this is the most immediate sense in which the *artes* of the Spanish missionaries could be understood. Yet the word *arte* also referred to a lie (*engaño*) or a fraud (*fraude*), particularly in the Middle Ages and in Spanish vernacular literature of the sixteenth century.[14] And the 1611 *Tesoro* of Covarrubias tells us that one who writes an *arte* is a kind of "mechanic who proceeds by the rules and measures of his *arte* and gives reasons for them."[15] One who writes an *arte* can therefore also be thought of as one who works a machine that spins out an elaborate series of artifices.

The very project of writing an *arte* brings up the contradiction between language as gift and language as machine. In so doing, it also problematizes the task of translation in that it raises the question: Who controls translation? Is it the missionary acting as an agent of God or is it language itself, dictating to the translator what can and cannot be said? If language is a gift, it must come from a prior source—in Father Blancas's case, a divine one. It follows, then, that composing an *arte* could be thought of as a ritual homage to this origin. The missionary's grammar book and the translations that result from it are thereby sanctioned by a transcendent source. But the other possibility also exists. Language can be a self-propelling ma-

13. Charlton Lewis and Charles Short, *A Latin Dictionary* (Oxford: Clarendon, 1969), p. 166.

14. Joan Corominas, *Diccionario crítico etimológico de la lengua castellana* (Madrid: Gredos, 1976), 1:290.

15. Sebastián de Covarrubias, *Tesoro de la lengua castellana o español,* ed. Martín de Riquer (Barcelona: S. A. Horta, 1943), p. 153.

chine and thus inhuman in neither a divine nor a demonic sense. Translation then becomes a matter of submitting to the indefinite play of its parts. Instead of reducing the parts of the vernacular into a whole capable of acknowledging its divine Author, the translator is instead reduced to the tedious enumeration and citation of examples of usage. Indeed, at certain points Blancas breaks off the enumeration of Tagalog's parts, remarking on the impossibility of taking a total inventory of its rules of transformation and pronunciation: ". . . but in the end, the rules of language cannot be treated mathematically [*no pueden ser de Matemáticos*] and one does what one can in such varied matters; and one speaks what one can after many years of practice; the Lord God will supply what's lacking" (p. 281).

Blancas makes *Dios* function alternately as an example and as an exemplar: as an arbitrary element in the work of codifying a language and as the One who completes the work and underwrites the author's mastery of grammar. In the interest of resolving this contradiction, the missionary accedes to the notion of language as gift, which is infused with the spirit of God. By metaphorizing language as a sacred blessing he can realign translation with ritual. In doing so, he can overcome, at least provisionally, the mechanical repetitiousness inherent in enumerating and exemplifying the various parts of the vernacular. That is, he is able to "reduce" its complexity at the same time that he privileges a certain notion of translation that is geared to the economy of divine gift giving. Seen in this way, translation converts the vernacular into a gift that contains the imprint of its source. The linguistic machinery of Tagalog is thus made to refer to an origin and destination beyond its community of native speakers—to God's Word as it is expressed in the discourse of Spanish Catholicism and in relation to the grammatical grid of Latin. It is as if Tagalog were alienated from the Tagalogs by the missionary-translator, who, after endowing it with a grammar and a lexicon in his *arte,* gave it back to them in the form of prayers, sermons, and confessionals. The vernacular is thus refashioned into an object to be classified and dissected, a gift to be circulated, and an instrument for the insertion of its speakers into a spiraling network of obligations with the Father.

To see translation as intending the ritual acknowledgment of one's indebtedness to God is thus to exclude the other possibility of translation as intending only language. It is to dominate the machine of the vernacular in such a way as to reformulate all its parts in order to make them available to convey the message of God. This mastery is never complete, however. The missionaries never managed fully to harness an important aspect of the vernacular: the precolonial Tagalog writing system called *baybayin*. In the end, as we shall see, the "failure" of native writing to yield fully to the demands of evangelization would result in its eventual replacement by Latin phonetic characters.

In order to appreciate how Tagalog script confounded missionary notions of language and translation, we must first consider the oral nature of evangelization. In the circulation of God's gift of tongues, what place did speech occupy in relation to the written word? As the raw material of conversion, what roles did voice and writing play in the dissemination of the promise of salvation? In what significant ways did the materiality of the letter as it is written and voiced in Tagalog affect the hierarchizing movement of Spanish ideas about translation and conversion?

The "Failure" of Native Writing

In the censor's letter of approval attached to Father Agustín de Magdalena's Tagalog *arte* of 1679, we read the following fragment: ". . . this *Arte* is an instrument for the use of the Ministers of the Faith who desire to preach to the pagans, that they may have persuasive and clear voices [*vozes vivas y claras*] with which to manifest God's doctrine."[16] Like Blancas, Magdalena sees the instrumental function of his work as subservient to its function of providing missionaries with "persuasive and clear voices" with which to convey God's Word. This priority is based on a pervasive assumption among Spaniards that the voice has primacy over writing in the transmission of the Gospel. As we saw earlier, conversion placed special stress on the activity of speaking and listening to God's Word. The voice was systematically ascribed a privileged position in the hierarchy of signs. Faith for this reason was based less on what one saw than on what one heard.

Reflecting the Spanish emphasis on the oral transmission of the faith are the various missionary accounts of seventeenth- and eigh-

16. Padre Agustín de Magdalena, *Arte de la lengua tagala sacado de diversos artes* (Manila, 1679), unpaginated.

teenth-century popular devotional practices cultivated among the native converts. The catechism, once translated into the vernacular, was periodically read out either by the parish priest or by clerically appointed native supervisors, called *fiscales,* to the prospective or recent converts of an area. The Creed, such basic prayers as the Our Father and the Hail Mary, and the commandments of God and the church were to be memorized. The natives were called upon to recite them frequently, while the parish priest jogged errant memories. The occasions for these recitations were the question-and-answer periods held after mass called *tocsohan* or *tanongan,* "in which those present are examined on the principal truths of the faith."[17] In addition, the litany of saints, the Angelus, and the rosary were regularly chanted at the town plaza by native choirboys receiving instruction from the parish priest. The hope was that such public displays of devotion would encourage others to perform similar rituals in their homes with their families. The church, nonetheless, was the locus of the collective voicing of the faith. The mass was not only said but sung in Latin; lengthy sermons in the vernacular were given in the middle and at the end of the ritual.[18]

There were, of course, pragmatic reasons for transmitting the doctrine orally. As John Phelan has noted, the expense of printing and the difficulty of preserving books of delicate rice paper in the humid tropical climate made it impossible to make devotional texts available to any but the Spanish priests and a limited number of native auxiliaries.[19] Yet other factors were also at work here. The tendency to favor voice over writing in conversion was related both to Christian tradition and to Spanish humanist conceptions of language.

The New Testament always speaks of Christ orally proclaiming the "good news" of salvation to those around him, just as he eventually sends out his apostles to preach his message.[20] Indeed, the term

17. Costa, *Jesuits in the Philippines,* pp. 530–531, culling from the account of the Jesuit Pedro Murillo Verlarde, *Historia de la Provincia de Filipinas de la Compañía de Jesús* (Manila, 1749).

18. See the accounts of Diego Aduarte, O.P., *Historia de la Provincia del Santo Rosario de la Orden de Predicadores de Filipinas, Japón, y China* (Zaragoza, 1693); Pedro Chirino, S.J., *Relación de las Islas Filipinas* (Rome, 1604; Manila: Historical Conservation Society, 1969); Francisco Colin, S. J., *Labor evangélica* (Madrid, 1663), passages of which are cited in Schumacher, *Readings in Philippine Church History,* pp. 44–48.

19. Phelan, *Hispanization of the Philippines,* p. 58.

20. See, for example, Matthew 4:23, 11:5; Romans 1:1.

"evangelist," from the Latin *evangelista,* referred in the early days of the church not only to an author of one of the Gospels but to any preacher of God's Word. And to preach (from *praedicare*) was always to proclaim or announce something publicly. The compulsion to preach the "good news" arises initially from hearing something said rather than from reading something written. Evangelization as the oral dissemination of God's Word is thus linked to a notion of conversion as that moment when the divine voice registers on human consciousness. Hence the exemplary case of Paul, whose conversion was occasioned first by a flash of light from the sky, then by the sound of Christ's voice saying, "Saul, Saul, why do you persecute me?" (Acts 9:4–6). Similarly, Augustine's "true moment" of conversion occurred when, while weeping alone in a garden, he suddenly heard a voice saying, *"Tolle lege, tolle lege,"* "Take up and read, take up and read." He interpreted this voice as none other than God's, commanding him to read, appropriately enough, the epistles of Paul,[21] which had been written for the express purpose of being read aloud to the people they addressed. In the Christian tradition, then, there is a pervasive sense that conversion is a matter of receiving and responding to God's call: that it can take place to the extent that the divine voice contained in sacred writing (for it is the divine voice that "sacralizes" the writing) can be heard conveying the message of salvation. For this reason, the apostles were granted the "gift" of speaking in tongues. It was only later that Christ's speech was codified into a body of sacred writing, standardized and translated over the centuries.

This stress on the oral dimension of conversion is echoed in the missionary *artes.* By learning the vernacular, the missionaries would be in a position to distribute to the natives the "bread of the doctrine" with which to "communicate to their souls the [message of] eternal life."[22] It was therefore essential that the "Divine Bread of the Doctrine be given to them in good portions, in small pieces, well chewed [*muy menudos y masticados*] with the force of explication, repeated through various modes of reasoning, similes, comparisons, and examples with moderate and gentle words that may manifest to the *indios*

21. *St. Augustine's Confessions* (1631), ed. and trans. William Watts (Cambridge: Harvard University Press, 1950–51), bk. 8, chap. 12.
22. Padre Marcos de Lisboa, *Vocabulario de la lengua bicol* (Sampaloc: Convento de Nuestra Señora de Loreto, 1754), *Prólogo,* n.p.

the anxious desire and love of the Father."[23] The imaging of a body of received writing—the Christian doctrine—as "sacred bread" underscores the ultimately oral process of delivering God's Word to those who "hunger" for it. In this sense, writing functions to conserve what has been proclaimed in the past. The Spanish priest, in mastering the local language, was performing his duty of transmitting the primordial Voice that had been received and recorded by the prophets, the apostles, and the evangelists before him. God's Word was translated into the vernacular in the hope that those who heard it—or "ate" a piece of it—would begin to return it to its source in the form of prayer:

Question: What is prayer?
Answer: It is to lift up the soul to God and ask for mercy.
Q: What is the most important prayer?
A: The Our Father.
Q: Why?
A: Because it was told by Christ to His Apostles in petitioning Him.[24]

Believing in Christ, asking him for mercy and favors, and petitioning him for assistance are all communicative acts that are carried out by oral means. The value of speech has to do with its proximity to the original teachings of God's Word and that of the church. Voice, like the metaphor of gift, is believed to transform the difference between languages into a progressive hierarchical flow of signs and obligations that pass through Christ, the apostles, the church, the Spanish missionary, and the convert, finally to be delivered back to its source: the Father. Insofar as translation was concerned, the special value of voice in conversion had an important effect. For translation always involved not only the transfer of meaning between languages but also the conversion of the written text of Christianity into a voice that would, in penetrating the ear of the listener, initiate its own voiced assent to the truth of God.

The desire for an unequivocal translation of God's words into the native language was thus, for the Spaniards, conjoined with a desire for a univocal transmission of those words. Blancas alluded to this

23. Sebastián Totanes, *Arte de la lengua tagala y manual para la administración de los Santos Sacramentos* (Manila: Convento de Nuestra Señora de Loreto, 1745), *Prólogo,* n.p.
24. Gaspar de Astete, *Doctrina cristiana* (Manila, 1777), pp. 26–28.

desire when he spoke of God's wisdom as shining "in the multitude of languages that are all so harmonious . . . in their marvelous difference of pronunciation proper to each one." The stress placed on the pronunciation proper to the native vernacular suggests the workings of the other factor that elevated voice over writing: Spanish humanist views on language.

While drawing on the writings of Plato and Aristotle, the Renaissance humanist Antonio de Nebrija nevertheless formulates the relationship between speech and writing in a way that dovetails with that implied in the Christian tradition of conversion: "The reason for the invention of letters was, first, to serve our memory, and later so that we could speak with those who were absent or who were yet to come. . . . Therefore, letters are nothing but figures that represent the voice . . . and voices signify, as Aristotle has said, the thoughts that we have in our soul" (*Gramática,* pp. 18–19). Following the models of antiquity, as he did in his discussion of Castilian, Nebrija gives writing a position subordinate to voice, and places voice ultimately in the service of the soul's thoughts.[25] It was for this reason that he undertook to standardize Spanish orthography so that it might function as the instrument of an instrument, as a guide for the voice which would act as a boundary across which the soul's thoughts could be transported in the absence of the speaker's body. Taking for his norm the orthography of Latin, Nebrija repeatedly insists that "in order to say better what we have here been presupposing, and all those who have written about orthography assume, we must write as we speak, and speak as we write; otherwise, all letters would be useless" (p. 23).

The importance of writing hence revolves around its double function of representing voice (and with it, thought) and regulating the diversity of voices. The move to standardize orthography is part of a larger interest in containing voice and stabilizing the modes of representing thought, particularly in one's absence. For this reason Nebrija's discussion of the sound value of each letter refers to the letter's

---

25. For one of the most persuasive and compelling critiques of this "logocentric" tradition in the history of Western thought, see the works of Jacques Derrida, especially *Of Grammatology*, trans. Gayatri Chakravorty Spivak (Baltimore: Johns Hopkins University Press, 1976); *Dissemination,* trans. Barbara Johnson (Chicago: University of Chicago Press, 1981); *Margins of Philosophy* (1982) and *Writing and Difference* (1978), both translated by Alan Bass and published by the University of Chicago Press. My understanding of these works has shaped much of the following discussion on writing and voice in Spanish and on Tagalog signifying conventions.

oficio or office, as if letters were bureaucrats charged with maintaining purity of thought. Far from being a trivial concern, the office of writing in relation to voice and to thought constituted an important segment of Spanish colonialism.

The Tagalog *artes* and *vocabularios* display this humanist investment in the regulation of writing in the interest of guarding the reproduction of voice and the message it contains. This concern is registered in the repeated stress on rules of accentuation and pronunciation. In the *prólogo* of a 1754 *vocabulario,* for instance, we read: "The most arduous thing in this language is to give fixed rules of accentuation, a difficulty augmented by other authors with their explanations and with the variety with which they have numbered and noted them down."[26]

Earlier writers of *artes* all concur, however, on the relative importance of the old Tagalog script as a supplement to learning the correct voicing of the language. The local script called *baybayin* consisted of seventeen characters, which missionary writers of the early seventeenth century classified and designated as three "vowels" and fourteen "consonants." It was reportedly in wide use among the Tagalogs as well as other linguistic groups in the archipelago during the early period of colonization. The Jesuit chronicler Pedro Chirino, among others, noted that the Tagalogs "are much given to reading and writing, and that there is scarcely a man much less a woman that does not read and write in the letters proper to the island of Manila, which are sufficiently diverse from those to be found in China, Japan and India."[27] Such twentieth-century scholars as William Henry Scott and F. Landa Jocano have inferred that the ancient Tagalog syllabary is structurally related to those found in Sulawesi and conclude that the seafaring Buginese traders had probably introduced the alphabet to the inhabitants of the archipelago shortly before colonization.

Upon discovering the existence of these characters, the missionaries early on attempted to employ them in the translation of catechisms into the native idioms. Such efforts were quickly abandoned, however. The Spaniards found the Tagalog script to be "inadequate" to the demands of an unequivocal translation of Christian doctrines. In their place the Spaniards attempted to institute the phonetic script characteristic of Latin and Castilian.

26. Padre Juan de Noceda and Padre Pedro Sanlucar, *Vocabulario de la lengua tagala* (Manila: Ramírez y Giraudier, 1860), *Prólogo,* n.p.
27. Chirino, *Relación de las Islas Filipinas,* p. 45.

Though largely marginalized in the three and a half centuries of colonial rule, local writing never completely disappeared. These ancient characters, in fact, sporadically resurface in the Spanish accounts of precolonial native customs, as "signatures" appended to some seventeenth-century documents, and as objects of scholarly inquiry in a number of late-nineteenth-century essays on Philippine languages by Spanish, French, and even Filipino writers. At present, *baybayin* is still used in limited ways by the unchristianized Hanunoo and Tagbanua tribes of Mindoro and Palawan, respectively, two islands off the coast of Manila. William Henry Scott has marveled at the "wealth of documentary testimony spread across four centuries" accorded to the Tagalog script as well as at the remarkable "consistency—from the *Doctrina Christiana* of 1593 to Mangyan love letters of 1967"—of the formal features of this script.[28] No less remarkable, however, is the rapidity with which *baybayin* was displaced by romanized phonetic writing among the Christianized natives. This shift had to do partly with what the Spaniards considered to be the "incomplete and unintelligible" nature of the script, particularly in light of the imperative of producing a univocal translation of the faith:

> Sometimes adjoining the Tagalog word written in Spanish letters I place the Tagalog characters with which the same word is also written, in order that through them whoever can read them can come to know the proper pronunciation of that word. . . . For which reason those who wish to talk well should learn to read Tagalog characters, since it is such an easy matter that they can be learned ordinarily in one hour, although reading the Tagalog language in its own characters without faltering as we read our own Spanish language no Spaniard will ever be able to do in all his life, though it might be as long as Adam's. The reason for this will be readily understood by anybody who takes just one lesson in it, and he will see it by experience even in the native speakers themselves, among whom even the most skillful grope through it, because after all, reading their characters is almost pure guessing. All this notwithstanding, I would ask the diligent student to learn such reading and he will see how it will help him perfect his pronunciation.[29]

. . . the Tagalog script . . . is so defective and so confusing (for not having up till now a way of writing suspended consonants, that is,

28. Scott, *Prehispanic Source Materials*, p. 60.
29. Blancas de San José, *Arte y reglas de la lengua tagala* (Bataan, 1610), *Prólogo*, n.p.

consonants that do not sound off vowels) so that even the most astute *ladino* [bilingual native] is detained by it and is given to a great deal of thinking in many words in order to be able to pronounce what the writer had tried to write.[30]

. . . although they [the Tagalog characters] are easy to write, it is almost impossible to read them because the consonant that follows when pertaining to an antecedent word is not written, so that one has to guess the circumstances in which they would appear.[31]

This script is as easy to write as it is difficult to read because it is to guess [*adivinar*] it . . . it helps to know the Tagalog characters in distinguishing accents.[32]

This script . . . cannot be any less than illegible . . . it presents great difficulties not for him who writes it but for him who reads it. . . . [We are thus] far from believing that this alphabet could provide the simplicity and clarity of Latin. Also it is absurd to say that with a few points and commas these characters can be made to signify everything that one might want to write as fully and as easily as our own Spanish alphabet.[33]

From these accounts spreading through the centuries of colonial rule we can glean, to paraphrase Scott, the remarkable consistency with which Spaniards read Tagalog script in terms of phonetic writing and concluded that Tagalog was inadequate to the task. At stake here is the accessibility of *baybayin* to phonetic transcription, which could then be translated into a voice that would carry with it a determinate meaning. Tagalog characters were written in such a way that each character ended with what the Spaniards referred to as a "vowel" sound: *a, e-i,* and *o-u.* A diacritical mark called *kurlit* (or at times *kudlit*) was placed above or below each character to modify its sound ending: a *kurlit* above signals the *e-i* sound, below the *ou* sound. Unmarked, a character ends with an *a* sound. The Spanish writers and later commentators found "completely wanting . . . a

---

30. Padre Francisco López, *Belarmino* (1621), quoted in W. E. Retana, *Los antiguos alfabetos en Filipinas, La Política España en Filipinas* 21 (May 1895): 6.
    31. Magdalena, *Arte de la lengua tagala,* p. 70.
    32. Gaspar de San Agustín, *Compendio del arte de la lengua tagala,* 2d ed. (Sampaloc: Convento de Nuestra Señora de Loreto, 1787), p. 155.
    33. Padre Cipriano Marcilla, *Estudio de los antiguos alfabetos filipinos* (Malabon: Asilo de Huérfanos, 1895), p. 19.

'rest' or 'stop' which cancels the vowel value of any letter and permits it to stand as a consonant alone."[34] This lack partly explains Father Marcilla's observation that "a few points and commas" above or below the characters would not suffice to make them readable in Spanish terms. For to read local writing phonetically would involve "guessing" the points or breaks in each syllable—those "suspended consonants" to which Father López referred—which would block the slippage of one signifier into another. Gaspar de San Agustín's example serves to illustrate the difficulties this script presented to the Spaniards:

> . . . these two letters ꜀꜀ can be read in eight ways, which are *lili* (side), *lilim* (shade), *lilip* (border), *lilis* (to raise), *lilit* (?), *lilim* (the act of shading something), *liclic* (to deviate), *liglig* (to drop something), and with all these they are understood. Ditto with △ Ꮛ , which can be read as *bata* (child), *batar* (?), *batac* (to throw away), *banta* (threat), *batay* (to fix on something) . . . [*Compendio,* p. 169].

The attempt to reinscribe *baybayin* into phonetic writing requires one to determine the specific "consonant" with which to tell one signifier from another and thereby arrive at its appropriate signified. But as San Agustín's example shows, there always exist several possibilities in the determination of a word's sound and accent. The effect of this "defect" is to render open-ended the process of signification in Tagalog writing. The *kurlit* or diacritical mark contributes less to the fixing of signifiers to signifieds than to the proliferation of signifying possibilities. This is not surprising in light of the fact that the Tagalog word *kurlit,* defined by the Spaniards as *acento* (accent), also means in Tagalog "a minor scratch" or "a small wound." Thus a *kurlit* not only marks the boundary where writing is given up to voice, that is, the line that by giving value or stress to a syllable determines the sound of the signifier, thus delimiting the range of signifieds that can be attached to it; as a "scratch" or "wound," it also calls forth a multiplicity of sounds and consequently other signifieds. Hence, *from the Spanish point of view,* the "illegibility" and "unreadability" of the script results from the lack of a direct and fixed correspondence between script and sound. It was precisely for this reason that reading *baybayin* phonetically seemed like "almost pure guessing."

34. Scott, *Prehispanic Source Materials,* p. 60.

Bā bē bī bō bū. Çā çē çī çō çū.
Đā đē đī đō đū. ſā fē fī fō fū.
Ᵹuan ᵹuen ᵹuīn ᵹuon ᵹun. ħā.
ħē ħī ħō ħū. Jā je jī jō jū. Lā lē.
lī lō lū. Māẟā mē mī mō mū. Nā.
nē nī nō nū. Pā pē pī pō pū. Q!.ā.
quē quī quō qū. Rā rē rī rō rū. Sā
sē sī sō sū. Tā tē tī tō tū. Ulā vē.
vī vō vu. Xā xē xī xō xū. Yā yē.
yī yō yū. Zā zē zī zō zū.

❦ El abc. en léguatagala.

❦ El paternoſter.

PADRE nueſtro que eſtas en

A page of *Doctrina Christiana* (Manila, 1593) shows the phonetic "reduction" of the precolonial Tagalog syllabary (*baybayin*) into roman letters. Toward the bottom of the page "the abc in the Tagalog language" is shown in the *baybayin* characters, followed by the title and first line of the Our Father in Castilian.

The inevitability of "faltering" as one reads Tagalog script, as Blancas remarked, obstructed the passage of a determinate thought that was believed to be contained within the hierarchy voice/writing. The ambivalence inherent in Tagalog script tended to defer sense in favor of the sensation of sound as one slid from one signifier to another. This tendency is further suggested by the very word for the script: *baybayin* means to learn the alphabet and to spell a word, but it also refers to the seacoast, or the act of coasting along a river. This sense of the word highlights the seeming randomness involved in the reading of the script as one floats, as it were, over a stream of sounds elicited by the characters. Perhaps this was why the natives, as Spanish writers and present-day historians have observed, showed little interest in employing the local syllabary for the "serious" preservation of historical and literary texts. Instead, writing on bamboo and other such perishable materials, Tagalogs used this script, as a nineteenth-century commentator remarks, for such things as "barely intelligible amatory verses written in hyperbolic style."[35]

With the introduction of paper in the late sixteenth century, however, some Tagalogs did take to recording land transfers in *baybayin*. Two such documents, each a page in length and dating respectively from 1613 and 1625, were reproduced together with their phonetic transcription and a commentary (in Spanish) by a Dominican archivist in Manila, Father Alberto Santamaría, in 1938. Interestingly enough, Santamaría found it impossible to ascertain the details of the records, so that he had to rely on another document written by a Spanish notary in 1629 which accompanied the *baybayin* documents. Yet the notary's attempt to read the documents is marked by a great deal of equivocation, owing to what he refers to as the "bad style that they have; they cannot be transcribed to the letter, but the substance of one of them is: It seems that in Tondo . . ."[36]

It seems, then, that the ambiguity involved in translating the native script spreads across the centuries. The relative undecipherability of these documents crystallizes particularly around the signatures attached to them. It is a feature of these records that the signatures are often at odds with the names that appear in the main text of the

---

35. Sinibaldo de Mas, *Informe sobre el estado de las Islas Filipinas,* 2 vols. (Madrid: I. Sancha, 1843), 1:26.

36. Padre Alberto Santamaría, "El 'Baybayin' en el archivo de Santo Tomás," *Unitas* 16 (February 1938): 448.

documents and with their phonetic transcriptions. The name of one of the signers, for example, appears alternately as "A Yi Ya," "Ba Yi Ka," and "Ba Yi Ya"; the Spanish notary renders it "Baycan." Such slippages abound in the specimen signatures that Santamaría reproduces as well. In addition, several of the signatures, as Scott remarks, appear to have been written "by the same hand, as if the testators could not sign for themselves."[37]

In an official contract involving the sale of property, one would expect—as the Spanish notary obviously did—that the person's name would be consistently rendered, so that the signature could be made to stand as a faithful representative of the contractor before the law. But the notion of "signature" did not exist among the Tagalogs before the coming of the Spaniards, as is evidenced by the fact that the Spanish word *firma* (rendered phonetically as *"pima"*) is used in the *baybayin* texts. The local script did not allow for a direct and unequivocal link between signature and name and between name and person.

The question then arises: What would a "signature" be which perpetually postponed the definitive location of name and person? In the case of *baybayin,* it was a series of marks that called forth sounds but whose referent had to be "guessed"—perhaps with a little help from God: "With respect to the inscriptions [*letreros*] [of the documents] we have transcribed them as God has given us to understand them," Santamaría explains (p. 30).

The peculiarities of the local script led at least one Spanish writer to remark in 1878 that "Tagalog characters are more like syllabic codes than letters. They are the transition from hieroglyphics to the perfection of phonetic writing."[38] The "perfection" ascribed to phonetic writing has to do, as we have seen, with its conceived proximity to voice and the perceived fit between the two. Tagalog script was consequently unsuitable to the Spanish demand for the kind of labor required by translation and conversion. In effect, Tagalog script undercut the efforts of both colonial officials and missionaries to return the local language triumphantly to its meaning and source (yet another meaning of the Spanish *traducir,* from the Latin *traducere,* to lead along, to conduct in triumph, to remove, to transfer from one rank to

37. Scott, *Prehispanic Source Materials,* p. 58.

38. Padre Toribio Minguella, *Ensayo de gramático hispano-tagalo* (Manila: Plana, 1878), pp. 9–10.

another). Being a "syllabic code," it could not be reduced to the conventions of a univocal reading. Marginalizing the local script into a merely supplementary position with regard to phonetic writing on the one hand and pronunciation on the other, the Spaniards, aided by the Tagalogs themselves, chose to write Tagalog in roman characters. By converting *baybayin* into phonetic writing, the Spaniards hoped to make the Tagalog language more "readable." And "readability" in this case implied the control of the differing and deferring movement of writing by the "persuasive and clear voices" of the missionaries who worked to ensure the passage of God's Word and the king's authority through the local idiom.

The transcription of Tagalog writing into roman characters with its accompanying accent marks—*agudo* (´), *grave* (`), *circunflejo* (^)—was intended to relieve the Spanish reader of the need to guess the link between signifier and signified. Phonetic writing effected the graphic suppression of the "vowel" which followed every consonant in *baybayin* (*b* instead of △, pronounced *ba*, for example) and replaced the *kurlit* with diacritical marks to distinguish between the syllables of a word. Yet even with the subsequent conversion of Tagalog script into phonetic writing, the Spanish voice found itself confronted with what it could only describe as a persistent "lack" in Tagalog phonetics.

The 1745 *arte* of Sebastián Totanes is symptomatic of the Spanish wishfulness with regard to the question of Tagalog writing. The first section of the work, titled "The Tagalog Alphabet in Our Castilian Characters," states that he no longer finds it necessary to illustrate *baybayin* characters because "rare is the *indio* who still knows how to read them, much less write them. All of them read and write our Castilian letters now."[39]

We would be hard-pressed to demonstrate the veracity of this statement precisely because of the problematic nature of reading and writing in Tagalog. Totanes's statement, like others that appear in the mid-eighteenth-century *artes,* is significant less for its description of what may or may not have been a historical fact than for the way it links up with the Spanish dream of a univocal speech and a transparent translation of Christianity into Tagalog. And it was in the process of acting out that dream in the texts of their *artes* that the

39. Totanes, *Arte de la lengua tagala,* p. 1.

Spaniards met up with the resistant turns of a difference that they had sought to domesticate by designating it as a lack. Hence, in Totanes's section on Tagalog phonetics, we read:

> They have no *F* but they supplement it with a *P* so that to say *confesar,* they say *compisal.* Nor *LL* to say *cavallo,* they say *cabayo,* because they substitute for it a *Y.* Nor do they have *X,* or *Z,* or *J,* substituting for them *S.* . . .
>
> Neither do they have a strong *R,* so that to say *ramo* they say *damo,* because they supplement it with a *D.* . . . Neither do they have *Ce* or *Ci* as we do when we pronounce the name Cicerón. . . . Neither do they have a *Ge* as in *general,* or *Gi* like Gines. . . . [Totanes, *Arte de la lengua tagala,* p. 2]

In this compilation of what Tagalog does not have in comparison with Castilian, the elements of Tagalog phonetics are seen as mere derivatives of Castilian sounds. In seeking to appropriate the native language, Spanish speakers were constantly confronted by what they perceived to be the absence of familiar consonants. In the place of those consonants Tagalogs inscribed supplementary approximations of them. This need to substitute Tagalog letters for "missing" Spanish sounds generated such anxiety in Totanes that he saw the substitutions as acts of violence against Spanish sounds:

> There are only three vowels: because *E* and *I* are commonly mistaken for each other and are used almost indifferently, now one, now the other, especially in writing; though in speaking they use the *I* more. At the beginning of the sentence, there is no need to look for *E,* owing to the barbarity of the Tagalogs. The same occurs with *O* and *U,* which are mistaken in speaking as they almost always are in writing, and they often convert one into the other, especially when forming the passive. For example, *arao,* day, they say *arauan* [to expose something in the daylight]; *litao,* to appear, *linilitauan ang catauan* &c. [the body is appearing]. *E* and *O* they call *malata,* i.e., soft [*blanda*]. *I* and *U* they call *matigas,* i.e., hard [*dura*]. Such is the explanation of the *indios* for violating our five vowels. [P. 1]

In an effort to ventriloquize the Tagalog voice, the Spanish writer runs up against the "indifferent" distinctions of "vowel" sounds among the native speakers in addition to the need to search out

Tagalog "consonants" that approximate the sound of Spanish ones. The natives' "barbarity" is regarded as the cause of the confusion encountered in the determination of a word's pronunciation. Rendered into phonetic writing, Tagalog "vowels" and "consonants" still manage to elude the Spanish demand for a direct, one-to-one correspondence between graphic mark and vocal sign. What was thought to be a defect of the local script—its failure to surrender itself to a determinate voice—is thus reenacted in the phonetic rendition of Tagalog. The native speakers, according to Totanes, account for the "indifferent" sliding of "vowel" sounds by distinguishing between the E-O sound and I-U sound, referring to them respectively as *malata* (from *lata*, soft, gentle, docile, flexible) and *matigas* (hard, rigid, tenacious, inflexible). From the Tagalog point of view, speech seems to be constituted by an opposition (soft versus hard) that stresses the physicality of sound—and one that is highly unstable, as E and O often slide into I and U. Thus written characters were not expected to point to a specific sound, which in turn would give way to an imperious message. Instead, they generated certain sounds whose possible range of meanings were evoked with reference to how they felt to the body that listened and spoke. Here we see something we have noted before: the tendency of *baybayin* to suspend sense in favor of sensation.

This is perhaps the reason for the bizarre last statement in the passage quoted above: "Such is the explanation of the *indios* for violating our five vowels." The *indios* are accused of transgressing the norms of Spanish phonetics precisely because they do not, as the Spaniards do, pronounce a word the way it is spelled and vice versa. The "violation" of native speakers thus consists of their insistence on maintaining a gap between writing and voice (and consequently between voice and meaning) which the conversion of *baybayin* into Castilian characters was supposed to close. Tagalog allowed for a continued investment in the sensuousness of language as it was converted from writing to voice, a sensuousness that came across the rift between a written word and its vocal reproduction. The implication is that voice had a different status among Tagalogs, one that ran counter to the hierarchy of signs that the missionaries set out to impose on them. The Spaniards conceived of the privileged place of voice in the circulation of signs in terms of its ability to efface itself, like the "fiery language" of the Pentecost or the host of the Eucharist, which disappeared as it delivered up the Sign of God into the person. The structure of the Tagalogs' language suggests that they related voice and writing in a different way. They valued writing precisely for the play of voices (rather than the emergence of *a* voice) to which it gave rise, thereby making of reading a process akin to guessing. And just as writing provided the condition of possibility for the reproduction of voice, voice did not exist in a relation of subservience to "meaning" or "thought" but was valued for its ability to generate sensations that, in effect, deferred the content of a message.

CHAPTER 2

Tomas Pinpin and the
Shock of Castilian

In the early seventeenth century a Tagalog printer, Tomas Pinpin, set out to write a book in romanized phonetic script to teach Tagalogs how to learn Castilian. His book, published by the Dominican press where he worked, appeared in 1610, the same year as Blancas's *arte*. Unlike the missionary's grammar (which Pinpin had set in type), the Tagalog native's book dealt with the language of the dominant rather than the subordinate other. Pinpin's book was the first such work ever written and published by a Philippine native. As such, it is richly instructive for what it tells us about the interests that animated Tagalog translation and, by implication, Tagalog conversion in the early colonial period. As we shall see, Pinpin construed translation in ways that tended less to oppose than to elude the totalizing claims of Spanish signifying conventions.

Syncopating Language

In his early-seventeenth-century work *Memorial de la vida christiana,* Blancas de San José remarks about the Tagalogs' talent and enthusiasm for phonetic writing:

> I am well aware that those who can read these characters of ours are not many; but I also know that there is hardly anyone who does not possess the aptitude or the talent for it, and to such a degree that I am amazed more particularly at what I have seen by experience among women, not just in one or another, but in many. . . . Their joy is particularly great

when they find those things written in clear characters and whole and complete readings, unlike theirs, which the best reader guesses rather than reads.[1]

Chirino, a few years earlier, had also noted the Tagalogs' enthusiasm for Spanish letters. "They have learned our language, pronouncing and writing it as well as we and even better, because they are quite skilled so that they can learn anything with great facility."[2] For all their skill and enthusiasm, however, and despite the schools established by the missionaries and the educational reforms instituted by Spanish liberals in 1863, the overwhelming majority of the Tagalogs, like other linguistic groups in the archipelago, never did become fluent in Spanish. At the close of the Spanish regime, only about 10 percent of the population could actually understand it.[3]

Historians concur that this lack of fluency in Spanish is tantamount to a failure of sorts and that it can be traced to pragmatic and extrinsic factors: a lack of adequate financial resources, the perennial shortage of Spanish clerical personnel to serve as teachers, and according to Phelan, the absence of "social and economic incentives" that would have encouraged Tagalogs to learn Castilian.[4] The Tagalogs' lack of fluency in Spanish makes it inappropriate to refer to them as truly bilingual; for most natives then, like their descendants today, possessed only what one Spanish priest in 1689 called a "rough comprehension" of Castilian.[5]

Perhaps inadequacy of funding and personnel to teach Spanish did play important roles in the failure of Tagalogs to acquire fluency in Spanish. But one would be mistaken to assert, as Phelan does, that incentives for learning Castilian were totally lacking. Such an assertion is unable to account for the appearance in 1610 of the perplexing book of Tomas Pinpin, *Librong Pagaaralan nang manga Tagalog nang uicang Castila* (The book with which Tagalogs can learn Cas-

---

1. Padre Francisco Blancas de San José, *Memorial de la vida christiana, en la lengua tagala* (1605), 2d ed. (Manila: D. Jose Maria Dayot, por Tomas Olivas, 1835), Preface, n.p.

2. Chirino, *Relación de las islas filipinas,* ed. Echevarría, pp. 46–47.

3. *Census of the Philippine Islands, 1903,* 3 vols. (Washington, D.C.: U.S. Government Printing Office, 1905), 3:594, 595, 687, 689; also Phelan, *Hispanization of the Philippines,* p. 132.

4. Phelan, *Hispanization of the Philippines,* p. 132.

5. Miguel de Pareja, S.J., letter of 15 April 1689, cited in Schumacher, *Readings in Philippine Church History,* p. 153.

tilian).[6] The assumption that most Tagalogs never learned Spanish is premised on a specifically Western notion of what it means to master a language. Pinpin's work points to a different kind of investment in a foreign language, one that aimed not necessarily at fluency but rather at pleasure and protection.

Tomas Pinpin is best known as the *ladino* printer of Blancas de San José's *Arte y reglas de la lengua tagala.*[7] Unlike the Dominican, Pinpin calls his work a *libro.* The Spaniard was concerned with the reconstruction of Tagalog grammar and its use in the conversion of the local populace; Pinpin seems to have had another aim. He hints at his purpose in the prologue of the work, headed "*Paralang sulat ni Tomas Pinpin tauong Tagalog sa manga capoua niya Tagalog na nagaabang magaral nang dilang macagagaling sa canila,*" or "The letter delivered by Tomas Pinpin to his fellow Tagalogs expecting/waiting to study the tongue that will cure/do them good." Studying a language is here likened to waiting or expecting its delivery. The value of the language lies in its capacity to serve as a curative or as a source of good. Throughout the *Librong,* Pinpin refers to Castilian as a "thing," indeed the "inside" (*laman*) of all things Spanish, that which lies beneath the outward manifestations of Spaniards' dress and demeanor:

> Di baquin ang ibang manga caasalan at caanyoan nang manga Castila
> ay inyong guinalologdan at ginagagad din ninyo sa pagdaramitan at sa

6. The first edition of this book—the only book-length work Pinpin is known to have written—appeared in 1610. A second edition appeared in 1752, this time as an appendix to Blancas de San José's *Arte de la lengua tagala,* a copy of which is in the microfilm collection of the National Library in Manila. The edition that has been used here and to which all page numbers refer is a facsimile edition contained in Manuel Artigas y Cuerva, *La primera imprenta en Filipinas* (Manila: Germania, 1910), pp. 135–259. Little is known of Pinpin's life. He was born in Laguna, a province south of Manila; we do not know the date. As a printer in Bataan and Manila, Pinpin worked on a significant number of missionary works and devotional books in both Castilian and Tagalog until around 1639. Artigas speculates that Pinpin probably learned his trade from the Christianized Chinese Juan de Vera, who is credited with having printed missionary works in the vernacular in the sixteenth century.

7. Bienvenido Lumbera defines a *ladino* as a bilingual native who worked mostly with Spanish missionaries during the early period of colonization. *Ladino*-style poetry appeared sporadically throughout the seventeenth century and the first half of the eighteenth. See Lumbera, "Tagalog Poetry during the Seventeenth Century," *Philippine Studies* 16 (June 1968): 99–130. Most Spanish dictionaries define *ladino* as "one versed in an idiom, speaking different languages fluently," and as an adjective (interestingly enough for our purposes), as "sagacious, cunning, crafty."

nananandataman at paglacadman at madlaman ang magogol ay uala
rin hinahinayang cayo dapouat macmochamocha cayo sa Castila. Ay
aba itopang isang asal macatotohanan sapangongosap nang canila ding
uica ang di sucat ibigang camtan? . . . Bancay na nga cayo, con anong
dating nagbisting Castila ang taou, cun ualang asal asal na tantong
icamuchang Castila niya? Caya nga ang iba, y, baquit na cacasti-castila
nang pagdaramit na ualang di cacastila ang asal solual: bago con saca
sila dologui,t, paquiusapan nang uicang castila ay totongog tongog na
sa hahangal. Ay condi gayon nga,y, ano? . . . Bagcos nanga ito ang
naguiguing puno nang ibang marami at paran laman ito, at ang iba,y,
cabalat cayohan lamang. Di con magcamomocha nang tayo nila nang
pagdaramit ay con ang pangongosap ay iba, ay anong darat-
ing? [Pinpin, *Librong*, pp. 142–143]

No doubt you like and imitate the ways and appearance of the Spaniards in matters of clothing and the bearing of arms and even of gait,
and you do not hesitate to spend a great deal so that you may resemble
the Spaniards. Therefore would you not like to acquire as well this
other trait which is their language? . . . Would not a person who
dressed like a Spaniard but did not have the other trait of the Spaniard
be like a corpse? So why should you bother to appear Spanish in your
dress if you do not have the traits of the Castilian: so that when you are
spoken to in Castilian, you merely gape like fools. And if this happens,
then what? . . . Therefore it is this [Castilian] that is the source of a lot
of other things and it is like the inside of things, and everything else is
only its external covering. So if we look like them in our manner of
dressing but speak differently, then where would things come to?

As Castilian is at the "inside" of Spanish appearances, learning it
becomes a means of consolidating and further adding to those other
signs that one has already acquired from the Spaniards. Castilian is
regarded thus as a "source" for the acquisition of other things Spanish. Like dress, weapons, and behavior, it may be appropriated to
enable one to engage in some kind of exchange with colonial authority. This is perhaps why one who has gone to great lengths to look
Spanish but does not have Castilian is compared to a corpse, that is, a
dead body that is incapable of exchange, linguistic or otherwise. The
acquisition of Castilian, the Spanish object par excellence, was thus a
way of amassing a surplus of word objects that would enable one to
feel alive in the face of a representative of the colonial hierarchy.
Without some Castilian, one would risk the danger of being startled

by the sudden appearance of the Spaniard. Gaping with astonishment and terror, one would fail to understand the Spaniard's words and thus would incur only his laughter and wrath. One who learns Castilian is prepared to respond and thus to avoid the shock of being assailed by something one can neither recognize nor contain.[8]

In stressing the materiality of Castilian, Pinpin values it less for its ability to communicate a metalinguistic content than for its capacity to extend what one has already acquired from the Spaniards. Knowledge of Castilian provides the Tagalog with a position from which to engage in a linguistic exchange with them. The native who finds such a position is relieved of the fear of being overwhelmed and thus of appearing like a corpse in the face of the other. This is perhaps the reason for Pinpin's delight when he thinks of other Tagalogs learning Castilian. He registers his joy in an *auit,* or song:

Ay ano, baquin ang ibang manga tauo capoua natin Tagalog ay silang maralan co niton manga catha cong ito ay di na taonan ay magsialam na ang dami nang naalaman nila. Caya nga sa natanto co yaong canilang caronongan, na dito rin sa manga gaua cong ito napaquinabang nila ay aco,y, matoua ngani at mangbanta na acong isalimbagan itong madlang aral: nang paraparang magsipaquinabang nito cayong lahat na magaacalang magsicap nang camahalan at dili aco nacabata, na di aco mag auit na gayon.   [Pp. 147–148]

8. As we shall see, the shock of colonization never fully disappeared. The colonizer never became wholly familiar to the Tagalogs but remained irreducibly alien. To the Filipinos, the figures and signs of colonial rule continued to bear the traces of a prior shock; hence the continued capacity of those signs, if uncontrolled and untranslated, to arouse fear and terror. In this context, one can begin to understand the perennial observations of Spanish writers regarding the tendency of many Filipinos to respond to Europeans with either overwhelming alacrity or inexplicable dread. A late-nineteenth-century description of the "moral physiognomy" of the "civilized *indios*" written collectively by a group of Jesuits in the Philippines refers to the "fear . . . that totally disconcerts and stupefies [the natives] . . . so that they sweat and tremble with anguish. The very presence of a European alone puts them in this state, even though they have not been threatened or castigated. It is enough that the [tone of] voice be changed or raised, or that they be argued with, or pressed with questions for this fear to change into real terror, especially among the *indios* little accustomed to dealing with foreigners. This fear or terror of the natives is perhaps a satisfactory explanation of the absurdities and disparate and contradictory responses to which they at times are prone and which otherwise would remain inexplicable" (*El Archipélago Filipino: Colección de datos,* por algunos padres de la Misión de la Compañía de Jesús en estas islas, 3 vols. [Washington, D.C.: U.S. Government Printing Office, 1900], 1:213). It is precisely those reasons "which otherwise would remain inexplicable" that I seek to examine by referring to colonization as a shock experience.

Is it not that other fellow Tagalogs were the same ones whom I taught with these writings of mine so that in barely a year they were able to learn so much? This is why, upon seeing their learning, which came from this work of mine, I was delighted and attempted to publish these collected lessons: so that like them, you can also benefit, all of you who have wanted to obtain this valuable language; and I can no longer restrain myself from singing in this way.

The *auit* that follows is the first among several such songs that Pinpin inserts between lessons. In standard *ladino* fashion, Castilian follows Tagalog on the same line, serving as a semantic approximation of the Tagalog words. It reads:

> Anong dico toua, Como no he de holgarme;
> Con hapot, omaga, la mañana y tarde;
> dili napahamac, que no salio en balde;
> itong gaua co, aqueste mi lance;
> madla ang naalaman; y a mil cossas saben;   5
> nitong aquing alagad, los mis escolares;
> sucat magcatoua, justo es alegrarse;
> ang manga ama nila, sus padres y madres;
> at ang di camuc-ha, pues son de otro talle;
> na di ngani baliu, no brutos salvages.   10
>
> Totoo ding sucat. Cierto que es bastante;
> ipagparangalan, a hacer de ello alarde;
> ingatan nang Dios, mi Dios me los guarde.
> Magcanomang gogol, por mucho gaste;
> sa pag lilimbagan, en hacer estampar;   15
> nitong aral co, aquesta mi arte;
> san libo mang ganito, aunque cien taes;
> na pauang dalisay, de finos quilates;
> gaoin cong sangsaga, seran un adarme.
> At malauon man, aunque mas se tarde   20
> dili aco oorong, no he de quedarme atras;
> anoman ang pagal, por mas que trabaje;
> matutuloy din, ha de ir adelante;
> ang ganitong gaua, obra de este talle;
> di sucat itahan; no es bien que se ataje.   25
> Acoy mangangahas, quiero abalanzarme;
> mag catha nang aral, a hacer una arte;

na icasaysay, que mucho declare;
nang uicang mahal, el rico lenguaje.

O Ama con Dios, o gran Dios mi Padre;   30
tolongan aco, quered ayudarme;
amponin aco, sedme favorable;
nang mayari ito, porque esto se acabe;
at icao ang purihin, y a vos os alaben.

[P. 148]

The following English translation follows as literally as possible the
Tagalog, then Spanish lines.

Oh, how happy I am, why shouldn't I make merry,
when afternoon and morning, morning and afternoon,
no danger occurs, it was not in vain,
this work of mine, this my transaction.
So much will be known, and a thousand things will be known   5
by my followers, those my students.
Such is their joy, they do right to rejoice,
their parents, their fathers and mothers,
and even those not like them, for they are of another kind,
they are not crazy, not savage brutes.   10

It is truly fitting. Surely it is right
to dignify this, to boast of this,
God protect [them], my God guard them for me.
Whatever may be spent, though much be spent,
in impressing, in printing   15
my lessons, this my grammar,
even a hundred of these, though a hundred taels
of purest quality, of the finest degree of purity;
I will make them equivalent to one weight of gold/silver,
    they will be half a dram,
And even if it takes long, although much it be delayed,   20
I will not retreat, I must not fall behind;
however long it takes, however much the work,
it will go through, it has to go forward;
this kind of work, a work of this sort,
should not be stopped, is not to be cut off;   25
I will dare, I want to venture,

to compose an *aral,* to make an *arte,*
that will tell, that declares much
of the valuable language, of the rich language.

O God my Father, O great God my Father;   30
help me, please help me;
adopt me, be favorable to me;
that this be accomplished, so that this can be finished;
and you will be praised, and you will be glorified.

In the last lines of the *auit* (30–34) Pinpin seems to be mimicking the Spanish pattern of returning language to God in the form of an offering: his book. Yet, in the light of the preceding lines, one might justifiably suspect that this gesture is not necessarily a recentering of the divine Father in the movement of language. The appeal to God may have been a figural ploy to placate the Spanish censors and priests without whose approval the book could not have been printed or circulated. Pinpin uses a textual convention derived from the Spaniards. Nevertheless, the style of the *auit* results in the decontextualization of this convention. How so?

First of all, some of the prosodic features of the *auit* are worth noting. Like the other songs that sporadically surface in the book, both the Tagalog and Castilian lines follow typically assonantal rhyme schemes, each line consisting of five to eight syllables.[9] The Tagalog lines rhyme not with the Castilian but only with other Tagalog lines; similarly, Castilian is made to rhyme only with itself. In listening to the *auit,* one hears two languages separated by a regular rhythmic interval, so that the sound of Tagalog is counterpointed by that of Castilian. Tagalog is brought into association with Castilian to the extent that both are subordinated to the same acoustic beat. That is, both vernaculars are made to refer neither to a master language such as Latin nor to a single message such as the promise of salvation, but to the persistence of rhythm and rhyme.

By the same token, the rhythmic correspondence between the two languages is not always coincident with a semantic one. Indeed, the meaning of a Castilian line is often linked only tenuously to that of the Tagalog line that precedes it. Acoustic consonance, then, is privi-

9. Lumbera, "Tagalog Poetry," p. 119.

leged over semantic fit. In the first three lines of the *auit* above, for example, the Tagalog *toua* (joy) is rendered as Castilian *holgarme* (to disport oneself, to make merry); *hapot, omaga* (afternoon and morning) is inverted as *mañana y tarde* (morning and afternoon); and *napahamac* (to come into danger) becomes *en balde* (in vain, to no purpose). The result of eliding strict semantic correspondences between the last words of the two languages, however, is the occurrence of a consistent rhyme in Castilian: *holgarme, tarde, en balde.* The same holds true for line 10. The Tagalog *baliu* (crazy) is strangely rendered as *brutos salvages* (savage brutes). This semantic drift is then productive of an acoustic fit between *salvages* and the dominant *e* rhyme of the preceding nine lines. In fact, this same pattern may be discerned in many of the other lines in Pinpin's songs. Again, the relationship between Tagalog and Castilian is cast in terms other than those obtaining in the Spanish notion of translation. It appears that by eliding a more exacting "fit" between signifieds in favor of producing regular acoustic correspondences between lines, Pinpin brings the two languages together in what we may call a relation of syncopation.

The *Oxford English Dictionary* defines *syncopation* in this sense as the "contraction of a word by omission of one or more syllables or letters in the middle"; in music it is "the action of beginning a note on a normally unaccented part so as to produce the effect of shifting back or anticipating the accent." In Pinpin's song, the semantic progression of Tagalog is repeatedly contracted by the recurrence of what to non-*ladino* Tagalogs would have been largely incomprehensible though rhythmically predictable Castilian lines. It is as if the punctual insertion of the sound of a second language acts to interrupt momentarily the sense of the first. Cut up and suspended periodically from final completion, the Tagalog creates an opening for the appearance of Castilian. Castilian is made to occur in the interval—the *loob* or *laman*—between fragments of Tagalog. The *auit* thus raises the possibility of hearing in one's own language the recurrence of a foreign one. Through the *auit,* the return of Castilian is set within a regular pattern. Hence listeners attend to the song in a condition of expectation—*nagaabang* (waiting, expecting), as Pinpin puts it. They are led to anticipate the reiteration of Castilian on the basis of the spacing provided by the Tagalog.

Conversely, recognition of the sounds of Castilian brings native listeners to the next line in Tagalog. From there, they can then look forward to the occurrence of yet another set of rhymes in Castilian. Hearing the *auit,* one is constrained to shift between the sense of one language and the sound of another. On the one hand, the rhyming sounds of Castilian reproduce a kind of percussive effect tangentially related to the message of the song. On the other hand, the regular recurrence of the familiar Tagalog words provides listeners with a sense of relief from the task of anticipating the resurgence of the unfamiliar Castilian words. In this way, native listeners habituate themselves to the sound of a language other than their own and can then recognize Castilian as that which results when the sense of Tagalog is deferred.

The structure of the *auit* thus suggests a mode of translation distinct from that of the Spaniards. Pinpin's song indicates that the comprehension of a foreign language was predicated neither on its reduction to a grammar wholly external to it (such as Latin or the Word of God) nor on its semantic continuity with one's own language. Instead, the possibility of translation was based on one's capacity to anticipate the serial displacement of one's first language by a second, and concurrently to see in the acoustic recurrence of the second the possibility of crossing back to the first. Castilian was thereby reconceptualized: it was no longer merely a jumble of incomprehensible and unknowable sounds that threatened to overwhelm the native listener but a series of ordered sounds in the *auit.* This is why the song could be a source of pleasure. Castilian could, like Tagalog, be subjected to the special fit of rhythm and rhyme; its apprehension did not after all depend, as the Spaniards seemed to think, on the fixing of semantic effects.

Rendered into a series of ordered sounds, Castilian is made to act as a syncope of Tagalog. In interrupting Tagalog, it produces a series of mild shocks. The appearance of Castilian mimes in benign form the appearance of its original speakers. The *auit* draws attention to Castilian as the trace of something from the outside which seems to have no immediately recognizable place in the "inside" of one's own language. Hearing Castilian, one is thus reminded of that which does not belong and is alien to Tagalog but nonetheless insists on lodging itself there. But by casting Castilian into a set of ordered sounds, the *auit* also raises the possibility of translating this insistence into a set of "shock effects," that is, into the signals with which to anticipate the dangers of its source. In this way, Castilian is given a place in Tagalog discourse: as something that can be recognized apart from Tagalog, that signals the appearance of the figures of colonial authority, and that can be appropriated so that one may respond to their demands. Perhaps this is why Pinpin constantly warns the Tagalogs in the latter sections of his book of the perils of learning Castilian, stressing the physical arduousness involved in its acquisition. But by the same token, the shock value of Castilian gave it its privileged place in the realm of Spanish signs. By exposing themselves to the hazards of Castilian, natives could immunize themselves against those real shocks that might come at any moment from the Spanish priest, official, or soldier. More, they could carry on an exchange with the authority figures in a way that would not impinge directly on them as speaking subjects, just as the Tagalog lines of the *auit* elude the pull of direct semantic correspondence with the Castilian.

Hence if a Tagalog notion of translation could be said to exist in Pinpin's song, it is one that is determined by, to borrow a term from Walter Benjamin, a "principle of interruption."[10] Translation in this sense is not designed to coincide with ritual in that it is not meant to recall the promise of speaking a purely transparent language. Rather, it is meant to alert and habituate the natives to the interruptive effects of Castilian. Tagalogs such as Pinpin would thus have at their disposal a way of inoculating themselves against the larger shock of conquest. By interspersing Spanish sounds as discrete fragments among the Tagalog words, the *auit* made available a way of signaling the potentially dangerous intrusion of an outside force. By doing so, it posited a position where natives could protect themselves against the threat of being engulfed by a flood of unreadable signs.

Thus the implicit politics of the *auit:* it furnished the Tagalogs with a mode of resisting, in however local a fashion, the insistent pressures from above. By giving what looked like enthusiastic assent to the phonetic script and to the Castilian language, Tagalogs such as Pinpin

10. See Benjamin's essays "What Is Epic Theatre?," "On Some Motifs in Baudelaire," and the classic "Work of Art in the Age of Mechanical Reproduction," all in *Illuminations*, ed. Hannah Arendt, trans. Harry Zohn (New York: Schocken, 1969).

could at the same time circumvent the hierarchizing force that the signifying conventions of colonial Christian authority sought to impose on them.

Counting and the Evasion of Grammar

The evasion of the force of Spanish signification in Pinpin's *auit* is complemented by the setting aside of grammar in the *aral* or lessons that follow. These *aral* are divided into nine chapters or *cabanata*. Five *cabanata* are irregularly divided into a series of five to nine *aral* each. The *auit* are similarly spread out: four in the third chapter, one each in the fourth and fifth chapters.

Again a cursory comparison of these *cabanata* and *aral* with the chapters and lessons of the Spanish *artes* is instructive. Unlike the chapters of the *artes,* which bear such explanatory headings as "*De las declinaciones de los nombres*" and "*Pronombres primitivos,*" each *cabanata* or *aral* is assigned only a number: "The first *cabanata,*" "The second *aral,*" and so forth. One gets no sense of progressing from elementary to more complex lessons, as each section proceeds in random fashion. The reason may lie partly in the meaning of the word *cabanata.* The mid-eighteenth-century *vocabulario* of Noceda and Sanlucar defines *cabanata* as a chapter (*capítulo*) in a book; but it also denotes a frame for catching fish (*un armazón de pescar*). In the early seventeenth century, when Pinpin's work was published and printed books were still relative novelties to the natives of the archipelago, there was thus a latent sense that a *cabanata* served as a kind of device for trapping Spanish words the way a frame was used for catching fish. Learning Castilian, like fishing, then involved skill and patience, as one had to stand poised for those random moments when Spanish signifiers flashed forth from the stream of each chapter's discourse.

The first chapter of the *Librong* is the longest, running some fifteen pages. Curiously, it displays no concern for the basic divisions of Spanish grammar. Pinpin prefers to begin, instead, with numbers:

> Dito sa unang cabanata, isisilid co ang manga pagbilang nang dilan bilang na, munti, t, marami; ang sa pilac at ang sa dilan tinatacal: at an siya ngang naiibig ninyong pagaralan. [Pp. 148–149]

Here in this first chapter, I will insert the numbers for counting everything, be it little or a lot; for silver and for everything measurable: for this is what you love to study.

Why does Pinpin begin with counting? The immediate reason seems to be that this is what his readers "love to study." The first lesson proceeds to enumerate the Tagalog numbers and their Spanish equivalents:

Isa, uno; dalaua, dos; tatlo, tres; . . . Maycaliman isa, cuarenta y uno. Ang ibang isusunod dito ay ualang liuag; yayamang manga camucha din nitong sinabi ngayong pagbubuhat nang pagtuturing nang bilang hangan sa limang puuo, cincuenta; anim na puuo, sesenta. . . .

Saca naman labi sandaan isa, ciento y uno; labi sandaan dalaua, ciento y dos; at gayon nang gayon, mapanibagong tumuring ninyo na unang bilang at idagdag sa ciento.   [P. 149]

One, *uno;* two, *dos;* three, *tres;* . . . Forty-one, *cuarenta y uno.* The others that follow are not difficult, as they are similar to those that have already been mentioned regarding the marking of numbers up to fifty, *cincuenta*, sixty, *sesenta.* . . .

Also one hundred and one, *ciento y uno;* one hundred and two, *ciento y dos;* and so on and so forth, just remember the numbers mentioned and add them to *ciento.*

As we have seen, the Spanish *artes* always began with the classification of nouns, pronouns, verbs, and so on. Numbers were such a minor concern in the learning of Tagalog that they were usually relegated to the last section of the missionaries' works. Pinpin's decision to begin with numbers suggests that the Tagalogs' conception of the place of counting in language differed from that of the Spaniards.

The recounting (*saysay*) of something—here the Castilian language—in terms of numbers has the effect of avoiding reference to the mechanism—Spanish grammar—which constitutes it, for a number has no intrinsic content: "four" is "four" because it is neither "five" nor "three." It is this highly arbitrary character of number signifiers in any language that gives them the aspect of pure externality. In the context of everyday discourse, the appearance of a number normally raises the expectation that there is something beyond it to which it refers. In Pinpin's case, however, one number in

Tagalog is followed by its equivalent in Castilian, in a potentially infinite running on of a numerical series on two linguistic registers. The numbers point to nothing beyond themselves.

The running on of numbers is further stretched out by Pinpin's insistence on the specification of quantities:

> Datapouat con di matanto ang calalabhan sa sangdaan, ay ang uica,y, mas de ciento . . . . Datapouat con matatanto na munti ang cahigitan sa balang namang bilang ay ang uica. Poco mas de veinte, poco mas de ciento. . . . At con maalaman baga na munti na ang caculangan doon sa bilang ay an uica. Cerca de diez, cerca de ciento, cerca de quinientos. . . . At gayon caya poco menos de doscientos, etc. . . . At ito cayang uican casi. Con baga cincuenta, casi ciento, casi mil, siyarin cerca de ciento, cerca de mil; con ibig ninyong pacatibayin ang uica, na dili rin lumalo doon sa bilang na yaon, ay gayon ang uicain. Iisa lamang, uno solo, uno solamente. Iisa isa lamang, tan solamente uno, uno solo y no mas. Daralana, dos solamente; daraladalana, dos solamente que no pasan de ahi; tatatlotatlo lamang, tan solamente tres y de ninguna manera mas. Hindi lomalo, hindi comolang, ni faltan ni sobran de alli. . . .   [P. 150]

> If it cannot be ascertained how much more than one hundred, one says *mas de ciento* . . . . And if it can be seen that there is a slight excess in the amount being counted, one says: *Poco mas de veinte* [a little more than twenty], *poco mas de ciento* [a little more than one hundred]. . . . And if it can be known that the amount being counted is slightly less, one says: *cerca de diez* [about ten], *cerca de ciento* [about a hundred], *cerca de quinientos* [about five hundred]. . . . And also *poco menos de doscientos* [a little less than two hundred], etc. . . . And this word *casi* [almost]: With *cincuenta* [fifty], *casi ciento* [almost a hundred], *casi mil* [almost a thousand], which is the same as *cerca de ciento* [nearly a hundred], *cerca de mil* [nearly a thousand]; if you want to determine the number so that it does not exceed what you are counting, you can say: Only one, *tan solamente uno, uno solo y no mas.* Only two, *dos solamente;* two and only two, *dos solamente que no pasan de ahi;* only three, *tan solamente tres y de ninguna manera mas.* No more, no less, *ni faltan ni sobran de alli.* . . .

The Tagalog propensity for numerical specification had been noted by various Spanish writers of *artes.* Yet, despite the concern for specifying quantities, nothing in either Pinpin's *Librong* or the Spanish *artes* indicates the presence of an arithmetical system for summing up quantitative relations. In fact, Gaspar de San Agustín's 1703 *arte* states that Tagalogs were not arithmetically inclined (*"los Tagalos son pocos aritméticos . . . en el contar, son varios y malos aritméticos"*).[11] This absence of arithmetic can be seen if we turn back to Pinpin's *aral*. In lieu of an arithmetical system for specifying quantitative relations, Pinpin inserts [*isisilid*] Spanish words that indicate the "more or less" quantity of whatever it is that is being counted. There is a sense, then, in which the heightened fascination with the determinativeness of quantities is in inverse proportion to the specification of anything beyond numbers. Throughout his section on numbers, Pinpin is far more concerned with the listing of the number signifiers themselves. Only rarely does he give examples to illustrate the use of these numbers; and when he does, the examples tend to underscore the Tagalog investment in numbers:

> Yaon namang uicang yaon (que), pagmamacalauahan co yaon, dos veces mas que el; at turan con ano yaong gauang inilalo. Pinagmamaicatlohan ni Pedro si Juan nang dunong; sabe mas Pedro tres veces que Juan. Pinagmamacaapatan cata nang pagcain, como yo cuatro veces mas que tu; Pinagmamacailanan nang langit ang lupa nang laqui? Cuantas veces es mayor el cielo, que la tierra? Pinagmamacapopouan, diez veces mas. Dalaouang ganganito: dos veces mas que esto. Sang puuo pang gaito nang laqui: diez veces mas grande que esto.   [P. 154]

> That word there (*que*) I have twice more than that, *dos veces mas que el;* and it refers to what it is that is in excess. Pedro is three times more learned than Juan; *sabe mas Pedro tres veces que Juan.* I eat four times more than you do, *como yo cuatro veces mas que tu;* How much bigger is heaven than earth? *Cuantas veces es mayor el cielo, que la tierra?* Ten times more, *diez veces mas.* Two more than this: *dos veces mas que esto.* Ten times bigger than this: *diez veces mas grande que esto.*

Such examples of Tagalog counting appear also, with slight variations, in the *artes'* sections on numbers. We may infer, then, that for Tagalogs an important way of indicating the quality of something is to refer to quantity. The absence of arithmetic allows for the ready conversion of quality to quantity. The process is further facilitated by

11. San Agustín, *Compendio* (Manila, 1703), pp. 133, 136.

the Tagalog tendency to use numbers not simply as "adjectives" but as "verbs" and "nouns" as well, as in *Tinatlo co ang saguing,* literally, "I threed the banana," *Bigay sa akin ay tatlo,* "I was given three," and *Tatlong tao ang dumating,* "Three people arrived." It should also be noted that before the arrival of the Spaniards, the Tagalogs did not have a system of numerical notation with which to abbreviate quantity. The coming of the Spaniards thus tripled the possibilities for denoting numbers. Aside from Tagalog signifiers, Spanish numbers in romanized script and arabic and roman numerals brought in by the Spaniards were now also available to the native enterprising enough to learn Castilian or at least phonetic writing. Castilian along with phonetic writing promoted the opportunities for counting, while the absence of arithmetic as an organizing principle of quantification made the prospect of learning Spanish numbers into a process of indefinite counting.

The sheer enumeration of quantities meant that one could speak Castilian without having to sum up the totality of one's intentions. Counting alone tends to elude the pressures attendant upon learning grammar as much as it eliminates the need to subordinate the meaning of one's discourse to the terms of the other's. Translating Tagalog into Castilian in this section then becomes only a question of marking numerical differences rather than seeing in the second language a quality that is missing from the first. Just as the *auit* reorders both languages in terms of a rhythmic pattern, counting establishes equivalences between Tagalog and Castilian in relation to a numerical series that avoids reference to something else outside of it.

The pleasure that the Tagalogs derived from this process had to do with their interest in acquiring fragments of Castilian that did not require them to give up the self that spoke Tagalog. In learning Castilian numbers, one gave up only their equivalents in Tagalog. One could then keep on counting without the worry of following the rules of grammar or conforming one's intentions to those of the other. For to the extent that whatever was being signified could be deferred in favor of extending the means for signifying them—that is, numbers— the self that counted could distance itself from the thought of having to be accountable to someone else. In Pinpin's *Librong,* translation tended to relieve one of the need to distinguish between the counting subject and the counted object. Given the absence of arithmetic, the extended treatment accorded to numbers allowed for the substitution of one language for another while suspending the necessity of acknowledging their qualitative differences, that is, the sense that Castilian could say what Tagalog could not. Thus counting loosened the linguistic hierarchy that the Spaniards sought to impose on the natives.

Such is of special importance where the language of authority is concerned. The focus on numbers allows the native to acquire fragments of Castilian while simultaneously eluding its grammatical and political constraints. The reader's/listener's dealings with the language of authority is kept from being an antagonistic confrontation so long as one's attention is deflected to numbers. For had it been otherwise, the learning of Spanish would have called for a self that in apprehending the language of the other would have sought to master it as well. Instead we see the drawn-out "love" for numbers which made the question of fluency irrelevant, for grammatical and arithmetical considerations had been brushed aside. In this *cabanata,* the self that "fishes" faces Spanish only randomly.

Gambling on Castilian

Within a colonial context, attempts to elude the full weight of linguistic hierarchy constitute one important moment in the practice of Tagalog translation. The wish to appropriate Castilian in terms of an *auit* or through counting is never fully realized, however, to the extent that such a wish can emerge only in relation to a prior anxiety—in this case, the possibility of being overwhelmed by Spanish words that one cannot recognize, much less appropriate. It is in this light that the fascination with numbers tends to give way to another concern over the meaning (*cahulugan*) of Castilian words. The "enjoyment" attached to the accumulation of foreign signifiers is countered by the imperative to take into account their corresponding signifieds. It is during these moments that Pinpin seems to be deferring to Spanish signifying conventions and the hierarchy of voice/writing that they imply. In such cases, we can sense not only the pressure of Castilian words but the entire conceptual machinery of Spanish translation insinuating itself into Pinpin's lessons. Pinpin begins the second chapter, for instance, by trying to explain the peculiarities of Castilian phonetics:

Hindi magaling na itoloy co itong aral cong ito cundi comona cayo aralan manga capoua co Tagalog nang pagturing nang ibang letrang di natin tinotoran torang dati, at ang uala nga sa uica nating tagalog bago siyang maralas sa uicang Castila; ay maliuag mang maturan nang di dating namimihasa. Ay maliuag man ay mapagaaralan din ninyo con pagpilitan. Aba tayo na, at tandaan itong manga mahal na aral.   [Pp. 162–163]

It is not good that I continue this lesson of mine if I do not first teach you, my fellow Tagalogs, how to recognize and remember other letters that we are not accustomed to recognizing and remembering, and that are absent from our Tagalog language, but that are often used in Castilian; and that are difficult to recognize for one who is not used to them. Though they are difficult, you can learn them well if you force yourself. Well, then, let's get on, and mark out these valuable lessons.

The appropriation of Castilian, according to Pinpin, would be useless if one could not recognize (*torin*) those letters peculiar to Castilian but absent from Tagalog. Learning these letters involves a certain amount of difficulty, requires one to "force" oneself. Pinpin repeatedly writes about the need to "forcibly twist the tongue," "lower the teeth on the lip," "round off the mouth," and "gather the lips together," depending on the phoneme that is to be pronounced (pp. 163–166). Such effort is necessary because, "if the recognition of these letters is different, then so are their meanings in Castilian" ("*capag nagcaiba ang pagtoring nang manga letra, ay nagcacaiba naman ang manga uican yaong Castila at ang cahologan nila*" [p. 163]).

Yet the imperative to attend to the connection between Castilian phonemes and their signifying function goes beyond purely semantic considerations. For the danger involved in the mispronunciation and misapprehension of Spanish words stems from a real physical threat—that of incurring the laughter of the Spaniard with whom one speaks:

Dili nga matouid at tatauanang lubha nang Castila iton uica bueno casa es esto, cundi buena casa es esta. . . .

Ay ano mangyari cayang di tauanan iton uicang mucha palabras, at ito caya casa grandes at iba pang gaganito; at con pagpalitan caya, muchas palabras; casas grandes. . . .   [Pp. 171, 167]

It is indeed wrong, and the Spaniards will laugh a great deal at this statement, *bueno casa es esto,* which should be *buena casa es esta* [this is a good house]. . . .

Well, what else but laughter will meet this statement, *mucha palabras,* and this one, *casa grandes,* and others of this sort; and it should be changed to *muchas palabras* [many words] and *casas grandes* [big houses]. . . .

There is always a risk, then, that in return for the words one produces one will receive only laughter. And to get back laughter from above is to be deluged by a series of undecipherable signs that cut one off from further discursive exchange. In the passage above, translation comes across as a question of voice guarding over the transmission of sense, therefore closing the gap between word and referent. The turn to this notion of voice is a response to the prospect of incurring a severe loss on one's previous investments: the risk that instead of acquiring more words, one will end up with the ominous, scornful laughter of the Spanish interlocutor. This occasional attention to meaning is thus sanctioned by the fear of feeling the full weight of the colonial hierarchy implicit in Castilian, which in this example is figured as the laughter of the Spaniard. In other sections of the *Librong,* the failure of translation is imaged as a series of violent blows (*sontoc*) visited upon the native's body (pp. 200–203). Unable to anticipate Castilian, one is shocked out of speech altogether. Conversely, the ability to connect signifier with signified by voicing the appropriate Castilian forms allows one to occupy a position from which to carry out a return that will placate the person above and ensure a subsequent semiotic profit to the one below. Linguistic transactions of this sort require the marking out and remembrance (*toring*) of the phonetic distinctions in Castilian, so that the spoken words will "fall" (*holog,* to fall, is the root word of *cahologan,* to signify, to mean) into their proper referents.

But this concern for marking out Castilian phonemes in terms of their function to modify the meaning of any given word is not sustained. In the succeeding chapters, the logic of translation inscribed in the *auit* and in counting reemerges. The remaining *cabanata* shift their concern to re-marking Castilian affixes, which indicate noun gender, the augmentative and diminutive forms of nouns, and verb tenses, among other things. While these sections' stress on the remembrance of affixes does not altogether overshadow concern for the meanings of words, it does relegate that concern to the margins of the *aral*.

Pinpin's work never refers to Castilian in terms of "nouns," "verbs," "adjectives," or "cases." Just as he had earlier focused on the numerical series of Castilian without referring to their arithmetical formulation, Pinpin highlights affixes themselves while avoiding reference to a grammatical or syntactical schema. We can observe this process in several places in the *Librong*. With regard to gender distinction, for example, Pinpin writes:

> Maliuag mang saysaying itong iaaral co ngayon ay acquing pagpipilitan ding saysayin; opang mamalay malayan ninyo munti man. . . . Con lalaqui ang tinotoran nang Castila ay o nang o ang idinodolo at con babayi ay a nang a, caya nga ang manga ngalan nang manga babayi ay manga dorolohan nang a, Maria, Catalina, Lucia . . . at con cahi mat ngalan nang Santong lalaqui and ipangangalan sa babayi, at cahima,t, o ang dating dulo ay hinahalinhan din nang a, di baquin itong ngalang Francisco, ay con sa babayi itapat ay hindi na Francisco condi Francisca. . . .
>
> At dili sa manga ngalan lamang nang manga tauong manga lalaqui at nang babayi natatapat iton aral condi sa iba pa mang sinasabi, ay yaong uicang itinatapat sa caniya ay nadorolohan din nang o at con babayi ang sinasabi ay a, ang carolohan. . . . Si Pedro ay masama, Pedro es malo, ay con babayi, mala, si Ana ay masama, Ana es mala. . . .   [P. 168]

Difficult as it is to speak about this lesson, I will force myself to speak about it so that you may take note of it, even if only a little. . . . If it is a man that is being referred to in Castilian, *o* and only *o* is placed at the end [of the word] and if it's a woman, *a* and only *a;* that's why the names of women end with *a,* Maria, Catalina, Lucia . . . and even when names of male saints are used to name a woman, and even if these names end in *o,* they are replaced by *a* so that Francisco if it be given to a woman is no longer Francisco but Francisca. . . .

And is not this lesson applicable as well not only to the names of male and female persons but also to other things that are said of males and females? So that for words referring to males, one says them with an *o* at the end, and when referring to females, with an *a* at the end. . . . Pedro is bad, *Pedro es malo,* and with a woman, *mala,* Ana is bad, *Ana es mala.* . . .

And with regard to the first person plural, present indicative, he writes:

Manga caibang lubha ang tutungcol sa gauang guinagaua nang dalaua catauo at nang marami caya sa dalaua. Cayanga ang gaua nang dalauang catauo at ang marami caya sa dalaua ang sinasabi ay sila din at ang isa caya sa canila ang nangongosap niyon ay ang idorolo sa uicang yaong Castila ay amos, at emos caya. Ang manga dati ding uica ang ipaghalimbaua co. Anong gaua ninyo? Que haceis? Cami ay coma-cain, Comemos, tinatahi namin itong damit, cosemos esto vistido, nagiinom, bebemos . . . at minsan minsan namang hindi amos at handi emos ang dulo condi imos; cami naparito, nosotros venimos aqui. . . . Anopa,t, di cayanga an uica nating manga Tagalog ay cami at tayo caya ay yaong gauang sinasabing guinagaua namin at natin caya ay con sa Castila saysayin ay hindi sasala na di ang idorolo ay ang isa dito sa tatlo con amos caya, at con emos caya, at con imos caya. . . .   [P. 182]

There are important differences that exist with words that refer to the actions carried out by two or more people. That is why, when the actions of two or more people are spoken by either all or one of them, then the ending that is placed [on the word] in Castilian is *amos*, or *emos*. I will give a few examples. What are you doing? *Que haceis?* We are eating, *Comemos*, We are sewing this dress, *Cosemos esto vestido*, We are drinking, *Bebemos* . . . and other times, it is not *amos* and it is not *emos* that is placed at the end [of the word] but *imos*; We come here, *Nosotros venimos aqui*. . . . That is why in our Tagalog language, *cami* and *tayo* are used to refer to the actions performed by *namin* and *natin* [us] so that when they are said in Castilian, one cannot go wrong if one appends at the end of the word one of these three, either *amos* or *emos* or *imos*. . . .

As these passages show, for Pinpin the acquisition of Castilian requires one to note the various affixes that can be pinned to Spanish words. It is as if the learning of Castilian involved the play of detach-able and reattachable signifiers—*a, o, emos, amos, imos*—which by themselves signify nothing. In this procedure the *Librong* is in marked contrast to the Spanish *artes*. The *artes* classify the parts of Tagalog in terms of Latin grammar and Castilian discourse. The Tagalog alter-native might have been to use Tagalog terms to delineate the parts of Castilian. But Pinpin never makes such a move.

The absence of a Tagalog classificatory scheme for designating the grammatical machinery of the local language is not unique to the early seventeenth century. Not until the 1930s, during the Commonwealth regime, did an autonomous system of grammatical classification come into use, under the sponsorship of the Institute of National Language, a government agency bent on installing Tagalog as the basis for the emergent national language, Pilipino. From the late nineteenth century till then, Westernized Tagalog scholars had drawn on the classificatory schema that had been worked out by the missionaries of earlier centuries. But Pinpin's *Librong* not only conspicuously lacks a system of classifying the parts of Castilian in Tagalog terms but has no recourse to the organizing grid of Castilian itself. Instead it highlights the signifiers that, like numbers, are arbitrarily added to or subtracted from a word, enabling it to circulate in a chain of discursive exchanges between colonized and colonizer. Pinpin then enjoins the Tagalog reader to remember these marks, cautioning them to "set aside enough reserve so that one can keep supplying the necessary effort [to learn Castilian], lest it fall short" ("*mag palaan cayo nang bait at con ga mangyaring daragdagan ay dagragan din at maca colangin*"; p. 181).

What is the nature of the reserve and the mode of expenditure to which Pinpin refers? If we reread Pinpin's explanation of the first person plural, we note that the Spanish endings *amos, emos,* and *imos* rather than the Spanish pronoun *nosotros* (we) are equated with the Tagalog pronouns *cami* and *tayo*. The *cami/tayo* pair in Tagalog denotes a sense of "we" but in a somewhat oblique fashion. One of the characteristics that Tagalog shares with most other Malayo-Polynesian languages is the use of two pronouns to denote "we." One of them, *cami,* has been referred to by present-day linguists as the "first person plural exclusive."[12] *Cami* differs from the Spanish *nosotros* and English "we" in that it functions not to indicate a sense of shared subjectivity between speaker and listener but to exclude a third term in a given communicative exchange. It is on the basis of that exclusion that a sense of "we" arises from *cami*. When a Tagalog says, "Tagalog cami," "We are Tagalogs," the speaker's sense of belonging to the category "Tagalog" arises from having excluded the person addressed. "We" in the sense of *cami* therefore differentiates the person speaking from the person spoken to. *Tayo,* on the other hand, is often

12. Paul Schachter and Fe T. Otañes, *Tagalog Reference Grammar* (Berkeley: University of California Press, 1972), pp. 88–90.

referred to in the Spanish *artes* as closest to *nosotros,* as in "Cristiano tayo," "We are Christians," where both speaker and listener are subsumed in the category "Christian." When *tayo* is repeated (*tayo-tayo*), however, it shades off into the same meaning as *cami.* Hence even the so-called inclusive form of the first person plural can designate a "we" that arises from exclusion of a third party. There is then a significant gap between the Spanish *nosotros* and the Tagalog *cami/tayo,* in that in the latter case, the speaking subjects do not necessarily seek to include and thus speak on behalf of the person they address.

This detour into the Tagalog pronouns for the first person plural gives us a perspective from which to understand Pinpin's strategy for dealing with Castilian verbs. He does not bring up the problematic gap between the Spanish *nosotros* and the Tagalog *cami/tayo,* as the missionaries were wont to do. Furthermore, in talking about the appropriate forms of Castilian verbs to be used, Pinpin refers neither to their infinitive forms nor to the subject and case on which they are predicated. He seizes instead on the endings that are to be used in association with other word endings.

Pinpin talks, for example, about the endings for the second person plural (*ais, eis, is*) in relation to those for the first person plural (*amos, emos, imos*) and the third person plural (*an, en*) in the following way:

Datapoua,t, con may pinaquiquiusapan ang taou at dili iisang tauo lamang yaong causap niya cundi dalaua at marami caya sa dalaua, ay ang idorolo doon sa uicang yaon ay *ais* at *eis* caya. Congmacain cayo, comeis, nininom, bebeis . . . anong binibili ninyo, que comprais . . . anong uica ninyo, que hablais. . . . At maminsan minsan hindi *ais* at hindi *eis* ang dulo cundi *is* lamang . . . ilang cayong napadirito, cuantos venis . . . ay at nag lilingcod cayo sa Castila, porque servis al español . . . caya nga *imos* ang dulo, con tayo at cami caya ang uica maguiguin *is,* ang dulo, con iban manga tauo ang pinaquiquiusapan, at caya naman *amos* ang dulo con tayo at cami, caya ang uica ay maguiguin *eis* ang dulo con ibang tauo ang pinaquiquiusapan; datapoua,t, ang gaua gaua nang ibang manga taou di pinaquiquiusapan ang sinasabi ay alin alin man dito sa manga dulong ito,y, hindi natatapat, cundi *an,* at *en* caya . . . aba dili ang catongo nang *amos* ay ang *ais* at ang *an,* at ang casama nang *emos* ay dili ang *eis* at *en* at ang catapat nang *imos* ay dili ang *is* at ang *en* naman, inyo ngang pagpacasicapang pagaralan ito, cundi ang galing. [Pp. 183–184]

But when one is speaking to not one and only one person but to two
and even more than two, then what should be placed at the end of the
word is *ais* or *eis*. You are eating, *comeis*, drinking, *bebeis* . . . what are
you buying, *que comprais* . . . what are you saying, *que hablais*. . . .
And sometimes it is not *ais* and not *eis* that is placed at the end but
instead only *is* . . . how many of you came, *cuantos venis* . . . why do
you serve the Spaniard, *porque servis al español* . . . that is why *imos* is
at the end for *tayo* and *cami*, just as the word will end in *is* when one is
speaking to other people; and that is why *amos* is at the end for *tayo*
and *cami*, just as the word will end with *ais* when one is speaking to
other people; however, the actions of other people that one does not
speak to directly are said not with any of these endings, but with those
of *an* and *en* instead . . . well, then, the partner of *amos* is then *ais* and
an, and the companion of *emos* is none other than *eis* and *en*, and that
which faces *imos* is none other than *is* and *en*; you should try your best
to learn all this, for it would be terrific.

Pinpin proceeds by establishing a series of associative links: on the
one hand, between *amos, emos,* and *imos* with reference to *cami/tayo*
in Tagalog; on the other hand, between *amos, emos,* and *imos* with
reference to *ais, eis,* and *is,* the verb endings for the second person
plural. He then differentiates between these pairs of verb endings and
those that are used to indicate the third person plural indicative, *an*
and *en*. But in choosing not to coordinate these verb endings with
their appropriate pronominal subjects, he filters out the grammatical
opposition between subject and predicate. Instead he associates verb
endings in such a way that the appearance of one set elicits or refers
back to another set. Evading the transformational logic of Spanish
grammar, marginalizing the pronominal subject in Spanish, ignoring
the infinitive forms of verbs, Pinpin launches into a matching game,
pairing off affixes. Remembering the meaning of a verb is then a
matter of associating or matching one set of endings with another. It
is this ability to acquire Castilian while eluding its grammatical machinery and the subject or source of the utterance that makes the
language of authority "terrific" to learn.

Pinpin lays stress on a set of Spanish affixes which refer back to
each other, as in a series. Learning to speak Castilian then becomes a
process of trial and error, in which the meanings of words (and hence
their exchange value in a communicative act) are determined by systematic speculation on the correspondence of their endings. Such

speculation in turn is based not on the infinitive form of the verb or on a table of tenses and pronouns but on the place one occupies in a given communicative act: if one were to speak in the mode of *tayo* or *cami,* one would use *amos, emos,* and *imos;* if one were speaking of others, *en* and *an;* if one spoke with and to others, *eis, ais, is.* One's response in Castilian would then be in accordance with the verb ending one heard: for *eis,* one responds with the ending *emos;* for *ais, amos;* and so forth.

This sort of speculation makes the labor of the *aral* akin to gambling. The Tagalog who attempts to speak Castilian is constantly betting on the odds given by Pinpin in the form of a set of possible word endings. The wish contained here is that Tagalog speakers will manage to use the right affix, that is, to connect a *dulo* or word ending suddenly heard to the appropriate *dulo* to use in response, and thus to avoid laughter or blows from above. One learns from Pinpin's lessons not the rules of Castilian grammar but the means for anticipating the combinatory possibilities of its affixes. Translation then proceeds as if by chance—which endings connect with which at any given moment?—rather than, as with the Spaniards, as a matter of systematic investment in articulating the ultimate Sign ruling over all other signs. The Tagalog faces language as a gambler confronts a game of chance, concerned not with a historically constituted past or a teleologically oriented future but with how much he or she stands to win or lose in a particular discursive match.[13] By highlighting this kind of confrontation with language, Pinpin's *aral* sets aside the authority figure in control of its words, just as it loosens the grip of grammar on the construction of speech. By following Pinpin's lead, one can increase the semiotic capital with which to deal with the Spanish authorities who may address one at any moment in Castilian.

The payoff of this *aral* comes in the form of an *auit.* The fact that translation works, that one can confront Castilian and manage to contain its potential for shock, becomes an occasion for celebration. The songs that are interspersed among the lessons make Castilian a source of pleasure as well as of protection. The person who becomes accustomed to Castilian can then begin to take delight in its use. At

13. On the nondialectical nature of gambling and the way it contrasts with the conservation of historical consciousness attendant upon nonmechanized labor (and by the same token, the way mechanized work, once dehistoricized, mimes gambling), see Benjamin, "On Some Motifs in Baudelaire," pp. 176–180.

the end of the *aral* that explains the *a* and *o* endings specifying noun gender, we read the following:

> At nang may icahalata cayo nitong manga aral cong ito ay aco,y, magdirito nang manga uicang Castila na ang iba ay o ang dolo at ang iba ay a, aquing pag babalquin, at gagaouin co nang auit Castila nang mamihasa cayong malogod sa Castilang auit.

Auit

> Ang tauo, el hombre, ang ulo,y, cabeza; ang utac, los sesos, ang tayinga, oreja; ang mata, los ojos, ang quilay, las cejas; ang ilong, narices, ang tanda, las pecas; ang bibig, la boca; ang dila, la lengua; ang labi, los labios; ang susu, las tetas; ang licod, la espalda, balacang, cadera; ang tuhod, rodilla, ang paa, las piernas, ang ngipin, el diente; ang bagang, la muela; ang camay, la mano; ang canan, la diestra, ang hita, el muslo, caliua, siniestra, ang galanggalangan ang ngolo,y, muñeca, ang palad, la palma, bayiqui, papera, ang bao, el casco, bonbonan, mollera, ang pigi,y, las nalgas, ang tae, la mierda, anopat di ang puit, la parte trasera, ang Bayan, el pueblo, ang bacod, la cerca, ang cuta, el fuerte, ang pinto, la puerta, ang malayo, ay lejos, ang malapit, cerca, ang panulat, pluma, ang sulat, la letra, ang bangbang, el foso, halamanan, huerta, ang parang, el campo, ang bondoc, la sierra, ang balon, el hoyo, ang pangpang, ribera, bilangoan, carcel, ang dusa, la pena, ay ang tanicala ang ngala,y, cadena, gab,y, na malinao, la noche serena, canlang ay tambor, calasag, rodela, at ang labin dalaua, son una docena.   [P. 169]

And so that you will take note of this lesson of mine, I will place here some Castilian words, some of which end in *o* and others in *a;* I will arrange it and make it into a Castilian song so that you will get used to enjoying Castilian songs.

Song

The man, *el hombre,* the head is *cabeza;* the brains, *los sesos,* the ear, *oreja;* the eyes, *los ojos,* the brows, *las cejas;* the nose, *narices,* freckles, *las pecas;* the mouth, *la boca,* the tongue, *la lengua;* the lips, *los labios;* the breasts, *las tetas;* the back, *la espalda,* hip, *cadera;* the knee, *rodilla,* the legs, *las piernas,* the tooth, *el diente;* the gum, *la muela;* the hand, *la mano,* the right, *la diestra,* the thigh, *el muslo,* the left, *siniestra,* the wrist and ankle, *muñeca,* the palm, *la palma,* mumps, *papera,* the skull, *el casco,* the pate, *mollera,* the buttocks are *las nalgas,* shit, *la mierda,* and the ass is what else but *la parte trasera,* the town, *el pueblo,* the fence, *la cerca,* the fort, *el fuerte,* the door, *la puerta,* what is far is *lejos,* near, *cerca,* a pen, *pluma,* the letter, *la letra,* the marsh, *el foso,* garden, *huerta,* the field, *el campo,* the mountain, *la sierra,* the well, *el hoyo,* riverbank, *ribera,* prison, *carcel,* punishment, *la pena,* and chains are called *cadena,* the night serene, *la noche serena,* a drum is *tambor,* shield, *rodela,* and a dozen, *son una docena.*

As Pinpin indicates, the purpose of the *auit* is to habituate the Tagalogs in taking pleasure (*logod*) in Castilian. In this particular song, he gathers together Spanish words, featuring those that end with the *a* and *o* sounds. In the process he free-associates along a stream of signifiers. He begins with a metonymic series—the parts of the body—which is broken up by shit attached to the buttocks. This image then gives rise to the juxtaposition of the words for "town" and "fence," "far" and "near," "pen" and "letter," interspersed with kinds of buildings and features of the landscape. The word for "riverbank" then wends its way to "jail," "punishment," and "chains"; then the sudden interpolation of "the night serene," "drums," "shield." It ends abruptly with a quantity, "a dozen." The metrical beat of this song is shorter (three syllables) than that of the song discussed earlier, so that one tends to scan the lines more rapidly—and all to the good, for only alternate Spanish words rhyme. A shorter beat allows for the same rhythmic flow as we find in the earlier *auit,* and consequently produces a similar shock effect attendant upon the appearance of similar-sounding Castilian words. Caught up in this acoustic regularity, one drifts, as it were, from word to word, borne by the expectation roused by the measured displacement of Tagalog and Castilian signifiers. Pinpin thus lavishes on his readers a collection of arbitrarily related words that are linked only acoustically. This device allows the reader to partake in the *frisson* created by the slippage of words, both Castilian and Tagalog, from their referents. It is therefore fitting that such a song should end with an empty signifier, "a dozen," and that it should immediately lead to two more *auit.* The *auit,* rather than illustrating a grammatical rule of Castilian, results in the displacement of that rule, fragmenting it in the gleeful celebration of sound. Whereas the *aral* had called for the body's investment in the arduous task of marking out and remembering the combinatory possibilities of Spanish affixes, the *auit* peel away from the labor of the lessons. In Pinpin's songs, the hierarchical distinction between the Tagalog and Castilian languages—a distinc-

tion that the missionaries' *artes* constantly invoked—is flattened out.
The perilous task of appropriating Castilian and keeping it in reserve
leads sporadically to the expenditure of language in songs. At the end
of the ninth and final chapter, Pinpin writes:

> Dunong aya ninyong lahat na mababait na manga tauo con itong lahat
> na manga sulat dito sa cabanatang ito ay macamtan ninyong maubos.
> Sucat na pala cayong mangahas magtipontipon ng manga uica uicang
> Castila at mangusap na nang mahahabang uica; caya yata nang may
> tonghan cayong nagaaralan at sampon tuloy catouaan ninyo ang in-
> yong carunungan, ay aco,y, susulat na ng isang auit. . . .   [P. 200]

> How learned all you good people will be if you can acquire everything
> that has been written down here in this chapter, and may you be able to
> exhaust it all. Then you will be prepared to dare to gather bits and
> pieces of Castilian words and to speak in long sentences; and so that
> you may have something further to study as well as take pleasure in
> your learning, I will write here an *auit*. . . .

By the early seventeenth century, Pinpin's *Librong* had taken its
place in a series of developments in the consolidation of Spanish rule
among the Tagalogs, among them the natives' considerable exposure
to Christian discourse and clerical authority, increasing exaction of
tribute and forced labor, and their recruitment to fight against other
groups in the archipelago, such as the Muslims and, in Pinpin's time,
the Dutch. Pinpin's statement may be read as a distinctly Tagalog
response to these pressures. It seems to embrace the signs of the
colonizers with enthusiasm, but that enthusiasm stops short of ac-
quiescence in total subjugation.

Pinpin expresses the hope that his Tagalog readers will be able to
exhaust (*maubos*) the *cabanata,* and by implication all that precedes
it in the book. This exhaustion is figured as the gathering (*magtipon-
tipon*) of bits and pieces of Castilian that can be strung together to
form "long sentences." But as the rest of the passage implies, the
project of forming "long sentences" is not geared to translation in the
Spanish sense of the word. Rather, it ends up, as it invariably did in
the previous sections of the book, in the pleasure of an *auit,* where the
self that sings, like the self that counts, reconstitutes itself as one that
is "somewhere else," borne away by the potentially interminable
expenditure of words, both Tagalog and Castilian.

The Tagalog response to Castilian thus differs considerably from that of the Spanish to the local language. The missionaries accorded language a value insofar as it could be used as a ritual prop for the conversion of the natives and the return of their souls to their proper owner, God. As we had occasion to see earlier, the Spaniards' belief in a hierarchy of languages had the effect of introducing into the history and culture of the Tagalogs a different kind of power relation. It was premised on the reading of signs, which, in subordinating signifier to signified, also privileged a dominant voice that could decipher and control the movement of writing. From the Spaniards' point of view, their language established them in a position of authority where they could arrogate to themselves the right to speak about and to the natives.

But for the Tagalogs, as Pinpin's *Librong* suggests, the appearance of Castilian triggered the desire for its fragmentary and random accumulation. "Castilian" in this case rendered problematic the historical distinction between ruler and ruled in the early period of colonization. While Castilian made apparent the Spaniards' power to move up and down the linguistic hierarchy, it could also be used— fished out or gambled on—by those in the lower ranks of the colonial hierarchy to evade the full force of the Spaniards' demands. Thus Pinpin's fascination with counting at the expense of grammar and arithmetic, his marginalization of meaning and referent in favor of acoustic fit, and his practice of fragmenting Spanish words by "betting" on the correspondences of affixes. Whether in the mode of syncopation, counting, or gambling, to translate was to acknowledge the hierarchical relationship between Castilian and Tagalog but in ways that undermined the missionaries' totalizing claims to political and linguistic authority. For to Pinpin and other Tagalogs, to understand Spanish was to be able to anticipate and thus defer to Castilian in the interest of warding off the threat of a violent and undecipherable return. And just as Pinpin's lessons underscore the value of the other's language as a source of protection, his songs take pleasure in the ability to recognize Castilian's translatability and thus celebrate the success of efforts to mark it off from Tagalog. Hence the plausability of reading in Pinpin's enthusiasm for Castilian the signs of resistance to its other political and linguistic constraints.

CHAPTER 3

Conversion and the Demands of Confession

To what extent do Spanish missionary ideas about translation help us to understand the process of evangelization and colonial subjugation? How indicative was Tomas Pinpin's book of a mode of Tagalog response to the Spanish presence, at least during the early period of colonial rule? Did other ideas about translation and the submission it entailed emerge among the Tagalogs? If so, when and under what conditions?

As we shall see, the contradictions inherent in translation came to the fore in the context of conversion and conquest. Similarly, the Tagalog translation of Castilian typified by Pinpin's book finds its correlate in the natives' seemingly avid yet "inadequate" conversion to Christianity, as the missionaries remarked again and again. Just as Pinpin's translation project grew out of a set of interests separate from those of clerical-colonial authorities, conversion among the Tagalogs was predicated on conventions of signification, exchange, and authority distinct from those of the missionaries. Hence, while translation was linked to conversion and submission among both Spaniards and Tagalogs, the structure and effects of that connection tended to vary between the two. The result was a colonial order that seemed to be premised on a mutual misreading of each other's intentions rather than on the unambiguous imposition of the ruler's will over the ruled.

The "Inadequacies" of Tagalog Conversion

"They readily receive our religion," asserts the Jesuit missionary Diego de Bobadilla in his 1640 account of the Tagalogs. Yet the sentences that immediately follow seem to be at odds with his claim: "Their meager intelligence does not permit them to sound the depths of its mysteries. They also have little care in the fulfillment of their duties to the Christianity they have adopted; and it is necessary to constrain them by fear of punishment and govern them like schoolchildren."[1] These remarks seem astonishingly contradictory, yet they are by no means unusual in a Spanish account of native conversion. More than a century later we find the following enthusiastic report of another Jesuit, Pedro Murillo Velarde, regarding the natives' zeal for confession:

> And at the season of Lent it is heartbreaking to see the confessor, when he rises from his seat, surrounded by more than a hundred persons . . . who go away disconsolate because they have not obtained an opportunity to make their confessions; and in this manner they go and come for eight or ten days, or a fortnight, or even more, with unspeakable patience, but with such eagerness that when the confessor rises they follow him throughout the house, calling to him to hear their confessions . . . and hardly with violence can they be made to leave the father and they continue to call after him and some remain in the passages, on their knees asking for confession, so great is the number of penitents.[2]

Yet the contents of the natives' confessions cause Murillo considerable befuddlement:

> No one save him who has had this experience can state the labors it costs to confess them; and even when the sin is understood in general, to seek for a specific account of circumstances is to enter into a labyrinth without a clue. For they do not understand our orderly mode of speech, and therefore when they are questioned they say "yes" or "no" as it occurs to them, without rightly understanding what is asked of them—so that in a short time they will utter twenty contradictions.[3]

Contradictions seem to have characterized conversion. By the first half of the seventeenth century the Spaniards had converted more than half a million Filipinos while maintaining fewer than three hun-

---

1. Diego de Bobadilla, S.J., "Relation of the Philippine Islands, 1640," in *Philippine Islands,* ed. Blair and Robertson, 45:295. (This 55-volume compilation of documents is hereafter cited as *BR.*)

2. Pedro Murillo Velarde, "Jesuit Missions in the Seventeenth Century" (Manila, 1749), in *BR,* 44:32.

3. Ibid., p. 30.

dred missionaries in the field and using far less military force than they had used in the New World.[4] Any reluctance on the part of the non-Islamicized lowland populace, particularly of the Tagalogs in the vicinity of Manila, seems to have been overcome rapidly. We see their acceptance reflected in the last section of Tomas Pinpin's book, where he offers them a confession manual. Written by the Dominican Blancas de San José, it consists of a long series of questions in Spanish and Tagalog which the priest was to ask the penitent to facilitate confession. Pinpin's remarks concerning this text give us a sense of the Tagalog enthusiasm for confession:

> Ah, and what I will write here will surely delight you, it is just that confession manual which was hidden from you in my opening letter at the beginning of this book; I put it here so that if you find no priest to whom you can confess in the Tagalog language, then you may know the priest's questions in Castilian. You should continuously study these questions of the priests; though they may not use them all up on one person; but you should know the way they like to ask questions of each and every person, and it will be up to them to observe the behavior of each and every one that confesses, and to decide which among these questions would be appropriate to ask each and every one. Esteem these valuable words . . . and do not make a joke of learning them. [Pp. 203–204]

Confession, then, is yet another occasion when one may be confronted by a Spaniard and find oneself with nothing to say. One is urged to "continuously study" the questions while leaving it up to the priest to determine which of them are to be asked. Nothing is said about the doctrinal content of these questions, nor does Pinpin give any indication what appropriate answers to such questions might be. Instead, Pinpin asks the Tagalogs to "esteem" the "valuable words" contained in the confession manual, just as earlier he asked his readers to treasure the Spanish words they had acquired. In both cases, the value of words lay in their perceived nature as objects of circulation and exchange with the Spanish father. Just as the acquisition of Castilian entailed for Pinpin the evasion of grammar and the syncopation of languages, the act of confession was a matter of anticipating questions to which a variety of responses—"yes," "no," or "twenty contradictions"—could be given. This is why Murillo Velarde calls hear-

4. Phelan, *Hispanization of the Philippines*, pp. 8–9, 56.

ing Tagalog confessions akin to "entering a labyrinth without a clue"; and why Bobadilla notes that though "they readily receive our religion," they remain incapable of—or perhaps resistant to— "sounding the depths of its mysteries." For it seems that for the Tagalogs, confession, the very epitome of Christian conversion, had little to do with comprehending the message of God by incorporating His Law.[5] Indeed, conversion occurred with astounding rapidity precisely because the majority of the people did not, from the Spanish point of view, seem to understand the faith they were accepting.

The missionaries tended to resolve the ambiguities of Tagalog conversion along two lines. On the one hand, they saw the rapid spread of the faith as the inexorable manifestation of divine will pulling to itself the diverse peoples of the world. On the other hand, they regarded the natives' apparent lack of doctrinal comprehension as a result of their "lack of intelligence," their "childish impressionability," and their consequent eagerness to be awed by the appearance rather than the substance of things.

Both ways of rationalizing the nature of Tagalog conversion served the purposes of a power bent on establishing for itself the privilege of speaking of and for the subordinate natives. In doing so they elided other complex forces that may have been at work in native conversion. The rapidity of conversion may also have meant that the Tagalogs had their own way of appropriating Christian signs, which to the Spaniards appeared to indicate an insufficient grasp of doctrinal subtleties. In order to explore this proposition, we must first reconstruct the logic behind the Spanish notion of conversion from the perspective of conquest and translation.

Reducing Native Bodies

For the Word of God to be delivered, the site of its exchange and circulation had first to be circumscribed. In order to delimit the physical space of conversion and the imposition of colonial rule, Spanish missionaries and officials were driven to reorganize the pattern of native settlements. Before the arrival of the Spaniards, the Tagalogs, like other linguistic groups in the lowlands, lived in dispersed villages.

5. "Confession" is from the Latin *confessio,* a creed, avowal of belief, and in ecclesiastical Latin, an acknowledgment of Christ. Thus all aspects of conversion are forms of confession.

In the late sixteenth century, most of these known settlements were strung along the coasts, and virtually all trade and political contacts were carried out by sea.[6] It is not surprising, then, that native communities bore the same name as the largest type of boat, *barangay.*

William Henry Scott has put together a remarkable picture of late-sixteenth-century Philippine lowland settlements, which served as transshipment points for the movement of goods ranging from food, gold, iron, and porcelain to slaves. "If there were any Filipino communities which supplied all their own food, clothing, tools, and weapons," Scott says, "Spanish accounts do not describe them. Rather the total impression is one of continual movement."[7] This continual movement of goods and people placed a certain kind of economy—one based on the sea rather than one oriented toward a centralized realm in the interior—at the forefront of precolonial interisland relations. It stressed mobility and deemphasized territorial boundaries.

The mobile and dispersed nature of native villages tended to obviate Spanish attempts at colonization and conversion. To counter this tendency, both officials and clergy sought to reorganize the natives into administrative units similar to those that had been established in the New World. While maintaining the *barangay* as the smallest territorial unit, they eventually imposed other territorial divisions that followed a centralized bureaucratic scheme: the *visita,* the *cabecera* (or *población* in later years), the *pueblo,* and the *provincia.*[8] In Manila, the colonial capital, a walled city was erected over several decades along the lines laid down by Philip II in the Law of the Indies. It was consciously modeled after the urban centers of the Roman empire and influenced by architectural ideas of the Italian Renaissance.[9]

These administrative divisions systematically ascribed a special site for the church.[10] As the symbolic expression of the power of Spain,

6. Scott, "Boat Building and Seamanship in Classic Philippine Society," in *Cracks in the Parchment Curtain,* p. 95.

7. Ibid., pp. 87–88.

8. See Phelan, *Hispanization of the Philippines,* p. 124.

9. John Reps, *Town Planning in Frontier America* (Columbia: University of Missouri Press, 1980), pp. 27–30; see also María Lourdes Díaz-Trechuelo Spinola, *Arquitectura española en Filipinas, 1565–1800* (Seville: Escuela de Estudios Hispano-Americanos de Sevilla, 1959), chap. 1.

10. See Zelia Nuttall, "Royal Ordinances Concerning the Laying Out of New Towns," in *Hispanic American Historical Review* 5 (May 1922): 249–254, for the

the church was to be constructed at the center of each *cabecera* and
pueblo (the smaller *visitas* were so called because each contained a
small chapel that the parish priest in the *cabecera* visited periodically). Spanish urban planning emphasized a grid plan with a
plaza at the center of the town; the church was to occupy one side of
the plaza. People who lived outside of the towns were to be settled
bajo de la campana, within hearing of the church bells.[11]

It was in this connection that the Augustinian priest Tomás Ortiz
wrote to other missionaries about the "dangers" of population
dispersion:

> Regarding the dispersed state in which the natives live away from the
> towns, placing their houses and habitations far from the churches:
> Among these natives much spiritual and temporal damage occurs and
> those who live in this way are often Christians in name only. For this
> reason, the ministers are obliged to preach to them and admonish them
> continually to confine themselves [*que se reduzcan*] to a town and to
> put their houses near the churches of the *cabeceras*. . . . No little harm
> is occasioned in those *visitas,* where the natives often live with too much
> liberty of conscience. Therefore ministers must not permit them to pick
> up and leave for a new *visita* . . . without first securing the expressed
> and written permission of the superiors in Manila.[12]

As late as the first half of the eighteenth century, then, the Spaniards' attempts to resettle the native populace in compact administrative units had not yet been fully realized. Some groups in the
archipelago—the Muslims in the south, the hunters and gatherers in
the jungles, and the mountain peoples of northern Luzon—resisted
resettlement as persistently as they refused conversion.[13] Lowland
coastal dwellers, however, despite their initial reluctance, were
eventually prevailed upon to resettle, just as they had been induced to
convert. Adherence to the law required them to become accessible to

---

pertinent sections of Philip II's ordinances concerning the locations of churches in the
colonies.

11. Phelan, *Hispanization of the Philippines,* pp. 48–49.

12. Padre Tomas Ortiz, *Práctica del ministerio que siguen los religiosos del orden
de N. S. Agustín en Filipinas* (Manila: Convento de Nuestra Señora de los Ángeles,
1731), p. 43.

13. Phelan, *Hispanization of the Philippines,* chap. 10; William Henry Scott, *The
Discovery of the Igorots* (Quezon City: New Day, 1974).

the representatives of God and king. Missionaries and bureaucrats arrogated to themselves the privilege—or "obligation," as Ortiz put it—of regulating the placement, location, and movement of the converted populace with reference to the larger concerns of evangelization and colonial administration.

The relocation of native bodies—or at least the designation of their areas of residence as parts of a larger administrative grid—permitted them to be identified in Spanish political and religious terms. Resettlement and evangelization were consistently denoted by the same term used for translation: *reducir*. To reduce a thing to its former state, to convert, to contract, to divide into small parts, to contain, to comprehend, to bring back into obedience: the multilayered definitions of *reducir* allow for its application in a variety of contexts. It thus sums up the thrust of Spanish colonization as both a political and a moral undertaking designed to reconstitute the natives as subjects of divine and royal laws. Bodies were to be "reduced" to centralized localities subject to the letter of the law, just as Tagalog was to be "reduced" to the grammatical terms of Latin in Castilian *artes*. The conversion and colonization of the local populace necessitated their physical relocation. Natives had to be taken by either force or persuasion from their dispersed villages and made available to the law's representatives. The hierarchical organization of settlements functioned as terminal points into which natives could be inserted and thereby reduced to the terms prescribed by law. This task in turn required the work of a certain kind of translation: the recording of names on tribute rolls, the accounting of native domiciles, and the differentiation of the populace into discrete categories (e.g., those liable to and exempt from tribute and labor requirements, those baptized and unbaptized, those dead and alive, etc.). In short, the imposition of Spanish power was propelled along the same lines as the capturing of the vernacular languages. "Reducing" the natives to towns, like "reducing" their language to grammar books and dictionaries, entailed the fixing of names to things and the recording of those names in administrative lists and records. The process would result, as far as the colonizers were concerned, in converting the colonized into arbitrary elements that could be made to fit into a divinely sanctioned order characterized by the hierarchization of all signs and things in the world.

Spanish colonialism thus presupposed the possibility of establishing a hierarchical relationship between all things "Spanish" (and therefore already "Christian") and all things "Tagalog" (yet to become "Christianized"). That is, the Tagalog language, culture, and social organization could be encoded, by virtue of being named and translated, as distinct but derivative aspects of the Spanish order. The elements of the codes could then be ordered by reference to God, the acknowledged source and destination of all signs in the world. This was why confronting the natives became for the Spaniards a question of "reducing" them: of mastering their signs and bodies within the confines of Spanish discourse. From this perspective, it was appropriate that Spanish writers of Tagalog *artes* also wrote and often appended devotional texts in the vernacular to their books. These texts consisted of prayers in verse, confession manuals, and manuals for the administration of the sacraments. Endowing the native language with a grammar was linked to the activity of supplying native souls with Christian signs. Christian signs in turn derived their efficacy from their ritual articulation. They were assumed ultimately to originate from and lead back to God's Sign, Christ. The Sign's representative, the priest, in possessing the language of God, initiated as he regulated the articulation of Christian signs in Tagalog. As the sign of the Sign, the priest had the words and gestures that could be placed into circulation for the sake of those who lacked them.

Evangelization therefore unleashed a spiraling movement of Sign and discourse. For the Sign to be known, it had to be talked about; and talk was valid only if it had the imprint of the Divine Sign. Such a movement generated as it mystified the power relationship between those who had and those who did not (yet) have God's Word. This dialectic between Sign and discourse and the politics of exchange and indebtedness to which it gave rise is best exemplified in the Catholic practice of administering the sacraments. The sacraments, in turn, hinged on the imperative to confess, which, as I shall try to show, was structured in ways remarkably analogous to the process of translation.

Confession and the Logic of Conversion

Christian conversion can be said to repeat the process of translation, at least where the missionaries were concerned. Both processes involved the sublation of all signs and speech to the sacred Sign of

God, Christ. As the Sign of the Father, Christ stands at the apex of all creation insofar as He is the perfect fusion of the Father's will and expression. In Christ one has the image of perfect speech, in that in Him everything that has been and will be said has already been spoken. To be converted is to recognize the Sign as the sole and authentic representation of the Father. It is to acknowledge one's words and intentions as therefore derivative of a prior Word. Put another way, conversion may be said to involve the translation of the person into a sign of the Sign of God. Just as God speaks to men and women through Christ, converts address God only through His Word. Christ therefore translates, in ways that are meant to be more than metaphorical, between the realms of the divine and the human.

This process of translation is carried out most explicitly in the administration of the sacraments. Catholic theology regards Christ himself as the source and author of all the sacraments, codified into a set of seven distinct rituals by the Council of Trent. Their crucial importance lies in their function of bringing God's gift to bear on the convert. Sacraments are signs valued for their capacity to make transparent the Source of all gifts. Their power is such that in accordance with the Thomistic formulation, "they effect what they signify; they are signs that cause what they signify and cause by signifying."[14] In their ritual performance, sacraments are thus the codes that constitute their own utterance so that the articulation of each sacrament brings with it the articulation of the entire history of Christianity.

Participation in the sacramental life of the church was a key feature of the Spanish project of evangelization. The discourse of the priest in initiating the dissemination of God's signs also had the task of regulating their reception by the converts. For the sacred and "secret" nature of sacraments meant that their efficacy hinged on their proper administration by the priest.[15] The privilege accorded to the missionary of administering the sacraments had to do with ensuring their proper reception. Missionary discourse often underlined this concern.

14. A. M. Amadio, "Sacraments of the Church," in *New Catholic Encyclopedia* (New York: McGraw-Hill, 1967), 4:808.

15. In ecclesiastical Latin, *sacramentum* was something that was to be kept sacred; it also meant a secret, a mystery. In nonecclesiastical Latin, however, *sacramentum* was defined juridically as "the sum which the two parties in a suit at first deposited, but afterwards became bound for, with the *tresviri capitales;* so called because the sum deposited by the losing party was used for religious purposes, especially for *sacra publica*" (Lewis and Short, *Latin Dictionary*). In military terms, it pertained to an oath of allegiance, a solemn obligation.

For example, in the *Prólogo* of *Librong Pinagpapalamnan yto nang aasalin nang tauong Cristiano sa pagcoconfesar at sa pagcocomulgar* (Book that contains the proper behavior to be observed by the Christian in confession and communion), by Father Blancas de San José, the following is addressed to the Tagalogs:

> The reason that this book [*sulat*] was composed by the reverend Fray Francisco De San Joseph [sic], my brothers, was so that you can study the proper way of confessing and receiving communion; otherwise these beloved medicines [*gamot*] might end up being poison [*lason*] for your souls were you to receive them in error: that is why this book teaches you about all the benefits that a Christian can derive from these two Sacraments.[16]

The *sulat* or book of the priest ensures that the sacraments will have a curative rather than a poisonous effect on the convert. Discourse details the proper administration and reception of signs so that in receiving them, one incorporates God's gift of mercy. As Blancas's text implies, qualifying oneself for the efficacy of God's signs pivots on confession and communion. These sacraments comprise the negative and positive poles in the dialectical assent to God's Word. Each is already implied in the other precisely because both emanate from the same source:

> Confession indeed is like the sacred spring of water that came from the side of our Lord Jesus Christ when he was nailed to the cross; and it is that which bathes our souls every time they are dirtied [*malibagan*] by sin. . . . This is the true cure for all the wounds of the Christian, no matter how rotten and smelly they may be; and it is also that which brings life back to those who died in sin; and it is also the payment of our debts [*otang*] to Him.   [*Prólogo,* n.p.]

Confession as the "holy blood" that cures the soul of sin is also construed as the payment for a debt. Submission to the cure is conjoined with the payment of debts, which entitles one to receive God's gift in the form of communion:

16. Padre Francisco Blancas de San José, *Librong Pinagpapalamnan yto nang aasalin nang tauong Cristiano sa pagcoconfesar at sa pagcocomulgar; nang capoua mapacagaling at capoua paguinabangan niya ang aua nang P. Dios,* 6th ed. (Manila, 1792), Preface, n.p. As Blancas died in 1614, this book was probably written within the first thirteen years of the seventeenth century.

And if one were to speak of Communion, the holy sacrament on the
altar, is it not the most sacred and most holy of all the sacraments, and
the source of all their power? . . . This most elevated of sacraments
gives one total grace along with all the blessings of God the Holy Ghost;
and the great mystery of our Lord Jesus Christ is in this sacrament,
body and soul, as well as in divine form.   [Ibid.]

Communion is presented as the symbolic culmination of conversion. The "holy sacrament on the altar" is made to stand for the Sign
of the Father. In receiving communion, the convert is said to incorporate the very Word of God Himself, which contains within it the
totality of His gifts. The ritual of communion is thus invested with the
sense of reaffirming something that has already occurred: the prior
profession of one's indebtedness to the Father. It is this act of admit-
ting one's dependence on God that validates communion. Such is the
object of confession: to elicit from the convert a voiced acknowledgment of what he or she owes to the Father. Hence, while communion
marks the closure of the relationship of indebtedness between God
and the convert, confession, the negative moment of this relationship,
enjoys a certain primacy in the project of evangelization.

Confession as the proclamation of one's faith, the admission of
one's fallenness, and the assertion of one's desire to be reinserted into
the network of divine commerce undergirds all other sacraments.
From baptism to extreme unction, confession informs the giving and
receiving of God's signs. Indeed, even a cursory glance at the missionary literature published between the seventeenth and early nineteenth
centuries reveals the prominent place assigned to confession in both
the performative and the institutional senses. Pinpin's insertion of a
confession manual in his book and missionaries' accounts of native
enthusiasm for confession further evidence its key role in conversion.
It would therefore not be inappropriate to assume that in the context
of conversion, confession functioned as one of the dominant modes of
discursive exchange between Spanish missionaries and Tagalog converts.

Ever since the eighth century, confession had taken on the specific
meaning of an oral rather than a written disclosure of one's sins to a
priest. It is associated particularly with the sacrament of penance,
though the apotropaic move implicit in confession—the turning away
from a sinful past dominated by a Satanic figure toward the gift of

God—permeates the other sacraments as well. The ritual of baptism, for example, in rehearsing the myth of the fall, reminds the participants of their primordial inheritance, which is loss. Original sin handed down from Adam and Eve signifies the inherited failure to appreciate the consequences of what one lacks. Renouncing Satan in baptismal rites is thus a way of representing that loss by acknowledging its cause as well as assuming the debt attendant upon that realization. Confession in baptism thus entails acknowledgment that one is born without something and that one has the duty to recover the *sense* of something missing, turning it into an opportunity to regain what has been lost.

Converting loss into an opportunity for gain: such is the logic of confession as it is encoded in baptism. In order to effect this purpose, a certain mode of remembering the past is essential. Past events are seen to take their places in a chain of indebtedness. We get a sense of this perspective in the section on baptism in Sebastián Totanes's bilingual manual. The priest speaks to the godparents of the child: "Listen to me . . . explain to you what you owe your godchild. It is your duty when he [she] has grown up to teach him [her] the doctrine, and all the duties of a Christian, including all the proper behavior that would improve his [her] life as a Christian."[17] Baptism establishes an obligation between godparent and child. The former owes to the latter the proper learning of Christian doctrine and the behavior appropriate to a Christian, based presumably on the understanding of that doctrine. Yet what the Christian doctrine obliges us to know is that we owe all things to God. It is His mercy and grace that constitute the world, which comes to us as a kind of gift:

> You must always remember to appreciate the manifold mercy [*aua*] and blessings given to you by our Lord God. Didn't He make you, both your body and soul? Didn't He baptize you? Didn't He take care of you so that your life might not be in danger?
>
> And if you were to look up to the sky, and notice everything above the earth: aren't they also blessings from God—the sun, the moon, and the stars, all our food and all our clothes . . . ?

17. Padre Sebastian Totanes, *Manual tagalog para auxilio a los religiosos de esta provincia de S. Gregorio Magno de Descalzos de N.S. Padre S. Francisco de Filipinas* (Sampaloc: Convento de Nuestra Señora de Loreto, 1745), p. 304. Like the other missionary texts of conversion cited here, Totanes's was reissued several times well into the nineteenth century.

And if I were to speak of even more sacred things: didn't God give
you the Sacraments as blessings for the life and benefit of your soul?
And what about the incomparable suffering of our Lord Jesus Christ,
who do you think that was for? . . . For you, who else! For it was for
you that He died on the Cross . . . and all His sufferings and pains were
gifts for you. [Blancas, *Librong*, pp. 44–47]

The world is seen as a catalogue of God's gifts. Encompassing life
and death, heaven and earth, God's mercy comes to converts, though
they do not deserve it. Indeed, just as the Divine Creditor is infinite,
so is the convert's indebtedness to Him. What lends one's debts this
sense of infinity is not merely the fact that God's blessings comprehend the lived world; more important, Christ's "incomparable
suffering" and death constitute the most precious gift against which
all other gifts in the world are to be measured. Christ's death is
memorialized because it is God's supreme recognition of the be-
liever's irredeemable debt. Through the Son, the Father makes a gift
of Himself to men and women, and he expects them to reciprocate in
turn: that is, to acknowledge divine redemption as the basis of all
human indebtedness. To say that "Christ died for you" is to say that
you are perpetually indebted to God insofar as you have become a
recipient of a gift so enormous as to defy equal return. "God Himself
makes payment to Himself":[18] such is a debt that can never be fully
repaid.

Sacramental ritual, in recalling the pivotal importance of God's
incommensurable gift, is meant to elicit the sense of one's perpetual
indebtedness to the Infinite Creditor. In partaking of the sacraments,
one avails oneself of the signs that allow one to remember what one
owes to one's Creditor: a debt that is beyond life and death. The
sacraments are thus intended not only to define the ultimate nature of
human indebtedness but also to regulate the specific means for remembering it. Indebtedness and memory are reconceptualized in
terms of their putative source and ultimate referent. Hence remembering one's lack simultaneously reflects God's infinite surplus. Memory in this case is productive of a hierarchy in which God as omnipotent provider stands over human beings as perpetual receivers of gifts.
By giving voice to this hierarchical order, sacraments can protect

18. Friedrich Nietzsche, *On the Genealogy of Morals,* trans. Walter Kaufmann and
R. J. Hollingdale (New York: Vintage Books, 1969), p. 92.

against the danger of forgetting what one does not have. They are gifts that signify one's indebtedness to the Father at the same time that they point to another time and place where indebtedness as such would have been fully repaid. By reenacting the divine giving back of itself to itself, the sacraments signal God's bounty at the same time that they remind one of one's lack.

To the extent that a sacrament recalls the significance of God's supreme gift, it can be seen, as the missionaries were wont to see it, as analogous to translation that seeks to reiterate in the vernacular the meaning of God's Word. Just as the sacraments redefine indebtedness as they reorder memory, translation reclassifies the vernacular as a gift within a hierarchy of other gifts at the same time that it regulates speech. Both involve the ritual reduction of all things native to the divine by the Spanish priest-translator.

One of the most instructive ways of seeing the link between conversion and translation is by examining the discourse of confession, particularly as it was institutionalized in penance. The centrality of confession, I suggest, lies in its requirement that the convert reformulate his or her past in a narrative of sin and repentance. In confession, one's remembrance of the past is translated into an accounting of one's accumulated failings. In this way, the past can be "sanctified." That is, to say aloud what was once hidden is to make a payment of sorts to the extent that one's confession can be brought in touch with God's Sign and thereby directed back to the Divine Creditor in recognition of His infinite benevolence.

The obligation to avail oneself of the sacrament of penance at least once each year was set forth by the Fourth Lateran Council of 1215. The council prescribed auricular as against written confession, because speech was seen as crucial in the submission of one's sins for judgment. Aquinas later concurred, and the Council of Trent reaffirmed this rule in 1551, insisting on the divine origin of confession and its necessity for salvation. It also ascribed to the priest, by virtue of the "Church's power of the keys," the role of a judge who "without knowledge of the case cannot exercise the office of judge inherent in the sacramental process."[19] Hence from its inception penance bestowed on the confessor a juridical function. It made him not only an

19. See E. F. Lakto, "Confession, Auricular," in *New Catholic Encyclopedia*, 4:131–132; also *Dictionnaire de théologie catholique*, ed. Alfred Vacant and Eugène Mangemot (Paris: Letouzey & Ane, 1911), 3:920, 132.

active interlocutor but an interested one as well. The priest as judge is
not an impartial arbiter; his investment in the narrative of sins is
clearly indicated from the start. The priest's interest in hearing and
pronouncing upon sin is concomitant with a desire to consolidate his
position in the hierarchy of divine commerce.

The juridical inflection of confession in penance made it necessary
to regulate the accounting of sins. The proper procedures for a "good
confession" were detailed in various missionary writings addressed
not only to native converts but to newly arrived missionaries as well.
The Augustinian Tomás Ortiz, for instance, says in his *Práctica del
ministerio* that priests ought to

> occupy themselves in teaching [the natives] and preaching to them all
> the things necessary for a good confession, and in particular explain to
> them not only the mode of examining their conscience; and about the
> acts of contrition and attrition and the diverse effects that each causes;
> but also the things that they have to value, and the way in which they
> have to value or think about them in order to excite and to move their
> hearts to feel sorrow for their sins.[20]

The existence of such categories as "good confession" and "bad
confession" simply underscores the necessity of installing the priest as
the special arbiter in the communication of the gifts contained in
penance. It was not enough merely to elicit confessions from converts; they must also be instructed in the thoughts, emotions, and
words appropriate to confessional discourse. Elsewhere we get a
more detailed account of such prescriptions, this time addressed to
the Tagalogs in their language. In Totanes's *Manual tagalog,* "contrition" and "attrition," the two acceptable modes of repentance, are
explained in terms of love and fear of God:

> 72. Repentance of the Child [*Pagsising Anac*], that is to say, the repen-
>   tance of the child for having sinned against its Father, is for the
>   sake of its love and desire for Him. . . .

20. Ortiz, *Práctica del ministerio,* pp. 7–8. Note that Catholic rhetoric about
penance remains essentially unchanged through 500 years. In N. Halligan's piece
"Frequency of Confession" in the *New Catholic Encyclopedia* we read the following:
"The sacrament of Penance was instituted to restore the holiness of life forfeited by
grievous sin and to deepen it through a livelier sorrow for sin and an earnest desire to
purify one's conscience as a worthy preparation for Eucharistic Communion"
(4:132).

73. So great in potency is this Repentance of the Child, which is called Contrition [*contrición*], because it brings with it the love and desire for our Lord God.

74. . . . [Whereas] the Repentance of the Slave [*Pagsising Alipin*] is that which comes only from the fear of punishment that awakens the soul [*loob*] to repentance like that of the slave fearing its Master. [Totanes, *Manual tagalog*, p. 74]

Totanes goes on to valorize the first type of repentance over the second. Sorrow for one's sins based on a childlike love for the Father is far more valuable than sorrow stemming from the slave's fear of punishment from the Master. The worst and virtually invalid motive for confession is the prospect of social censure—"natural repentance" (*arrepentimiento natural*). In this case, one's sorrow is based on the judgment not of God but of other people. Even repentance had to be ordered hierarchically. "Supernatural" rather than "natural" motives were stressed, and within the former, "love of the Father" was preferable to "fear of the Master." Blancas repeats this valuation: "And the reason one repents deeply for one's sins is that one has offended one's Lord who has made one. And the fear of hell should not be the only reason for repenting one's sins, and neither should it be the glory and rewards of heaven that should force one's soul [*loob*] to go back to God, but only one's love for Him above anything else" (pp. 121–122).

Even before the revelation of sins, a "good confession" requires the proper intention to set the tone for repentance. Fear of hell or the prospect of obtaining heavenly rewards are inadequate motives. "Real" sorrow and "real" repentance can grow only from the love [*pagyybig*] of the Father. The contrite child must therefore not simply accept its position of dependence but actively want it. In this sense, "real" repentance situates the Father as the locus of human desire. A "good confession," one that accrues to the benefit of the faithful, is fueled by the desire to be desired by God. For it is in repenting that one reorders one's desires with reference to the desire of the Father, which is no less than to be loved by the child. The logic of contrition is such that human desires should consist entirely of desiring God's desire. Forgiveness can come only after desires have been restructured so that the desire for the Father has been linked to the desire of the Father. Thus repentance becomes a matter of so conflating "for" with "of" that the confession of sins assumes the sense of an offering chained to a circle of divine love. The valorization of the notion of "love" in a confessional context reproduces on the level of wants the same tautological drift implicit in the relationship between Sign/discourse and giving/receiving which sacraments trace around and through the converts' bodies.

Even before repentance can be enacted and voiced, however, one must actively search through one's memories to recall one's sins. This process is referred to in missionary texts as *examen* (in Tagalog, *pagaalaala*), that is, the examination of conscience. Blancas gives us a vivid description of what it involves:

> By way of example, imagine many pictures [*larauan*] or say writings [*sulat*] piled up one on top of the other, or inserted in this and that: if one were to look at this pile, would one be able to tell each from the other? How else would you know about all those other things buried underneath this pile unless you were to go through each thing one by one? That is like the soul [*loob*] of a person who has many sins and is not used to examining them; the soul is so full of sins that he is unable to recall any of them, and thinks that he has no sins. . . . So why don't you unearth, my brothers and sisters, the multitude of sins buried in confusion in your souls, and if they are folded away, you should unfold them, and if they have gotten lost, you should search them out. [Blancas, *Librong,* p. 133]

The examination of conscience requires an accounting of past events piled up like undecipherable signs inside oneself. Recollecting one's past sins is thus analogous to the sifting and classification [*pagbuncalin*] of interior representations. This process assumes that in the penitent there exists not one self but two: one that bears the undecipherable marks of an unexamined past and another that reorders and reads those marks. The examination of conscience therefore splits the convert into a hierarchical opposition between a past, sinful self and a present, interrogating conscience. This temporal splitting of the self into one that reads and one that is read is at other times figured as an opposition between a body that speaks and one that is spoken to. Father Pedro de Herrera's *Meditaciones* recommends the following interior monologue to the penitent: "Oh, what a fool [*ol-ol*] I've been for loving my body! Woe is me, I still worship and adore this body of mine! Oh, what will I come to? I must keep destroying, keep forcing, keep invading, keep fighting this body of mine, which is truly my enemy. I will capture it, I will raid its forts, and this is because only the strongest conqueror can reach heaven."[21] There is a remarkable imaging of violence in this passage, suggesting the kind of repression the self was to exercise on itself. Here the metaphorics of repentance is brought in touch with the metonymic imaging of conquest in which one wars against oneself. In this way preconfessional practice constrains the individual penitent to internalize the established power relationship between priest and convert. This internalization of an exterior hierarchy consists of two interrelated procedures: the accounting of past events and the reproduction of the discourse of interrogation contained in the confession manuals.

First, the process of accounting. All confession manuals contain the unconditional demand that all sins be revealed. Over and over again, the convert is urged to tell all. To account for one's sins is to recount not simply sinful acts but all the clusters of desire that inform those acts and so obstruct the full insertion of the individual into the circuit of divine desire. Memory in this case becomes a tool for recollecting the sinful signs that constitute the past:

> . . . one must ask oneself when one last confessed, which year, month, week . . . was one's last confession. So that it can be known at what point one should start one's confession of one's new sins. . . . And if one knows of the utter uselessness of one's last confession, then one must force one's self to move further back in one's search for one's last good confession . . . and until one can remember this, well, one just has to keep moving back as far as one's memory will allow in recalling all the sins that must be declared in this new confession.   [Totanes, *Manual tagalog*, pp. 66–67]

To examine one's conscience is to remember as far back as one can to the last "good confession" that one had. Remembering necessitates not only the division of the past into discrete moments of acts and desires but the potentially endless accounting of all those moments. Once remembered and accounted for, the sinful past is then to be converted into a total discourse of repentance:

21. Pedro de Herrera, *Meditaciones cun manga mahal na pagninilay na sadia sa Sanctong pag exercicios* (1645; Manila: Compañía de Jesús, por Don Nicolas Cruz Bagay, 1762), folio 64.

If you want to be forgiven by God, you should confess well and say everything [*oobosin sabihin*] now, including all your evasions, and the number of times you committed them, and leave it to me to show mercy, and to pass judgment that may be to your benefit.   [Totanes, *Manual tagalog,* pp. 31–32]

You must declare all [*ybabala nang ybabala*], and serve all [*yhayin nang yhayin*] your sins to the Priest, reveal all in your soul [*loob*], do not be constrained by shame [*hiya*], do not cease from probing into your soul for its sins so that you can expend everything in speech [*paguubos ubosin sabihin*]. You must also recount the entire breadth, depth, and number of times you committed each and every sin. [Blancas, *Librong,* pp. 240–241]

The Spanish demand is that nothing be held back in confession. One is to expend all that memory can hold in a discourse that will bring together both the self that recalls and that which is recalled. The present self that confronts the priest in confession is thus expected to have managed to control his or her past—to reduce it, as it were, to discursive submission. Whereas the examination of conscience requires the division of the self into one that knows the Law and seeks out the other self that deviates from it, a "good confession" insists on the representation of a self in total control of its past. It is in this sense that confessional discourse imposes on the individual penitent what Roland Barthes called a "totalitarian economy" involving the complete recuperation and submission of the past to the present, and by extension of the penitent to the priest.[22]

Yet insofar as the ideal of a perfect accounting of sins also necessitated their recounting in a narrative, it was condemned to become a potentially infinite task. Given the limitations of memory, accounting "engenders its own errors." And the errors created by faulty accounting become further sins that have to be added to the original list. The very possibility of a correct accounting engenders an erroneous accounting, just as remembering one's sins would make no sense unless there existed the possibility of forgetting them. It is thus the guarantee of a faulty accounting of sins that makes conceivable the imperative

22. Roland Barthes, *Sade/Fourier/Loyola,* trans. Richard Miller (New York: Hill & Wang, 1976), pp. 39–75. My discussion of accounting in confession is an attempt to apply to the Spanish colonial context Barthes' remarks on the language of prayer elaborated in Loyola's spiritual exercises.

for total recall. Barthes puts it more succinctly: "Accountancy has a mechanical advantage: for being the language of a language, it is able to support an infinite circularity of errors and of their accounting."[23]

There is a sense, then, in which the demand for a total recollection of sins results in the unlimited extension of discourse purporting to extract and convey one's successes and failures in accounting for past acts and desires. Accounting thus allows confession to become a self-sustaining machine for the reproduction not only of God's gifts of mercy but of "sin" as well. For God's continued patronage—the signs of His mercy—requires a narrative of sins to act upon. The confessor who sits in lieu of an absent Father needs the penitent's stories, without which there can be no possibility of asserting and reasserting the economy of divine mercy. Without the lure of sin, the structure of authority implicit in this economy would never emerge. Confession was crucial because it produced a divided subject who was then made to internalize the Law's language. The penitent became "the speaking subject who is also the subject of the statement."[24] But confession was also important because it made for the ceaseless multiplication of narratives of sin through their ever-faulty accounting. In introducing the category of "sin," confession converted the past into a discourse that was bound to the Law and its agents. In this way the accounting and recounting of the past generated the complicitous movement between sin and grace.

These considerations bring us to the second moment in the interiorization of hierarchy prescribed by confession: the reproduction of the discourse of interrogation. The confession manuals written by the Spanish missionaries consist of a list of questions specific to each of the Ten Commandments. The confessor addresses the questions to the penitent, who then is expected to use them as the basis for an examination of conscience. As mnemonic devices for eliciting a narrative of sin, the questions are constructed in such a way that the penitent can respond simply yes or no. The commandments to which these questions are attached function as the all-encompassing code determining the kinds of discursive exchange that can take place within the confessional. God's Law furnishes the conceptual limit of

23. Ibid., p. 70.
24. Michel Foucault, *The History of Sexuality*, trans. Robert Hurley (New York: Vintage Books, 1980), 1:61. My discussion of the relationship between power and confession owes a great deal to Foucault's analysis of this phenomenon.

what can be said. Yet the Law can be known most forcefully only at the moment of its transgression. It is in the interest of guarding the sacredness of the Law that the priest probes into the penitent's life, demanding the oral recuperation of the sinful past. For the extent to which sin can be voiced to the priest is the extent to which it can be neutralized, that is, translated into a merely negative instance of the assertion of the Law's sway. Every admission of guilt signals a recognition of the Law. In this sense the notion of sin furnishes the manifold supports that enable God's signs to establish their authority to speak of and for the penitent. The utterance of transgressions within the framework of penance signifies the self's submission of itself to the demands of divine mercy.

Hence, just as the comprehensive accounting of sins was ineluctably attached to a faulty accounting of the past, the total retrieval of discourse in penance was conceivable only in terms of an ever-present surplus of discourse that could be brought back to the Sign and its Origin. The priest could hang on to his position of power in the circuit of divine commerce so long as there existed the possibility of a discourse that had not yet been reduced to the Sign; of a past that had not yet been converted into a set of interrogative propositions; of desires that had not yet been turned into secrets that could then be hunted down and transformed as offerings to the Father. The confession manuals clearly indicate that penance multiplied discourses emanating not only from the penitent but from the priest as well. In the process, the confessor's questions tended to take on the twists and turns of the very sins they sought to quell. This was particularly obvious where the Sixth Commandment was concerned. As the priest questioned the male penitent about any illicit sexual relations he might have had, clerical interest typically took on a certain luridness:

366. How many times did you sin with her?
367. You tell me that you always saw each other alone; well, then, how do you expect me to know how many times those were?
368. If you can't tell me the exact number of times, give me a rough estimate, tell me more or less how many times.
369. And if you can't tell me this, tell me how many years, or months, or weeks, or days has it been since you started sinning with her.
370. And during this entire period, how many times a week did you sin with her? Was it every day, or every other day, or what?
371. And aside from all those times you slept together, didn't you on

other days and hours also cavort [*nagbibiro*] and play around in a wanton manner?

372. And during those moments of playing around, didn't you at times just verbally joke around, and at other times embrace each other, and kiss each other, and touch each other, touching every single part of your bodies without reserve?

373. And did something dirty come out of your body? [*At nilabasan caya ang catauan mo nang marumi?*]

374. And did you cause her to emit something dirty, too? [*Pinalabasan mo naman caya ang catouan niya?*]25

375. How many times did you play around in this manner, for example, within a week? And how many times did each of you have an emission? Because this is not only a sin, but a very serious sin.

376. Aside from all this, I also suspect that every time you saw her or thought of her, you also lusted for her. Isn't this the case?

377. And because of your lust, did you do anything to your body, any kind of lewdness? And did your body emit something dirty? [Totanes, *Manual tagalog*, pp. 135–137]

Here the priest's discursive drift tends to mimic the sexual act it is decrying. Interest in the quantity of transgressions leads to a feverish desire to learn of their quality. This concern periodically climaxes, as it were, with the question "And did something dirty come out of your body?" The priest's power seems to come precisely from his ability to locate those moments when the convert has squandered what should have been held in reserve. Implicit in such exchanges is the sense of "You wasted yours while I still have mine"—that is, the sense on the confessor's part that he has the means to track down those occasions

25. In the Spanish text that accompanies the Tagalog, items 373 and 374 appear respectively as "Y tenías polución?" ("And were you polluted?") and "La hacías a ella tener tambien polución?" ("Did you also cause her to become polluted?") Seventeenth-century Spanish sensibility regarding sexual contact, at least within a confessional context, seems to have been concerned with the visible emission of certain bodily fluids from both the man and the woman rather than, as in the twentieth century, with the licit or illicit pleasure of the orgasm. The "sinfulness" of nonprocreative sex was indexed by the sight of something that should have been kept in reserve and out of sight but instead was released indiscriminately. Such fluids were then forms of "pollution" insofar as they were out of place. To the Tagalogs, however, the emission of bodily fluids in the sexual act did not entail "pollution." The ejaculation of semen, for example, was referred to then, as it is now, as *labasan*, literally the transfer of something from the inside to the outside. Hence missionary translations often had to modify this expression by appending the adjective *marumi*, "dirty," to *nilabasan* (as in *Nilabasan caya ang cataouan mo nang marumi?*).

when the convert lost his "property" plus the ability to recover discursively what has been misplaced.

The drive to overpower the penitent therefore is inextricably bound up with the desire to know of his most intimate acts and desires. Translating the past into a narrative of sin allows for the reduction of the penitent into discrete moments of his failings, which the priest-confessor can then appropriate.

The effects of the spiraling movement between the wish to know and the will to power in confessional discourse become even more significant when the past that is to be recovered appears to the Spaniards as an amorphous and ill-defined one. Such was the case with precolonial native culture. Like the local vernacular, Tagalog beliefs and customs had to be resituated within a coherent field that could be made available to Spanish discourse. In 1589, the Franciscan Juan de Plasencia had taken on the task of codifying Tagalog customs just as he had earlier written (though never published) an *arte* and a *vocabulario* of the local language.[26] His short treatise on marriage customs, slavery, burial rites, and "cults and superstitions" served as one of the bases for the subsequent missionary efforts at incorporating certain native practices that did not conflict with Christian notions while proscribing other aspects of the culture which did. The Spanish notion of translation as the reduction of native signs into a structure comprehensible in Spanish terms was very much at the root of the attempts to codify native culture. Translation was a process of making known the unknown, of distinguishing between "legitimate" and "illegitimate" native practices, and finally of harnessing native signs to further the spread of God's Word and consolidate its gains.

Unlike the Indian populations of the New World, the Tagalogs had neither temples to be destroyed nor pagan monuments to be smashed. The Hindu-Buddhist culture of other Southeast Asian countries, though not totally unfamiliar to the Tagalogs, never managed to exercise a definitive sway over the islands' populace. And by the second half of the sixteenth century, Spaniards found only vague Islamic influences among peoples north of the Sulu archipelago. It was as if the Tagalogs, along with the majority of other linguistic

26. Plasencia's treatise is reproduced in Padre Francisco de Santa Inés, *Crónica de la Provincia de San Gregorio Magno de Religiosos Descalzados de N.S.P. San Francisco en las Islas Filipinas, China, Japón, etc.* (1676; Manila: Chofre, 1892), 2:590–603.

groups in the Philippines, had remained outside of history—that is, history as it was known to the West. What the Spaniards saw was a mass of ritual practices that did not seem to be attached to any identifiable "civilization." Hence the project of evangelization involved the alignment of this cultural mass with the laws of Spanish-Catholic civilization. We have already noted the way the native settlements were incorporated in the Spanish geopolitical framework. Confession, by demanding the revelation of the past, further contributed to and reinforced the Spanish wish to bring the unknown signs of native culture into the known realm of Spanish knowledge and discourse. It is in the light of this project that Ortiz impresses upon other missionaries their duty to "examine their doctrines, customs, abuses, and superstitions, and, having examined them, impugn them and disabuse the said Gentiles of them because unless their roots are cut, the bad weeds will sprout again, no matter how many times you cut them" (*Practica*, p. 4).

It is worth noting that Ortiz makes a distinction between the natives' "doctrines" and "customs" and their "abuses and superstitions." This was a familiar move on the part of the missionaries in their effort to differentiate between Tagalog practices that could be incorporated into Christianity and those that would have a pernicious effect on it. The latter features of native culture then had to be weeded out. By designating such practices as *abusos* and *supersticiones*, the priests made their observance sinful. Thus they could be used as part of the scaffolding of sin on which the power of clerical discourse could be exercised. They were among the lawless elements that had originated in the Devil. Located outside of the Law, such practices were nonetheless situated within the Law's reach to the extent that they had been given a demonic author whose existence sprang from God. This is why missionary writers were compelled to render detailed descriptions of the *abusos* they sought to abolish. In some instances, the interest in such practices took on the lurid tone we noted earlier in the confessor's concern with the penitent's sexual history:

Although upon entering the obscure abyss of so much ignorance and idolatry, I find a disorderly confusion of things most vile, abominable, and worthy of their inventor: and although on scraping the wall within this infernal cave, I discover an infinity of obscene, filthy, and truly infernal pests: with the light of truth I offer to reduce them methodically so that we can praise the all-powerful God.[27]

This passage from a chapter on native *abusos* in Chirino's *Relación* is followed by a catalogue of "superstitious beliefs," "spirits," and "demons" in Tagalog culture. Such lists were typical of Spanish accounts as well as manuals for the administration of the sacraments. Just as they had endowed the Tagalog language with a grammar and a lexicon, the missionary writers sought to classify the confusion of spirits they heard of, construing them always and everywhere as the persistent murmurs of a diabolical past. Rendered in this way, *abusos* could then be recorded as variations of sins against the First Commandment:

180. Do you know anything whatever about the practices of sorcerers, or witches, who are all slaves of the devil?[28]

9. Did you worship anyone else aside from the true God, that is, do you make offerings to other spirits?
10. Whenever you are sick, do you have yourself treated by a sorcerer or by recourse to any other evil measures of the past?
11. Do you believe and swear by dreams, and do you tell them to others?
13. Did you make offerings to the spirits [*nono*], perhaps to the spirit of the earth; or perhaps you pay your respects to it and ask license from it?[29]

Penance furnished one of the most effective means of ferreting out Tagalog "superstition." It allowed the priest to subsume the myriad native beliefs in a set of fixed names and definitions and to locate their practitioners and followers. "Paganism" as a missionary construct gives the confessor the needed space to intervene in the natives' lives. A list of *abusos* ensured that there would always be more to confess, more of the past that could be made to speak, more "disease" to be cured by the priest-physician, who had a monopoly on the

27. Chirino, *Relación de las Islas Filipinas*, trans. Echevarría, p. 60.
28. Totanes, *Manual tagalog*, p. 103.
29. Gaspar de San Agustín, *Confesionario copioso en lengua tagala para dirección de los confesores, y instrucción de los penitentes* (1713), 2d ed. (Sampaloc: Convento de Nuestra Señora de Loreto, 1787), pp. 10–12.

prescribed medicine. In other words, the classification of Tagalog culture in segments falling within and without the Law, like the writing of *artes* and the resettlement of the natives, provided specific cognitive relays and physical points of transmission in the spread of Spanish power and knowledge among the Tagalogs.

All the preceding discussion, however, does no more than lay out the intricate and self-enclosed logic informing the relationship between conversion and translation. To leave things as they stand would merely reaffirm the Spaniards' claims of their dominance over the Tagalogs in the crudest possible sense and would beg the question of the native reception of Christian signs with which we began this discussion. For how is one to explain the persistent observation in seventeenth- and eighteenth-century accounts that although the natives "readily receive our religion," they still seem to be incapable of "sounding the depths of its mysteries"? If, as the Spaniards supposed, conversion is translation—"faith" being a matter of acceding to the language of the Law—then why was there so wide a gap between the Tagalogs' enthusiasm for the sacraments and their comprehension of their meaning? Was this merely a matter of the inadequacy of Spanish pedagogy, as most scholars tend to assume? Or was something else at work in the conversion of the Tagalogs?

The gap between response to and understanding of Christianity, I suggest, has something to do with the way the Tagalogs were constrained to negotiate with and around the totalitarian economy of divine mercy. The Tagalogs' notions of conversion and translation apparently diverged from those of the Spanish missionaries. In that case, we may assume that their ideas about exchange and hierarchy tended to differ as well from those that the Spaniards sought to impose on them. It is to these Tagalog alternatives that we now turn.

CHAPTER 4

Untranslatability and
the Terms of Reciprocity

Rereading Christianity

Earlier I mentioned that the Tagalogs were converted despite and because of the failure of the Spanish notion of translation to fully impose itself on the natives. The example of the people listening to the priest's sermon in Rizal's *Noli me tangere,* the persistence of the peculiar relationship between voice and writing in *baybayin,* Pinpin's *Librong,* and Spanish descriptions of native conversion all suggest as much. Tagalog responses seem to have been at odds with Spanish intentions. Their conversion to Christianity, like their learning of Castilian, occurred in ways that were not fully accountable in Spanish-Christian terms. It was as if the Tagalogs, in confronting the discourse of clerical-colonial authority, always had something else in mind which the procedures of missionary translation and conversion were unable to circumscribe. Some things in Tagalog culture could not be unequivocally restated in Spanish-Christian terms, just as some aspects of the vernacular exceeded the limits that the missionaries sought to set for it.

The vernacular's resistance to translation spurred further translations. The writing of *artes,* like the construction of confession manuals, was predicated precisely on the inadequacy of any given translation. The possibility that something might slip from their discursive grasp compelled the missionaries to keep talking, translating, and hearing confessions in the hope of finally mastering language—whether their own or the other's—and making it yield to the presence of the Same Truth.

For the Tagalogs, however, conversion to Christianity entailed attending to Latin and Castilian not only as they were spoken in the administration of sacraments and liturgy but as they appeared sporadically in the Tagalog of the priest who addressed them. As we noted earlier, the translation of Christian discourse into the vernacular necessitated as well the retention of Latin and Castilian words in their untranslated forms. Within a colonial context, Tagalog infused with untranslatable Latin and Castilian words now seemed not alien, exactly, yet not quite one's own language, either. The untranslated Latin and Castilian terms were the traces of an outside force breaking into the fabric of the convert's language. They made it necessary to translate within one's own language, that is, to distinguish between terms that had indigenous referents and terms whose meanings lay outside of what could be said in Tagalog. Thus the presence of Latin and Castilian terms in Tagalog opened up for the natives the possibility of finding in their language something that resisted translation. Their way of coming to terms with this resistance, however, differed from that of the Spaniards. It is on this difference in approach to the untranslatable—in ways of domesticating and thereby appropriating what seems to have no "natural" place in one's discourse—that I wish to focus. This difference enables us to posit a Tagalog alternative to the Spanish notion of conversion and the notion of reciprocity on which it insisted.

As a point of departure for comparing Spanish and Tagalog approaches to that which resists translation, we may look back to the native *abusos* and *supersticiones* detailed in numerous missionary accounts. A typical example can be found in Tomás Ortiz's *Práctica del ministerio*. In the chapter on the administration of penance, we find a long section on the various forms and manifestations of Tagalog "superstitions." A pervasive wishfulness infuses this lexicon of *abusos*: a desire to see them within the context of Roman and Chinese beliefs. Situated in this way, they could then be regarded as part of a familiar series of "fallen" customs that existed before the advent of Christianity:

The natives have many abusive practices that run counter to our faith and good customs, and among these are the following. First, the Idolatry of the *Nono*, about which it should be known that the word *Nono* not only signifies grandfather [*abuelo*] but also serves as a term of respect for ancestors and tutelary spirits (*genios*); those that the *indios* have under the name *Nono* are like those that the Chinese have under the name of Spirits [*Espíritus*]; and that the Romans had under the name of gods, which others called *Lares* or *Penates*, etc. With these tutelary spirits or *Nono*, the *indios* carry on frequent idolatrous practices; for example, they ask them for permission, help, aid, and that they not be harmed by them as well as by their enemies, etc., things that they do on so many occasions, and among these are the following: When they want to take some flower or fruit from a tree, they ask permission from the *Nono* or tutelary spirit; as when they want to pass through some field, river, brook, stream, or by a huge tree. . . . Whenever they are obliged to cut some tree . . . they ask them for pardon, saying among many other things that the Priest ordered it to be done, that it is not of their own desire to show lack of respect to them, or to go against their wishes, etc. When they fall ill with some malady . . . that they attribute to the tutelary spirit or *Nono*, they ask them for health, and make offerings of food, which they carry out on this occasion, among many others, in fields, on fishing boats, along riverbanks, at the foot of some big tree. . . . This kind of Idolatry is extensively rooted and quite ancient among the *indios*, and for this reason Ministers must exercise much care and force in extirpating them, without sparing diligence and effort until they are all rooted out.[1]

In reorganizing the structure of native beliefs, Ortiz follows standard missionary practice. His explication of these *abusos* is informed by a hierarchizing impulse that situates the *nono* at the top of a spiritual order, then positions this order as part of a set of perverted reflections of a distant, pre-Christian past. The coherence of *nono* comes through a received vocabulary: they are really no more than *genios*, that is, tutelary spirits similar to those of the ancient Romans; and being the spirits of dead ancestors, they resemble those worshiped by the Chinese. Yet when one examines the other connotations of *nono* in Tagalog, its insertion into a fallen hierarchy of pagan beliefs becomes highly problematic.

Nono, as Ortiz mentions, was (and still is to a large extent) used as a term to denote one's grandparents whether living or dead. It would seem, then, that the authority of the *nono* was derived from their ascribed place in a kinship network determined by time. But the Tagalogs' use of this term indicates otherwise. The difference between

1. Ortiz, *Práctica del ministerio*, pp. 11–12.

oneself and one's ancestors was reckoned instead by reference to the parts of the body. A Tagalog-Spanish dictionary lists the following terms: *nono sa tagiliran, nono* on the upper side of the body (great-grandfather/mother); *nono sa sinapupunan, nono* on the lap (great-great-grandfather/mother); *nono sa tuhod, nono* on the knee (father or mother of great-grandfather/mother); *nono sa sakong, nono* on the heel (grandfather/mother to the fifth degree); *nono sa talampakan, nono* on the soles of the feet (grandfather/mother to the sixth degree).[2] Equally worth noting is that like other Tagalog words, *nono* has no gender inflection. Thus one's ancestors were thought of as having a relation of contiguity with one's body rather than of temporal continuity evinced by the paternal name.

Similarly, *nono* in the sense of "spirits" were seen less as sacred figures from the past than as indeterminate auras emanating from certain objects in nature—trees, rocks, rivers, fields, even crocodiles. Missionaries construed the natives' ritual offerings to these spirits as signs of their respect. But to equate such signs of "respect" with idolatry was to conflate the nature of the natives' offerings with those of Christians. As Ortiz's text shows, the act of rendering "respect" to the *nono* was intended to appease them, not to conserve their authority by memorializing what one owes to them.

The *nono* have no fixed names. They are referred to simply as the *nono* of the mountain or of the tree or of the river. Partly for this reason there is no elaborate mythology surrounding them. From the Tagalog point of view, one comes to know a *nono* through the threat or promise it is said to pose. Offerings of appeasement, rendered arbitrarily from time to time and from place to place, were intended to ward off danger or to obtain one's desire. Here there is no question of resorting to a body of sacred texts, of uttering sanctifying formulas, or of unconditionally surrendering to the mediation of a figure in control of a ritual language. Offerings in this case are not sacrifices in the Christian sense in that they are not ordered to the conservation of an immutable hierarchy. Once one has eluded danger or obtained what one wants, one forgets about the *nono* until the next time they must be appeased: when one falls ill or must cross a river or a field or in any other way confronts a situation unknown or uncertain.

Given these considerations, Father Ortiz's attempts to put the *nono*

2. Pedro Serrano-Laktaw, ed., *Diccionario tagalog-hispano* (Manila: Santos y Bernal, 1914), p. 861.

at the apex of a hierarchy of tutelary dieties becomes a case of wishful mistranslation that spawns a multitude of other mistranslations. The Tagalogs understood the word *nono* in various ways that had little to do with the theological and historical implications of the category "paganism," in which the missionary sought to situate it. *Nono* always referred to something more than could be spoken of: spirits in nature and ghosts of dead ancestors.[3]

Like other Southeast Asians, the Tagalogs believed in the ability of spirits to cross the line between life and death, hence to remain unbound in either state. We encountered this belief in the Introduction, in Pedro Calosa's narrative of haunting and being haunted by the personalities of the past. Spirits could appear anywhere at any time. They had no specific names and their genealogies were indeterminate. Their places of residence varied and their origins were essentially unknown. *Nono* was thus one way of designating what eluded naming. It was a means of identifying the source of events and occurrences that seemed to defy explanation. Phenomena that cannot be accounted for are potential producers of shock in that they rupture the rhythm of everyday life. *Nono,* as part of the Tagalog lexicon of spirits, was one way of giving form to anything that threatened to confound all forms. Put another way, it was a means of localizing and hence dealing with what we may term untranslatable figures, that is, figures that could not be fully assimilated yet kept reappearing in the world. By referring to such figures as *nono* (or "Rizal," "Bonifacio," or a host of other names, for that matter), one begins to demarcate their heterogeneous quality. Herein lies the importance of token offerings to the spirits. Such occasional offerings were imperative in that they signaled one's ability to recognize one's place in relation to that which, by definition, had no specific place. They were thus a means of recognizing the existence of a difference between oneself and all those other things that seemed to be outside of one. In deferring to spirits, one was also drawing the boundary that kept them separate from oneself. Thus the untranslatability of spirits served as the basis of their authority. That is, one kept them apart only by deferring to them; and one had to defer to them in order to anticipate the unexpected and potentially shocking consequences of their appearance. A word such as *nono* therefore functioned to indicate the

---

3. The place of spirits in Tagalog culture is discussed further in chap. 6.

possibility of identifying what was untranslatable, and in so doing to render it separate and open to sporadic negotiations in the form of token offerings.

Spaniards' attempts to comprehend *nono* in terms of *genios, lares,* and *penates* reduced spirits to the categories of pagan beliefs. They had to do so if they were to identify *nono*, like other Tagalog *abusos*, in order to classify and oppose them dialectically to Christian practices as their "fallen" counterparts. But insofar as *nono* called to mind what resisted full translation and could only be alluded to in association with parts of the body and discrete aspects of nature, the word carried a reserve of referents that exceeded the limits of what the Spaniards could say about it.

However, for the Tagalogs to acknowledge the untranslatability of certain figures is, of course, already to embark on a form of translation in the sense of ascribing to such figures a place in relation to which one can assume a different position. Translation here is a matter of separating one's interests from the pull of an ill-defined outside rather than of privileging one set of meanings over another across languages. It is to know that one does not know and therefore to re-mark the difference between self and not-self, between the world of the living and that of the spirits (who are neither dead nor alive). This sort of translation recalls the syncopation, counting, and gambling at work in Pinpin's *Librong*. This mode of recognizing untranslatable figures—whether spirits signaled by such terms as *nono* or Spaniards signaled by the surge of Castilian words in Pinpin—was an important feature of Tagalog conversion. The sounding of untranslatable Christian terms breaking into the stream of missionary discourse stirred the Tagalogs in much the same way as the uncanny appearances of *nono* and the rush of Castilian in Pinpin's book. The signs of Christianity, like those of Castilian and often indistinguishable from them, were embedded in the vernacular. The grafting of Christian terms onto the vernacular introduced a new element of the uncanny into native discourse. Hearing missionary discourse in the vernacular, the natives were thus exposed to a series of shocks. In responding to these shocks, the Tagalogs sought to contain them in ways that left the missionaries puzzled and disturbed.

We can get a sense of the shock effect that Christian signs exercised over the Tagalogs if we turn back to Father Murillo Velarde's account. On the one hand, he complains about the "lack of seriousness" on the part of native converts attending distractedly to the priest's words:

> They attend with due seriousness only to certain undertakings; and the distractions of their disputes and business affairs and their indolence and the air of the country dissipate their attention beyond measure. Their imaginations, overborne with foolish trifles, accustomed to our voices become so relaxed that even the most forcible and persuasive discourses make little if any impression.   [*BR*, 44:33–34]

At the same time, he is amazed at the capacity of the Tagalog listeners to be suddenly roused simply by the sound of the priest's discourse:

> The marvel is that many *indios* and a great many Indian women, at the mere sound of the preaching in the mission and without understanding what they hear, are stricken with contrition, confess themselves, and receive communion in order to gain indulgences—to their own great advantage and to the unspeakable consolation of their confessors at seeing the wonderfully loving providence of God for these souls. [Ibid.]

The Jesuit Murillo, like other missionaries, explains the suddenness of the natives' conversion—that is, their turn to the sacraments—in terms of divine providence. A leap of faith comes as a result of ineffable illumination from God. One is struck, as he was, by the drastic reactions to the mere sound of the preacher's voice. From a state of pure distraction the natives are plunged into a concern bordering on obsession, apparently with no mediating cognitive process. Here the move from inattentiveness to repentance and confession has little to do with the understanding of the Law and the subsequent incorporation of its discourse. We have already seen the tendency of native penitents to answer "yes or no as it occurs to them" when the priest questions them. It is as if the Tagalogs respond not to the meaning of missionary discourse but to specific intervals in the flow of the priest's voice. What produces the abrupt turn to the sacraments?

To answer this question, it might be helpful to examine in more detail the effects of grafting untranslatable Christian-Spanish words onto a vernacular text. As we saw earlier, missionary writers were eager to safeguard the key words of the doctrine from confusion with native beliefs and terminologies. Hence in the liturgy and in the administration of the sacraments, ritual closure was always effected with blessings in Latin. This practice signified the presence of God Himself in His language. In the performance of other Christian rites, the crucial words were kept in Castilian. The validity of baptism, for example, especially when it was administered by a layman to a still-born infant, hinged on the use of the Spanish word *bautizar*. Missionaries explicitly cautioned against the use of what might have been its Tagalog equivalent, *binyag,* literally to give one a nickname.[4]

As we have seen, the practice of leaving certain words untranslated had important effects. For in any given discursive exchange between priests and converts, a sporadic rush of undecipherable words was bound to break into the fabric of the vernacular. The missionaries meant these words to ensure the orthodoxy of conversion texts in the native language; to the Tagalogs, however, they meant other things.

Pinpin's text, as I have argued, sought to habituate Tagalog readers to the intrusive presence of Castilian and in this way functioned to rehearse their response to the discourse of evangelization. Missionary descriptions of the natives' reactions to their preachings—often characterized by rapid shifts between distraction and avid attention—seem to confirm the workings of the sort of translation found in Pinpin's book. Hearing the untranslated terms of Christianity, native converts recognized them for what they were: opaque signifiers with no prior signifieds in Tagalog. Such terms formed momentary blanks in the semantic progression of the vernacular. To seize upon untranslatable signs was to mark the recurrence of such gaps and to see in them a whole range of possible associations that had only the most tenuous connection to the original message of the priest. In other words, the very untranslatability of Christian signs could be reread in different ways by native converts. Rather than making indisputably apparent the authority of God's Sign and that of the priest, such terms presented the possibility of dodging the full weight of the missionary's intent.

To get a sense of how this process might operate, we can turn to some of the passages in Totanes' *Manual tagalog* cited in Chapter 3. In this instance, it is helpful to reproduce both the Tagalog and Spanish sections of the text. The English translation follows the Tagalog as closely as possible. In addressing the native convert about to receive the last rites, the missionary is advised to say the following:

4. Totanes, *Manual tagalog,* p. 57; Serrano-Laktaw, ed., *Diccionario tagalog-his-pano,* p. 133.

Anacco, tayong lahat na Cristiano,y, ynootosan nang P. Dios at nang Santa iglesiang Ina nating maquinabang cun magcocomulgar touing mey panganib ang ating buhay. . . . Ytong paquinabang na yto,y, pinangalang Viatico, na cun baga sa uicang Tagalog ay Bauon nang mey paroroonang malayo. Pabauon nga nang Santa Iglesia sa tauong mey saquet na malubha ytong camahalmahalang na Sacramento nang pagcocomulgar, namacatatapang at macalalacas sa tauo sa pag-cacabanalan at sa paglalaban sa manga tocso nang diablong mar-aya. [Totanes, *Manual tagalog,* pp. 36–37]

Hijo mio, Dios nuestro Señor y la Santa Iglesia nos manda comulgar cuando hay peligro de muerte. . . . A este comulgar llaman Viatico, que quiere decir: Provision para el que tiene que hacer viaje largo. Provee la Santa Iglesia al hombre enfermo con este Santisimo Sacramento para el Viage de la eternidad para fortalecerle en la Fe, en la Esperanza, y en la Caridad, para que exercite las Virtudes y resista con valor a las tenta-ciones del demonio.

My child, all of us who are Christians are ordered by our Lord God and by our Mother Church to avail ourselves of communion every time our lives are in danger. . . . This useful thing is called *Viatico,* which in the Tagalog language is the *bauon* of those who are going on a long jour-ney. This is the provision that the Mother Church gives to the seriously sick person, this most blessed Sacrament of communion, which endows one with bravery and strength in order to reach holiness and to fight against the temptations of the devil.

The convert about to receive the last rites is bombarded by a re-markable number of untranslatable words. Against the impending threat of death, the Spanish text is unequivocal in situating ritual rhetoric as that which brings to the convert the Sign of God, the *Viático* or host. It is the host that ransoms the individual from the finality of death by fortifying the communicant in faith, hope, and charity with which to resist the devil.

In the Tagalog, however, while *Viatico* is retained, it slides into the register of *bauon,* which is the food that one takes on a journey. The nature of this journey is ambiguous. Whereas the Castilian speaks of it in terms of eternity (*eternidad*), implying the abolition of a prior history, the Tagalog is rendered as *paroroonang malayo,* long jour-ney, which leaves unspecified the points of departure and arrival. What the *Viático* as *bauon* does is similarly equivocal. In the Tagalog, it gives one neither faith, hope, nor charity (*Fe, Esperanza, Caridad*) but bravery and strength. Neither of the words used here, *tapang* and *lacas,* has any moral or theological connotation. Both words denote the capacity to release energy, which in the passage above is directed at achieving *cabanalan,* holiness, and resisting *tocso,* temptation. Yet the word *cabanalan,* from the root word *banal,* also means to become disconcerted, disjointed, and confused; *tocso* also refers to questions, interruptions, and jokes. The Tagalog text could be read, then, in a way that would be considerably at odds with Spanish expectations. The appearance of *bauon* leads one to think not of death as a passage to eternal life but of provisions that one can take on an indeterminate journey. These provisions could be valued for the protection they gave one against the danger of interruptions and confusions outside, particularly from the confusion of spirits believed to cause illness, and from the interruption of life by death.

In another passage, Totanes's Spanish text refers to the sacrament of extreme unction as *la gran virtud,* the great virtue. In Tagalog, however, it is referred to as *ang daquilang cabagsican,* that which gives great potency (p. 44). The semantic disparity between "virtue" and "potency" is similar to the gap separating bravery and strength from faith, hope, and charity. It is precisely the semantic interval created by the sounding of an untranslatable word that incites the convert to attempt its appropriation. Indeed, clerical discourse seemed to encourage this practice. In another passage, Totanes speaks of the "sweet names" (*catamistamisang pangalan*/*dulcisimos nombres*) of Jesús and María as weapons for resisting temptation. He urges the convert:

Gamitin mo't houag bitiuan itong sandata, at mananalo ca ngani sa lahat na manga caauaymo. . . . Si Jesus nang si Jesus, si Maria nang si Maria ang iyong uiuicain, ang iyong tuturan sa caybuturan nang loob-mo at sa bibigmo naman. . . . Magpajesusmaria nang Magpajesusmaria ca hangan sa dica mapatdan nang hininga. [pp. 50–51]

Usa de esta poderosa arma, no la sueltes, no la dejes, y venceras ciertamente a todos tus enemigos. JesusMaría, JesusMaría, es lo que en cada respiracion has de decir con el corazon, y con la boca tambien. . . . Repite continuamente estas Santisimos y Dulcisimos Nombres de Jesús y de María mientras tengas vida.

Use this weapon and do not let go of it, so that you may triumph against all your enemies. . . . Jesus and Jesus, Mary and Mary is what you will say, and what you will have in each breath of your soul and on your mouth as well. . . . Repeat again and again Jesusmaria, Jesusmaria while you have the breath to do so.

As Jesús and María are proper names, they of course are not translated in any language. They are "proper" precisely to the extent that they refer to no other words in any vernacular but to things—in this case people—outside of it. They seem then to be part of language, yet they stand at a remove from the linguistic system of both Castilian and Tagalog. Because they resist translation into other words, proper names cross linguistic boundaries without being assimilated or transformed. In this sense, they mime the approach of spirits moving back and forth between life and death.[5] This perhaps explains why the names Jesús and María could be invested with the aura of a "powerful weapon" (*sandatang matibay/segura arma*). Like amulets, they have the effect of distancing the speaker from the threat of death and the possible horrors that lie beyond it. The names exist as cult objects valued for their ability to convey the sacredness of their source.

But the transfer of Jesús and María from one language to another can have other consequences as well. Such occur when the names are repeated as one name over and over again until the one name comes to refer only to itself. In the Tagalog text, the act of saying the name is itself condensed into one word, *Magpajesusmaria;* and to this day, a common Tagalog expression to register shock or signify amazement is *susmaryosep,* a contraction of the names Jesús, María, and José. Contraction and repetition tend to drain the name of its extra-linguistic content and rob it of its aura. Thus it does not lead the convert to contemplate the promise of salvation contained in the name and the social hierarchy such a promise implies. Rather than become absorbed by the sacredness of the name, one takes to it mechanically. That is, one reproduces it automatically when shocked or confronted by external threats, out of habit. In this way the name's particularity is detached from its sacred referent. If the name of the Sign could be used as a sanctified weapon, it could also be converted

5. On the problem of proper names, see Jacques Derrida, "Des Tours de Babel," in *Difference in Translation,* ed. Joseph F. Graham (Ithaca: Cornell University Press, 1985), pp. 167–185; and Siegel, *Solo in the New Order,* pp. 303–304.

in ways that distanced the speaker not only from the claims of death but from the Law and the agents who claimed to control it.

The following pattern thus emerges: The appearance of untranslatable terms lodged in the vernacular triggered the interest of native listeners. They were roused by the imperative to anticipate the figures of colonial authority whose proximity was signaled by the surge of Castilian and the signs of Christianity lodged in their own language. By alerting themselves to the shock effects afforded by untranslatable terms, Tagalogs could find a place from which to deal with the demands of authority. The question of untranslatability is thus reformulated into a concern to protect oneself from the threat of being engulfed by the rush of undecipherable and hence uncontrollable figures from the outside. It meant reading into Christianity a surplus of referents with which to reserve for oneself a position from which to face those at the top of the hierarchy. Translating the untranslatable entailed deferring to the signs of authority while at the same time eluding the meaning and intent behind those signs.

The possibility of protection, however, raises the issue of what would happen if one were not able to "read" warnings into Christianity, that is, if one were unable to translate and appropriate its terms. What shaped Tagalog response to the untranslatable terms of missionary discourse, allowing for their conversion from sacred words to objects of protection? Where else could one look in early Tagalog colonial society to understand the interest informing native conversion?

The Imperative of Indebtedness: *Utang na Loob* and *Hiya*

The Tagalog appropriation of untranslatable Christian terms—in a sense, their translation—was predicated, as I have argued, on a certain anxiety about the success or failure of localizing the outside forces of colonial rule. In this case, translation and conversion were inseparable from the wish to contract colonialism in the double sense of circumscribing its reach and regularizing one's dealings with it. Contractual relationships of any sort entail a series of reciprocal exchanges. One way, then, of understanding the link between conversion and translation among the Tagalogs is to see it in conjunction with native concepts of exchange and reciprocal indebtedness.

The discourses addressed by the priest to the converts sought to use a notion of reciprocity that is culturally specific to the Tagalogs. In their desire to communicate the work of Christ in the insertion of the individual into the circuit of God's gifts, missionaries constantly employed the Tagalog idioms of indebtedness and shame: *utang na loob* and *hiya*.

> All of these things our Lord Jesus Christ gave me that I might have something to give God the Father every day in order to make up for my debt [*utang na loob*] and sins.[6]

> Such was the desire of the Lord God that I reach the greatest good that He gave up His life on the cross between the two thieves. . . . O my Lord God, how great is my debt [*utang na loob*] to you.   [Herrera, *Meditaciones*, f. 8]

> . . . and renew your repentance and your shame [*hiya*] at having offended God.   [Blancas, *Librong*, pp. 282–283]

> How will I manage to let you in, O Lord, when I have not the means, and the house of my soul [*loob*] is so disorderly? Truly I am shamed [*hiya na hiya*] in front of you, my God.   [Ibid., p. 370]

Such passages are found in all missionary texts in the vernacular. In prescribing the appropriate rhetoric with which to address God, missionaries invariably translated one's dependence on Him in terms of *utang na loob*, debt of gratitude or debt of the inside [*loob*]. Repentance and sorrow for one's sins were rendered as *hiya*, or shame.

But as we had seen earlier, the Spaniards insisted on "love" and contrition—that is, the conflation of human and divine desire—as the real basis for repentance and the appropriate stance for receiving God's gifts. Tagalog idioms of reciprocity were thus used as supplements to bring about the preferred basis for transactions with the Father. *Utang na loob* and *hiya* were made to occupy a conceptual space in the framework of evangelization analogous to that assigned to the native language: as the passages for the signs of God and the establishment of a Spanish monopoly on their circulation. Like the missionaries' efforts to reduce the vernacular to the margins of God's

6. Padre Alonso de Santa Ana, *Explicación de la doctrina cristiana en la lengua tagala* (1672; Manila: Amigos del País, 1853), p. 112.

language and Spanish discourse, however, their attempts to subordinate Tagalog idioms of reciprocity to Christian concepts were problematic and inconclusive. In the end, as we shall see, native conceptions of reciprocity tended to elide colonial-Christian notions of indebtedness and the submission they implied.

As part of a constellation of "values" among the peoples in the Christianized lowland areas of the Philippines, *utang na loob* and *hiya* have attracted considerable scholarly attention since the 1960s. Among the most influential such works were those of Charles Kaut and of Mary Hollnsteiner and the late Frank Lynch.[7] Set along the lines of structural-functionalist theory, their analyses of these "values" have been rightly criticized as ahistorical. As Reynaldo Ileto has cogently pointed out, by excluding history, studies of *utang na loob* and *hiya* end up depoliticizing reciprocity by failing to consider the place of conflict in processes of exchange and indebtedness. Ileto goes on to resituate these notions of reciprocity in late-nineteenth- and early-twentieth-century peasant movements. He convincingly demonstrates the revolutionary potential of *utang na loob* as it is constantly invoked in Tagalog literature of this period and in the writings of messianic leaders intended to rally their followers for a series of local revolts against Spain and later against the United States. While Ileto's work is a significant departure from those of Kaut, Hollnsteiner, and Lynch, it nonetheless tends to join them in regarding the *loob* in *utang na loob* as a privileged, a priori entity.[8] In this sense, *loob* assumes its coherence on the basis of a given ontological status as that which is part of yet apart from processes of exchange.

It is of crucial importance to hold on to Ileto's insight that reciprocity is always predicated on the possibility of conflict and disruption. But when we consider the historical effects of *utang na loob* and *hiya* in the context of conversion, we should initially try to circumvent

7. Charles Kaut, "*Utang na Loob:* A System of Contractual Obligation among Tagalogs," in *Southwestern Journal of Anthropology* 17, no. 3 (1961): 256–272; Mary R. Hollnsteiner, "Reciprocity in the Lowland Philippines," and Frank Lynch, S.J., "Social Acceptance Reconsidered," both in *Four Readings on Philippine Values,* ed. Frank Lynch and Alfonso de Guzmán III (Quezon City: Ateneo de Manila University Press, 1973), pp. 1–92.

8. Ileto, *Pasyon and Revolution,* esp. pp. 11–28. Ileto is more sensitive to the problem of *utang na loob,* defining *loob* as both the "inside of something" and the "inner self" (ibid., p. 331). Given the contexts he is examining and the apparently phenomenological thrust of his analysis, however, he tends to lean more heavily toward the latter definition.

both a phenomenological and a purely operational definition of *loob*—the "inside" that is staked in a debt transaction. It is helpful to reexamine *loob* first of all as a linguistic fact—as a signifier that attaches itself to a variety of signifieds. In this way, we can ask how *loob* gains value and force as a cultural term in a larger historical field.

The missionary texts make *loob* carry the weight of such Western concepts as soul, will, and conscience. The examination of conscience, for example, is said to entail a preparation of one's *loob* in expectation of God's judgment and forgiveness.[9] Thus the *loob* is seen as bearing the marks of a sinful past, as being opened up and offered to God in confession, and as affording a dwelling place for the Sign of God in communion.[10] In Christ, God is said to have given His own *loob* to the converts, and therefore he expects them to return their *loobs* to Him in payment. Damnation, in this case, is the permanent separation of human from divine *loob,* thus marking the end of all relationships of indebtedness (*utang na loob*) between the two.[11]

The aim of the missionaries' efforts to circumscribe the meanings of *loob* should be fairly clear to us at this point. *Loob,* along with a host of other Tagalog terms (*sisi,* repentance; *casalanan,* sin; *aua,* mercy; and many more) were meant to bear the burden of all those cherished metaphysical and theological concepts that would allow for the imposition of Spanish rule inside as well as outside the natives' minds. If we turn to other sorts of missionary texts, however—the *vocabularios* and the early-twentieth-century *diccionarios* modeled on them—we get a sense of the semantic instability of *loob.* Father Pedro de San Buenaventura's 1613 *Vocabulario de la lengua tagala* defines *loob* as "inside," "to go inside," "an interior room in a house," as well as the Spanish constructs "will" and "heart."[12] These connotations of *loob,* along with others, appear in Noceda and San Lucar's 1745 *Vocabulario de la lengua tagala* and Serrano-Laktaw's 1914 *Diccionario tagalog-hispano.* On the one hand, it is defined as *lo más interno,* the most inner part of the person, hence the seat of taste and desire. On the other hand, it is also the mere "inside" of any object, as

---

9. Totanes, *Manual tagalog,* p. 65.
10. Blancas, *Librong,* pp. 240–243; Herrera, *Meditaciones,* folios 4–8.
11. Santa Ana, *Explicación,* p. 112.
12. Padre Pedro de San Buenaventura, *Vocabulario de la lengua tagala* (Pila: Tomas Pinpin y Domingo Loag, 1613).

in *looban,* the inside of a house, the ground on which it is built, the floor of a building, the yard that separates the house from the street. In this sense, *loob* is not a privileged inside that grounds being but an inside that signals an interval separating one object from another or one part of the object from its other parts. *Looban* can also function as a verb to mean the act of attacking and sacking a house. Rendered as *ipaloob* or *pagpapaloob,* it pertains to the insertion of one object into another, its enclosure and concealment from the gaze of those outside. The verb form of *loob* indicates that it is thought of as the consequence of a prior displacement of objects from the outside, through either exchange or robbery. There is a sense, then, in which there is nothing natural or spontaneous about what is inside. For what is inside consists of things that have been shifted there from the outside or *labas.* Inside and outside thus tend to intermix. This sense is further reflected in the inflection of *loob* into *pangloob,* under-clothes, which serve as an interior layer of clothing between one's outer clothes and one's body. The same word is used to mean the inside of a fish pond along the bank of a river and for a kind of trap for rats. This is a further extension of the sense of *loob* as the space for the containment of things that come from the outside.

The inside of things, it is worth noting, is subject to a similar process of displacement outside. *Loob* is at the root of one of the words for "to give," *ipagcaloob,* and a gift itself is *caloob,* literally part of the inside of something. Thus inside is juxtaposed rather than dialectically opposed to outside. In being attached to the word for debt, *utang, loob* figures as both the site and the object of exchange. It consists of objects in circulation just as it functions to represent the desired form of circulation. *Utang na loob* from this perspective is not only a debt of gratitude but also a debt of, from, and for the inside, as indicated by the particle *na.* The *loob* that is staked in a debt transaction is therefore an inside that is also an interior surface, a container as well as that which is contained, but only to the extent that it is already oriented toward an external process of exchange.

Loob is important not because it invariably designated a "soul" (as the Spaniards wanted it to) at the core of being. The significance of *loob* lies in the fact that it marks out the space within which objects and signs from the outside can be accumulated and from which and toward which they can be issued in payment of a debt. In *utang na loob* transactions, the *loob* that one places in circulation is detachable and reattachable; it does not, as the Spaniards wished it to do, sum up the self in its totality. Where Tagalog notions of indebtedness are concerned, *loob* does not exist apart from the mechanism of debt transactions; it can be known and realized only in the process of indebtedness. To reduce *loob,* as the Spaniards did, to a question of intentionality and the locus of guilt and repentance is to assume that it stands behind and above the terms of reciprocity. But as the various definitions of *loob* suggest, *utang na loob* transactions imply neither an originary source of gifts nor a privileged interiority accountable for its debts.

If a sense of subjectivity is not what determines exchange, constraining one to enter into a reciprocal network of indebtedness with others, what does? In the context of *utang na loob,* it is the notion of *hiya.* From the early seventeenth century to the present day, *hiya* has been defined as the appropriate affect that accompanies indebtedness. Yet it is also the feeling that arises when one senses one's exclusion from a circuit of debt relations.

Often translated as "shame," *hiya,* like *loob,* can take on a wide variety of significations. *Hiya* is also irritation or vexation at being made an object of amusement or a foil for someone else's aggrandizement. To subject someone to this state of shame is *hiyaiin,* that is, to mock, to jest, to disconcert and confuse, and figuratively to slap and trample upon (*dar una bofetada*). To this extent, to be in a state of *hiya* is to be in a vulnerable position, available to receive another's blows, whether physical or figurative. For this reason, *hiya* is the embarrassment that arises from being overwhelmed (*empachado*). *Hiya* expresses the sense of one's inability to fend off the signs that come from outside by performing a response adequate to what one has received: that is, the sense of the unregulated and undeserved reception of signs and things from the outside. The displeasure produced by the feeling of *hiya* therefore comes from being made to think of all the things one would like to give back in return but cannot, as well as all the things one would like to receive but can no longer ask for.

But *hiya* also has a positive sense, as in *magbigay hiya,* to render respect, to consider and honor someone. The Tagalogs say, "Ang tauong kulang sa hiya, walang halaga ang wika": One who lacks *hiya* is one whose words have no value."[13] *Hiya* gives value to words

13. Serrano-Laktaw, ed., *Diccionario tagalog-hispano,* p. 333.

proffered in discursive exchange, just as it is the dominant affect that arises from the failure to return what one has received. Hence the ambiguity of shame. On the one hand, it is the condition of possibility for indebtedness, so that to have no *hiya* is to have no *utang na loob*. Indeed, as studies of Tagalog reciprocity indicate, the worst thing one can say about a person is that he or she is *walang hiya*, without shame, which is the same as to say that the person is *walang utang na loob*, without any sense of indebtedness. On the other hand, *hiya* also figures the rupture in debt transactions, filling one with confusion and a deep sense of helplessness in relation to the outside. *Hiya* thus colors the entire spectrum of indebtedness, signaling both its operation and its failure. It is out of fear of being publicly shamed, of being excluded from a network of exchange vis-à-vis the outside, that one accedes to *utang na loob* ties. For without the fear of *hiya*, the *labas* or outside would remain unknown. Consequently, the *loob* or inside could never be put into circulation. One can appropriate things from the outside only to the extent that one manages to block the surge of *hiya*. *Utang na loob* ties are valued precisely insofar as they allow one to contain the negative and undesirable affect and effect of *hiya*, converting it instead into an element that infuses what is given up in return. Reciprocity in terms of *hiya* and *utang na loob* thus becomes a matter of anticipating and domesticating the ever-present possibility of being overwhelmed by an uncontrollable rush of signs and things from the outside. For if one were incapable of knowing *hiya*, one would end up being "surprised" by its sudden surge to the point of being cut off from exchange. And without exchange, no sense of an inside or *loob* would emerge.

To the extent that Christianity was phrased in the idiom of *hiya* and *utang na loob*, Tagalogs felt constrained to attend to it. Caught up in what seemed like an unending stream of undecipherable words put forth in terms of reciprocal obligations, the natives "converted," that is, availed themselves of the sacraments as a way of entering into a debt transaction with the Spaniards and their God. The Tagalogs' interest in contracting Christianity and colonialism stemmed from their fear of being overcome by *hiya*, that is, of being barraged by gifts and signs that they might not be able to read and would be unable to control. Yet the terms of this contract, like the procedures of reading and assumptions about mastery, differed between the ruler and the ruled. The Tagalog notion of reciprocity spelled a crucial difference in terms of the indebtedness that conversion entailed. One way of getting a sense of the difference is to look back at the matter of confession. The validity of confession, as we had seen, depended largely on an accurate accounting of one's sins. The examination of conscience was thus a crucial prelude to confession. It allowed for a detailed recollection of the past events contained in the *loob* and their translation into a discursive offering to God. While insisting on a rigorous accounting of sins, the missionaries also demanded that they be converted into a narrative as straightforward as possible:

> He must straighten his sentences, open his *loob,* arrange his words, relate all of his sins, their number, their extent, their gravity; and if it were to be compared to walking, [the telling of sins] should take to the middle road rather than fork out in various directions; tell and relate everything so that the Lord God may know what is in your *loob* if you want to be forgiven everything by our Lord God.   [Totanes, *Manual tagalog,* p. 82]

In effect, the confessor expected from the penitent not only a comprehensive accounting of sins but also their recounting in a manner as free as possible from deviation. As it turned out, however, native converts tended to be much more interested in embarking on a discursive exchange than in getting to the point of that exchange. The reason has to do with the nature of payment involved in *utang na loob* relationships.

Studies of Tagalog reciprocity have stressed the inequality built into debt transactions. The hierarchy that is formed by indebtedness is based on the sensed incommensurability between the gift that is received and its return, particularly if the gift is unsolicited.[14] The prototypical debt of this sort is the debt one owes to one's mother. One has an *utang na loob* to one's mother (and never the reverse) by virtue of having received from her the unexpected gift of life. It is assumed that one will never be able to repay this debt in full, but instead will make partial payments in the form of respect (*paggalang*). But respect as a form of token recognition tends to be most explicit on the level of rhetoric. One uses such words of deference as *ho* and *po* in addressing one's mother—or any parental figure. These terms are usually attached to the words directed to the figure of authority, as in *Ano po ang gusto ninyo?* (What do you want, sir [madam]?) or *Oho,*

---

14. Hollnsteiner, "Reciprocity," pp. 75–76; Kaut, "*Utang na Loob,*" p. 262.

aco na po ang magluluto (Yes, sir [ma'am], I will be the one to cook).
By themselves, *ho* and *po* refer to nothing in particular. Only when
they are inserted between words directed to one's parents or elders do
they take on significance, and then they signal respect. To this extent,
they are also the signs of *utang na loob* ties that would otherwise
remain unarticulated. Children are usually given no set tasks around
the house. They are expected to serve their parents only after they
have become adults. The child thus accumulates a burden of indebtedness, and even after one enters adulthood one never stops owing
one's parent one's *loob*. As Mary Hollnsteiner has said, "nothing [the
child] can do during its lifetime can make up for what [the mother]
has done for it."[15]
The intrinsic inequality of debt relationships seems benign where a
mother and her child are concerned. It can take on much more pressing political overtones, however, when it is transferred to other social
contexts. Hollnsteiner makes the following pertinent observations:

> In the landlord–tenant relationship . . . the tenant knows he cannot
> approach anywhere near an equivalent return. As long as he fulfills his
> expected duties towards his landlord and shows by bringing a few
> dozen eggs and helping out at festive occasions that he recognizes a debt
> of gratitude (*utang na loob*), he may continue to expect benefits from
> his landlord. The tenant receives uninterrupted preferential treatment
> despite the fact that he never reciprocates with interest and never re-
> verses the debt relationships.   [Hollnsteiner, "Reciprocity," p. 74]

The hierarchical relationship between landlord and tenant arises
because of the tenant's inability to override the benefits bestowed by
the landlord. The continuation of exchange between the two is under-
written by the nature of payment. The tenant is expected to do no
more than render token signs of indebtedness to the landlord. Partial
payments ensure that a continuous flow of benefits from above will
accrue to those below. Such payments have no set form and are not
subject to a rigorous schedule; the nature and frequency of payments
depend largely on the creditor's whim and the debtor's resources.
Reciprocity in this case maintains a hierarchy to the extent that the
full payment of debts can always be—indeed, must be—deferred.
The imperative to defer full payment in favor of tokens of indebted-

15. Hollnsteiner, "Reciprocity," p. 76.

ness makes for a peculiar contract. Among the Spaniards, the contraction of obligations between two parties was always articulated with reference to a third term that stood outside of exchange yet determined its contours. Whether figured as God, the king, the state, or the law, this third term served as the central figure in all negotiations, acting as the origin, interpreter, and enforcer of the terms governing exchange. It was thus regarded as the source of hierarchy just as it was the source of all gifts. It was also within the province of the transcendent third term to insist on specific kinds of payment in return for benefits it had bestowed on its subjects. In the context of Spanish colonization, payments consisted of taxes, forced labor, the ritual observance of the sacraments, and the like. Furthermore, the specified amounts of payments were always coordinated with a time-table of sorts: monthly tax rolls, weekly masses, annual confessions, and so forth. This practice made for a system of indebtedness that was posited on the possibility and inevitability of full payment. For ultimately all debts contracted by the individual within the law culminated in death. Death was the last horizon of exchange. And where evangelization was concerned, it marked the moment of irrevocable reckoning of all of one's accumulated debts in the presence of an infinite Creditor.

By contrast, the tripartite structure of the contract gives way to a different configuration in *utang na loob* ties. The contracting of debts, given the nonoriginary source and destination of gifts (*loob*) and the practice of token payments, is premised not on the sanction of a transcendent third term but precisely on its elision. The possibility of eliding the third term has a linguistic basis. As we saw in Chapter 2, Tagalog has two pronouns to indicate the first person plural "we," in Spanish *nosotros: cami,* the exclusive "we," and *tayo,* the inclusive "we." *Cami* makes it conceivable to articulate a transaction between a self and an other which arises from the exclusion of a third party. In this case, one speaks of maintaining *utang na loob* ties that are predicated on a negative consideration of those who are outside such ties. Eighteenth-century *vocabularios* record such expressions as *Cami,y, nagpapapautangan nang loob,* "We are indebted to each other (and not to them)" or "We are contracting debts with one another (and not with them)" and *Hindi nagpapautang loob siya sa aquin,* "He does not want to be indebted to me." The forging of obligations thus

becomes a matter between *loob* rather than between individuals before the law.

The effect of this elision is to render the hierarchy found in *utang
na loob* ties explicitly arbitrary. This is to say that relationships of
indebtedness are not instituted by an Absolute Source of debts making itself felt through a progressive chain of signs. The arbitrariness of
hierarchy in this instance comes from the tenuous connection it is
thought to have with the figure of authority from which gifts come.
Token payments of debts are made not to memorialize authority (and
thereby to consolidate hierarchy) but rather, as in the case of offerings
proffered to the *nono,* simply to loosen the pressures from above (and
so to deflect the full force of hierarchy).

Conversely, failure to make partial payments signals one's failure
to read in the gift the return that is demanded, leading to an outbreak
of *hiya.* A violent onrush of things and signs from the outside makes it
impossible to have a sense of *loob* that could be offered in exchange.
Hollnsteiner, in discussing a Visayan analogue of *hiya, way ibalus,*
cites a popular saying: "A beggar prays for the good health of
whoever gives him alms, and a dog barks for his master, but a *way
ibalus* does not even have a prayer or a bark for his benefactor"
("Reciprocity," p. 78). The eruption of *hiya* leaves one speechless,
utterly unable to return even in words what one has received. In the
interest of containing *hiya,* one is thus constrained to reciprocate a
gift and thereby elude the potentially confounding and disconcerting
force of hierarchy. Reciprocity then is a matter of reading into the gift
one receives much less its source than the return that is expected.
Within a Christian-colonial context, the notion of *utang na loob*
furnished the Tagalog converts with a way of conceiving relations of
inequality that sporadically displaced the demands issuing from the
totalizing hierarchy of Spanish Christianity.

We can read the Tagalog response to confession in this light. At the
end of the confession manual in Pinpin's *Librong* we find the following remarks:

O my friends, aren't these questions wonderful [*galing*], and isn't it
good to go through them one by one; and if you can learn all these, then
you will be ready to confess to a Priest who does not speak Tagalog; for
someone asked me what this word *descubriste* means in the ninth com-

mandment of the Lord God, and there seem to be many words that the Spaniards speak that has this *des,* which this person doesn't know. So now I will teach you this because you, too, may not know it. [Pp. 234–235]

Pinpin celebrates here not the spiritual efficacy of confession but the accumulation of questions in Castilian and Tagalog. This move is consistent with what we saw in Chapter 2. The Tagalogs' fascination with confession, as with Castilian, had little to do with total submission to the Word of God.

It is instructive to note in this connection that the Tagalog word for asking forgiveness in confession is *tauad,* literally to bargain, to haggle, and to use evasions (in Castilian, *regatear*). In a sense, then, the Tagalogs saw confession as a means of bargaining with authority. And before one can bargain, one must have the appropriate resources. It was confession as a machine for producing signs that could be appropriated—displaced, as it were, from the outside to the inside—that attracted the natives. It provided an opportunity to hook onto the *loob* of Spanish discourse, to extract from it "untranslatable" word objects with which to perform the return demanded by the source of those words.

The interest in reciprocating the Spanish gift of words can be seen in Pinpin's evasion of any discussion of the meaning of confession. Instead, he slips into a discussion of the Spanish prefix *des.* He proceeds to list words in Castilian to which this prefix, indicating negation, can be attached. In the following three pages he discusses *con,* which signifies the preposition "with." Unlike the Spaniards, who were intent on orienting the flow of confessional discourse back to God, the Tagalogs were concerned with ensuring a continued proliferation of signs that would establish *utang na loob* ties with the authority figure and so multiply the possibilities for bargaining with him. The urgency of accumulating signs was due precisely to the insistent and exorbitant demand of the priest that penitents "exhaust" (*obosin*) themselves of all those signs contained in their *loob* as payment for their debts. Clerical discourse sought to theologize such debts as "sins." Yet the Tagalog word they used, *casalanan,* derived from the root word *sala,* denotes an error in counting. *Sala* is also synonymous with *ligaw,* to become lost, to become confused and disconcerted. Thus sin as *sala* receives the charge of *hiya*, that is, the sense of being remiss in one's acknowledgment of one's debt to another. The expenditure of sin in confession could then be thought of as a way of containing *hiya* within one's discourse. In so doing, one would avoid its sudden and uncontrollable eruption at the failure to perform a discursive return in exchange for the *loob* that one had been given. The idiom of *utang na loob* and *hiya* riveted the natives' attention not on the sacramental value of confession as a means of participating in divine commerce but on the discursive machinery of confession as a means of contracting and extending ties of reciprocity with those who had a surplus of signs. By availing themselves of the sacraments, particularly of penance, the Tagalogs seized the opportunity to maneuver around Spanish demands and thus to avoid the shock of *hiya* when they were confronted by them. It was perhaps for this reason that to hear native confessions was, as Murillo says, "to enter into a labyrinth without a clue." For the missionary who asked for an exhaustive accounting of the penitent's past was beset by digressions and non sequiturs. Blancas admonished the Tagalogs: "Why, despite all the admonitions and examples of the Priest, do so many of you persist in such twists and turns, in such obscurities and deviations in your *loob,* so that your sentences are contaminated by these same obscurities; you should be ashamed [*mahiya*] of yourselves for engaging in riddles [*nagbobogtongan*] during confession" (pp. 242–243).

Missionary lexicographers recorded native riddles (*bogtong*) to illustrate word usage in Tagalog. Such riddles seem to have antedated the Spanish conquest and they have continued to circulate, many of them unchanged, up to the present day. They were staples of Tagalog literature during the Spanish colonial period. Spanish accounts point out the *bogtong*'s popularity. Tagalogs were given to trading riddles in a game called *magbogtongan* at fiestas, wakes, and weddings, and even while engaged in such mundane tasks as tending their fields.[16] These games were not contests in the sense of having winners and losers. The delight in trading riddles came from the opportunity they presented for showing one's ability to decontextualize words from their everyday usages. What, for example, is "a little lake bounded by

16. Bienvenido Lumbera, "Poetry of the Early Tagalogs," *Philippine Studies* 16 (April 1968): 223–230.

a bamboo fence"? Answer: an eye. What is "by day a bamboo tube, by night a sea"? Answer: a sleeping mat.[17]

An eye and a sleeping mat have no necessary connections to a lake bounded by a bamboo fence or to a bamboo tube and a sea. The pleasure of such *bogtong* comes from the way they shift a word away from its functional connotations and create for it another constellation of associations. Hence, "mat" is seen not in association with sleeping but with the sea at night, and "eye" is brought in touch not with seeing but with the bounded area of a lake. By converting the discourse of sin into a game of *bogtongan,* native penitents displayed their ability to return conundrums in exchange for other conundrums they received from the priest. Instead of a straight narrative, the confessor got back what seemed to him like a bewildering show of the penitent's verbal dexterity.

Adding to the confusion was the natives' propensity to tell not their own sins but those of others: "And others seriously go astray when they announce to the Priest the sins of their wives, or their sons-in-law, or their mothers-in-law, while their own sins rarely cross their lips; the only reason they go to the Priest is to denounce to him all the people they dislike," Blancas complains (pp. 245–247). Rather than assume responsibility for their sins—as the acts that originated in their own *loob*—penitents appropriated the sins of others as offerings to appease the figure of authority. Blancas complains also of the tendency to blame others—a neighbor, one's spouse, even the devil—for one's sins. Tagalog penitents were far from inclined to claim ownership of their sins, for sins were attached to the *loob*, and everyone knew where the contents of the *loob* came from: outside. Thus the prescribed internalization of guilt and repentance was circumvented and confessional discourse remained suspended in the economy of *utang na loob* and *hiya.*

From this perspective it is not surprising to hear that confession served as well for displays of braggadocio. "One other great error that others commit in their confession," Blancas remarks, "is that they speak only of their great deeds, while never speaking about their sins. . . . The only reason they go [to confession] is to honor their own goodness" (p. 251). By bragging about one's "goodness" (*cabanalan*), one bypasses the demand for a narrative of sin. Bragging

17. Ibid., pp. 224–225.

in effect tended to subvert the entire conceptual apparatus of confession. Instead of submitting to the Law by recounting their accumulated transgressions against it, native penitents converted confession into an occasion for boasting and protesting their innocence. In this sense, the *loob* that is offered as payment for one's debt in confession ends up submitting to the representatives of the Law but at the same time relegating the Law itself to the margins of exchange.

To the Spanish demand that converts make their bodies speak the language of God, the Tagalog converts responded by performing token payments designed to appease the figure of authority and deflect the force of hierarchy. They eluded the interiorization of the interrogative language of the Law carried by the insistent voice of the dominant other. Confessional discourse, as with the sudden turn to the other sacraments, tended to be motivated, as I have argued, by the fear of *hiya* and the desire to establish *utang na loob* ties with those at the top of the colonial hierarchy. What emerged was confession without "sin," conversion in a state of distraction. Just as, in Pinpin's case, "Castilian" as the "inside" of things Spanish is acquired by the evasion of grammar, Christian signs occurring at intervals in clerical discourse were appropriated in the process of marginalizing their Referent. Conversion where the Tagalogs were concerned occurred as an *après-coup* response to the unsolicited and therefore shocking gift of signs that the Spaniards bestowed on them. To tame this shock, the Tagalogs had recourse to the familiar terms *hiya* and *utang na loob,* which accompanied the transfer of Spanish signs to the vernacular. Converting conversion and confusing confession, the Tagalogs submitted while at the same time hollowing out the Spanish call to submission.

CHAPTER 5

Translating Submission

The tendency to elude the all-inclusive hierarchy proposed by evangelization and colonial rule was one feature of Tagalog conversion. To recognize the authority behind the ensemble of Christian signs was not necessarily to accede to Spanish signifying conventions and the interests they implied. But the natives who accepted Christianity, many of them enthusiastically, did thereby submit to colonial authority; something about submission appealed to them. Thus arises the possibility of another kind of conversion in accord with Spanish intentions, one apparently consistent with the missionaries' assumptions in regard to translation. Such a conversion would entail deference to the other's language not simply in a state of distraction but submission to the intent behind it as well. Conversion in this sense brings with it a willingness to subordinate one's interests to those of others who are beyond one. Instead of evading the hierarchy of languages and the social order it set forth, one is led actively to incorporate it. Able to read Tagalog in terms of Castilian (instead of simply the other way around), converts could discern a commonality of interest between themselves and the missionary. Such a merging of interests resulted from the recognition of another realm that, by transcending the division between ruler and ruled, sanctioned its existence. It then became possible to construe an essential identity of interests between Tagalogs and Spaniards to the extent that both acknowledged the sway of an outside authority from whom all language and thoughts derived.

What are the conditions that make possible this other kind of conversion? How is it related not only to translation but also to colonial policies in regard to such things as patronage, submission, and class distinctions? How is "real" conversion among the Tagalogs, or at least among a certain class of them, understandable in the context of new social divisions instituted within colonial society?

To address these questions, it is necessary to probe further into the social and political effects of evangelization. Earlier I remarked on the intimate link between colonial politics and religious proselytizing. For the Spaniards, one grew out of the other. The resettlement of the natives into centralized administrative units was in an important sense a function of the missionary impulse to create coherent relays for the spread of the Gospel. The imperative to convert the natives—to situate them within a different field of power relations—necessitated the "invention" of Tagalog grammar as well as the relocation of Tagalog bodies. To sustain evangelization, Tagalog society and politics similarly had to be reformulated. An examination of this process of recasting—translating, as it were—native society into a different grid of social relations may help us understand why submission—to the extent of real conversion—may have seemed a desirable alternative to some Tagalogs.

Person and Status in Precolonial Society

In his brilliant essay on sixteenth-century Filipino class structure, William Henry Scott sums up the difficulty of identifying and categorizing Tagalog society in Western—be it Spanish or English—politico-juridical terms.[1] The difficulty is due mainly to the ambiguous nature of the sixteenth- and early-seventeenth-century Spanish accounts that provide the chief means for reconstructing the native social order. Scott's initial perplexity over these sources is worth citing at length:

> . . . any history teacher who has tried to use them to extract even such simple details as the rights and duties of each social class for purposes of

1. Scott, "Filipino Class Structure in the Sixteenth Century," in *Cracks in the Parchment Curtain*, pp. 96–126. The standard Spanish sources on the Tagalogs are Juan de Plasencia, "Costumbres de los Tagalos" (1589), in *Crónica*, ed. Santa Inés; Chirino, *Relación de las Islas Filipinas;* Antonio de Morga, *Sucesos de las Islas Filipinas* (1609), ed. Jose Rizal (Paris: Garnier, 1890). Other seventeenth- and eighteenth-century accounts are based on these sources and often quote whole passages verbatim, particularly from Plasencia.

his own understanding and his students' edification, knows how frustrating the exercise can be.

The problems are many. . . . They do not, for example, distinguish legislative, judicial and executive functions in native governments nor do they even indicate whether *datu* is a social class or a political office. On one page, they tell us that a ruling chief has life-and-death authority over his subjects, but on the next, that these subjects wander off to join some other chief if they feel like it. They describe a second social class as "freemen"—neither rich nor poor as if liberty were an economic attribute while one account calls them "plebeians" and another "gentlemen and cavaliers." The *maharlika* whom modern Filipinos know as "noblemen" show up as oarsmen rowing their master's boats or fieldhands harvesting his crops. And a third category called slaves everybody agrees are not slaves at all; yet they may be captured in raids, bought and sold in domestic and foreign markets or sacrificed alive at their master's funeral. Moreover, if the data as recorded in original documents are confusing, they are even more so by the need to translate sixteenth century Spanish terms which have no equivalent in modern English. Thus, *pechero* becomes "commoner" and loses its significance as somebody who renders feudal dues.   [Scott, "Filipino Class Structure," Pp. 96–97]

The confusion of data in early Spanish accounts stems from what seems like the inadequacy of Spanish political terminology, rooted in Roman law and European feudalism, to comprehend Tagalog social structure. There appears to be a lack of fit between Spanish descriptions and the Tagalog reality they seek to convey. Perhaps the difficulty may be attributed to the overdetermined nature of both Spanish political terminology and Tagalog designations of social status: the one is the product of a complex history of patronage and a century of imperial expansion, while the other is shaped by the vicissitudes of relationships of reciprocity and indebtedness carried out on a highly local level.

Spanish accounts generally distinguish among three "estates" (*estados*) when they refer to native social structure. These estates follow along the general lines of ruler, ruled, and slaves. Each estate is further subdivided into subgroups: the rulers into *datu* (chief) and his kin, called *maginoo;* the ruled into *timaua* and *maharlica;* and the slaves (*alipin*) into *namamahay* (literally, one who comes to another's house) and *sagigilid* (one who lives in another's house). Scott's patient reading of Spanish accounts makes it apparent that each estate was defined principally along the lines of relations of indebtedness.[2]

The head of a *barangay* or village was the *datu*. Only men could occupy this position. Spanish accounts indicate that the *datu* and his kin comprised an elite group called *maginoo*. Scott assumes that the *datu* came from the *maginoo* group, that is, that the latter category preceded the former. Yet as the *maginoo* group is never described as such in the accounts (Scott, p. 100), apparently membership in the village elite did not necessarily qualify one to be a *datu*. Rather, one who became a *datu* thereby became a *maginoo*. For while it was common enough for chiefs to inherit their positions from their fathers (so that the *maginoo* group appeared to be a birthright aristocracy), it was also common for nonelites to usurp village leadership and claim the position of *datu* for themselves.

One's claim to the rank of *datu* was conditioned largely by one's ability to attract a sizable following. "A powerful *datu* is . . . literally a popular datu," Scott tells us (p. 102). And popularity was based on one's ability to initiate the establishment of obligations with others. "To lead" in Tagalog is *mamono,* from the root word *pono,* "a leader who governs," but also a conduit of sorts, in that it refers to the roots and trunk of a tree. In the expression *Mamono ca,* "You lead," it implies beginning something. We may assume here that the *datu,* as the *pono* of the village, was able to lead his followers in war and trade with other villages. He would thus be regarded as the one most capable of securing the surplus with which to engage in a series of reciprocal exchanges with others in the community. As a *pono,* the

---

2. Scott, "Filipino Class Structure," pp. 99–111, 122–126. Given the tendentiousness of Spanish descriptions of Tagalog social classes, it would be impossible to extract from them a "pure" image of precolonial Tagalog culture and society. As Scott indicates, Tagalog social structure was already undergoing changes during the years (1590s–1630s) when the Spaniards were beginning to describe it. The causes of these changes are difficult to ascertain except with reference to the establishment and eventual consolidation of the Spanish presence in the islands. It is worth keeping in mind, however, that precolonial Tagalog society was far from static. Spanish accounts, always informed by a specific cluster of interests, invariably affect the terms of any discussion of native society still outside the control and influence of colonial authority. Thus Scott's aim of arriving at a "distinct, non-contradictory, and functional meaning for each Filipino term used in Spanish accounts" (p. 89) runs into difficulties at the outset. One cannot speak of a "precolonial" or "prehispanic" Tagalog social structure without factoring in the historical effects of the Spanish presence already at work in the very documentation of this society.

datu was the initiator of indebtedness, but was himself indebted to no one outside the *barangay*.

It was perhaps for this reason that the *datu*'s role was never specified in juridical or executive terms. True, he did play a role in the settling of village disputes. Yet he had no special power to resolve such conflicts, for they were often referred to a council of elders (which itself had no Tagalog designation—an indication of the looseness of arbitration procedures). The village chief enjoyed no special prerogative to pronounce judgments on cases brought before him. The accepted procedure for settling cases was to submit the accused to a trial by ordeal or divination. The resolution of conflicts was thus a matter of the random determination of blame and responsibility rather than the ascertaining of guilt on the basis of a moral calculus and legal precedents. Neither the *datu* nor the council of elders had full control over the outcome of litigation procedures, as conflicts were submitted to the rule of chance. Each act of meting out "justice" was thus discrete, resulting from an unpredictable conjunction of signs and events in divinatory practices or trials by ordeal.

The *datu*'s status was confirmed by the deference and respect that he could command from others in the village. The signs of deference included the limited rendering of labor and goods on the part of his followers. He was given part of the annual harvest, aid in feasts, maritime expeditions, war, and trade. Access to certain fields, fisheries, river passages, and the like was reserved primarily to his kin. The deference rendered to the *datu* also had a rhetorical aspect, indicated by the way in which he was addressed by others:

> The respect is shown by such deferential behavior as covering the mouth with the hand when addressing him, or contracting the body in a profound bow on entering his presence indoors, and raising the hands alongside the cheeks. The same deference is shown to his family and descendents . . . to all *maginoo*, in short—and slander against any of them is severely punished.   [Scott, "Filipino Class Structure," p. 103]

The tokens of respect rendered to the *datu* and other *maginoo*—whether economic or rhetorical—are reminiscent of the tokens of inequality exchanged by patron and client in an *utang na loob* relationship. Submission to the *datu*'s authority consisted of acknowledgment of his position as the initiator of obligations among others in the village. Particularly in riverine communities, the *datu* led the people in trading and raiding, that is, in the appropriation of the surplus goods and slaves that made for the formation of réciprocal ties among those whom he ruled. This is not to say that the *datu* caused exchange. The substance of his position as the *pono* and his designation as a *maginoo* was his reputation for acting in a way that allowed for the operation of exchange and indebtedness. In other words, being a *datu* depended on being recognized as such not by an authority outside the *barangay* but by those within it.

We may clarify this matter by taking a look at the inflections of *ginoo*, the root word of *maginoo*. Noceda and San Lucar's *Vocabulario de la lengua tagala* defines it as a "principal member," whether male or female, of a community. *Maginoo* is also an honorific title of sorts that was used to address a member of the village elite of either gender. Rendered as *guminoo*, it meant to refer to someone as *maginoo*; as *ginooin*, one who is addressed as *maginoo*. To act or carry oneself as if one were a member of the elite is *mag-ginoo* or *mag-maginoo*, while to insinuate oneself in the company of other *maginoo* is *maquiginoo* (in Castilian, *meterse con los principales*). As mentioned earlier, the Spanish acounts never describe *maginoo* as a distinct class, perhaps because they did not comprise a birthright aristocracy or an exclusive elite endowed with a set of economic and political prerogatives. Any privileges the *maginoo* enjoyed were consequences of a prior recognition by others in the village of their place on the social map. Anyone who could solicit recognition from the villagers could become a *maginoo*. There is a sense in which being a *maginoo*, and presumably a *datu,* was inseparable from being treated and addressed as such on the basis of one's relationships with others in the *barangay* rather than on one's attachment to a structure of authority emanating from another realm. What is important here is the apparent arbitrariness of the *maginoo* rank. For to be a *maginoo* and by extension a *datu* was to act like one; that is, to elicit signs of deference from others in the community.

Rank in this case does not pertain to what "naturally" belongs to one by virtue of a genealogy[3] or the sanction of an outside power.

3. Morga's and Chirino's accounts indicate the practice of teknonymy—the custom of taking the name of a father from that of his child—among the Tagalogs, which, as both Spaniards concede, made it difficult to locate the "head" of a family and much more so to trace the genealogical descent of an individual by means of the father's name.

Any man, conceivably, could be a *maginoo,* given the ability to solicit the recognition of others.[4] Status was thus the consequence rather than the determinant of a certain way of relating and exchanging with others. In this sense, we may postulate that *maginoo* referred less to a distinct social class than to a code of behavior attendant upon a certain position on the map of debt transactions. The acquisition of rank hinged on the sorts of exchanges one carried out with others within the village and the sorts of recognition that was accorded to one as a result of such exchanges. Perhaps this was the reason that ruling dynasties and supra-*barangay* politics never developed. The ranks of *datu* and *maginoo,* as highly localized designations, did not fall back on an outside source that might have sustained their privileges, perpetuated their rule, and expanded their claims to other villages. Instead, the position of *datu* represented an instance, albeit a privileged one, of social relations within the *barangay* rather than the sum total of those relations.

We may get a better sense of the nature of status in sixteenth-century Tagalog society if we consider the other "estates" recorded in the Spanish accounts. The clients or followers of the *maginoo,* Scott tells us, were called *timaua* and *maharlica* (pp. 104–106). The Spaniards perceived them as analogous to vassals in that they occasionally rendered agricultural and maritime labor to the *datu* and his kin. Their status designation supposedly depended on the form of services they rendered. *Timaua* were said to perform mainly agricultural services, *maharlica* military ones. Both groups, however, were expected to contribute manpower in fighting wars, constructing boats, and raiding and trading with other villages. Hence the division of labor between the two groups was somewhat vague. In fact, Juan de Plasencia (1589) and Antonio de Morga (1604) refer to these groups as *la gente común* (common people) or *plebeyos* simply to distinguish them from the *maginoo.* And by the early seventeenth century, Spanish *vocabularios* so faithfully reflect the increasing ambiguity of these categories that their definitions tend to shade off into one another. San Buenaventura's 1613 *vocabulario,* for example, gives the word for ransoming one from slavery as *timauain,* as in *Titimauaiin quita,* "I will set you free." This expression, Scott says, is synonymous with *Minaharlica aco nang panginoon co,* "My master set me free" (pp.

---

4. The reason for the exclusion of women from the position of *datu* cannot now be ascertained, given the nature of the documentation available.

105–106). And Noceda and San Lucar define *timaua* simply as one who is no longer a slave. In this sense, this "second estate" emerges from Spanish records as a vaguely articulated group, defined negatively as neither *maginoo* nor *alipin* (slave). In one sense, this situation was brought about by the steady encroachment of colonial rule among the Tagalogs. The Spaniards' interest in recording the social structure of *los gentiles* (the pagans) had to do with locating clear-cut and usable divisions between masters and slaves. One of the effects of colonial rule, as we shall see, was to retain and consolidate the status of *maginoo* while flattening the distinctions among *timaua, maharlica,* and *alipin.*

Spanish writers consistently distinguished between two types of slaves. There were the *namamahay,* who lived in their own houses and tended their own fields apart from their master's; and the *sagigilid* or "hearth slaves," who lived in the master's house and could be bought and sold. *Alipin* status was acquired through birth (*gintubo*), failure to pay debts, or capture in war. *Maginoo* and *timaua/maharlica* had *alipin,* and it was not uncommon for slaves to have other *alipin* beholden to them. It was also common for people deeply in debt to seek *alipin* status from their relatives (hence the term *nagpapaalipin,* to seek enslavement) because it would provide them with the means to repay their debts. Conversely, it was always possible for slaves, whether *namamahay* or *sagigilid,* to purchase or marry their way out of slavery.

The *alipin namamahay,* San Buenaventura says, are "almost free for they serve their master no more than from time to time and they say he almost has to beg them to go with him to other places or to help him with something, the same as he does with the freemen. . . ; and if he calls on them too often, it is considered an abuse." The key to this type of slavery seems to be the phrase "from time to time." Slave labor of the *namamahay* variety was performed irregularly, not in accordance with an externally imposed timetable. In fact, Father Plasencia underlines the ambiguity of *namamahay* status when he refers to this group simply as *pecheros,* tribute payers.[5] The tribute they rendered to their masters usually consisted of half of their harvest. *Namamahay* slaves were expected to help out at feasts, like everyone else in the *barangay,* and in the building of their masters'

---

5. San Buenaventura and Plasencia are cited in Scott, "Filipino Class Structure," pp. 107, 103.

houses and boats. That they could and were expected to render tribute was due to their possession of houses, fields, and heirlooms, such
as gold and Chinese porcelain.

At the lower rung of the slave hierarchy were the *alipin sagigilid*.
Though they could be sold, Tagalog masters rarely did sell them.
Scott describes *sagigilid* slaves as being as "dependent upon their
masters as his own children" (p. 109). It was common for them to
move out of their status by marrying people of other social groups or
by purchasing their way out with earnings from trading, raiding, or
hunting.

As in the case of *maginoo, timaua,* and *maharlica,* one's status as
an *alipin* was determined by the degree of one's indebtedness. Anyone
was liable to fall into *alipin* status if one was unable to repay one's
debts, just as anyone could become a *maginoo* if one could elicit signs
of deference.

The *namamahay/sagigilid* distinction referred to one's residence
and the amount of labor service one was expected to perform.
Namamahay (from *bahay,* house) frequented their master's house but
resided somewhere else. They rendered service only sporadically,
their status as slaves coming to bear only at the moments when the
master summoned them. Thus one's submission was called for randomly; it was not constantly invoked. The fact that in addition one
could shift the terms of one's enslavement meant that while the contours of social hierarchy were accepted, they were not internalized
and made coterminous with what one was.

The same may be said of the *sagigilid* slaves. *Sagigilid* comes from
gilid, meaning the edge of something, the entrance to a house, or the
border of a river. *Sagigilid* lived close to the master, literally on the
threshold of the master's house. They were more readily available to
the master than the *namamahay* and could be called upon more often
to perform a variety of tasks. There was thus more pressure on the
sagigilid. Yet they, too, could always purchase or marry their way out
of enslavement. In addition, *sagigilid,* like *namamahay,* could take on
their own slaves and pass the burden of their servitude to someone
else.

Within these two categories of slavery there were finer gradations
of servitude. Depending on the status of one's parents—say a
namamahay father and a *timaua* mother or a *maginoo* father and a
sagigilid mother—one could be considered half *namamahay* and half

timaua or any of a variety of mixtures. Even finer gradations of servitude were further indicated by the term *bulisic,* literally "vile," in reference to the *alipin* of an *alipin.* And one who was dependent on a *sagigilid,* Scott tells us, was called *bulislis,* "to be exposed like the private parts of the body when one's clothes are hitched up" (p. 110). One could well imagine that a person who was *bulislis*—the slave of a slave of a slave—was *walang hiya,* without shame. The word denotes less a rank than the absence of rank by virtue of one's exposure to an indiscriminate flurry of demands by others. To be *bulislis* was to be almost totally without protection, as indicated by the word's root, *lilis,* used to refer to the stripping away of one's skin, as in *"Nasilat aco sa sahig, ay nalilis ang balat nang aquing paa,"* "I tripped on the floor and stripped the skin off my feet."[6]

Yet, while *bulislis* takes on the connotations of *walang hiya* on the basis of one's status as a slave of a slave, it is also synonymous with *aba,* poor, unfortunate, wanting. *Aba* also functions as an interjection to call attention to one's misery and to solicit aid, as in *"Aba co!"* (Poor me!) or, in a later Christian context, *"Aba Ginoog Maria!"* (Pity me, Blessed Mary!) *Bulislis* is thus double-ended: while it points to a situation of extreme marginality in the social hierarchy, it is also associated with the solicitation of pity. To be *bulislis* and thus *walang hiya* was nevertheless to have a place of sorts in the circulation of debts, for one could elicit someone else's pity, which could mitigate the oppressiveness of one's condition. One therefore had a place in village society: one owed labor and deference to others and had a right to their pity.

Sixteenth-century Tagalog class structure thus was characterized by forms of indebtedness and servitude that were transferable and negotiable, allowing for random submission to authority. We might infer that rendering tribute and performing labor were less signs that memorialized one's submission to the master than ways of bargaining with him, of plugging into a circuit of indebtedness in which one could hope to accumulate the means to shift social registers. By moving from a lower to a higher rank, one could expect to reduce the amount of labor one had to render, thereby reserving part of oneself from the demands of authority.

These considerations shed some light on the relationship between

6. Serrano-Laktaw, ed., *Diccionario tagalog-hispano.*

person and status in Tagalog society at the onset of colonial rule. Rank was bound up with degrees of indebtedness. Yet indebtedness was in constant circulation, ever displaceable: the burden of payment could always be shifted to someone else in the hierarchy, while payment itself could be deferred. The link between person and status was therefore far from stable. Notably missing from descriptions of Tagalog society are elaborate mythologies purporting to relate social divisions to a natural or cosmological order. Nor did meticulously compiled genealogies establish the historical basis for the privilege of one group or family over others. Social hierarchy instead was generated by the give-and-take of obligations. Status distinctions emerged as the products of reciprocal ties that were not guaranteed by a source external to the *barangay*. Village society owed its apparent mobility to the displaceability of obligations. Status reflected indebtedness, not the person. Self and status were not "naturally" related but explicitly constructed on the basis of a series of asymmetrical exchanges— marriage alliances, usurpations of authority, trade relations, war, and so on. Indeed, the possibility of shifting from one rank to another—as evidenced by the remarkably fine gradations of servitude—bespoke the tendency to dissociate status from the person. While status functioned to locate one on the social map, it did not sum up the self in a hierarchy of obligations.

With the steady entrenchment of Spanish power over the archipelago, Tagalog society was to undergo drastic changes. Based on open-ended dyadic ties of indebtedness, the native social hierarchy was to be relocated in another order premised on the notion of a divinely ordained system of patronage whose effects came through the operations of an extensive bureaucracy. The *barangay* would henceforth cease to be a politically autonomous unit. Christianity and the colonial state apparatus incessantly sought to bind it to an outside realm where all gifts and punishments, and hence all forms of authority, were believed to originate. This transition was historically abrupt and uneven. The question is how and why it happened.

The Reach of Imperial Patronage

One of the most instructive documents related to Spanish rule in the Philippines is the massive compilation of the Laws of the Indies,

Recopilación de leyes de los reynos de las Indias,[7] first published in 1681. Its three volumes abridge some 400,000 edicts and ordinances into 6,400 *leyes* and *títulos* designed to govern the Spanish possessions in the New World and the Indies. These laws, formulated by the King's Council in Mexico, sought to regulate life in Spain's colonies in minute detail, though a great number of them were not enforced.[8] Many of the laws read like variations of the Ten Commandments. We find, for example, laws that order the preaching of the Gospel, attendance at mass, and the administration of sacraments to the natives; laws that prohibit the taking of God's name in vain; and laws that command the extirpation of all forms of idolatry beyond the church's tolerance.

The king's laws appear to be cast in the image of God's. Their ideological basis is the repayment of the monarch's debts—originally contracted by his progenitors—to the Father. What the king owes to God is the care and maintenance of the vast dominions' native populace.

This patron/client relationship between God and king has a long history, stretching back to the *Reconquista* of the Middle Ages. With the Spanish discovery and conquest of the New World, the relationship was institutionalized in the form of the *Patronato Real,* or Royal Patronage, first granted by Pope Julius II to Ferdinand and Isabella. It charged the Spanish kings with providing for the military and financial support of the missions in the colonies and empowered them and their representatives to appoint colonial bishops, abbots, canons, and holders of other ecclesiastical benefices.[9] This privilege implied that the king, as the patron of the church, was an exemplary Christian. His position as patron resulted from his prior submission to another patron, God. The king's authority over his realm was thus premised on the existence of a higher realm beyond his own which served as the focus of all forms of submission. The enforcement of his

7. A facsimile edition of the 4th ed. is used here (Madrid: Consejo de la Hispanidad, 1943).

8. Stanley G. Payne, *A History of Spain and Portugal* (Madison: University of Wisconsin Press, 1973), 1:256.

9. Horacio de la Costa, S.J., "Episcopal Jurisdiction in the Philippines during the Spanish Regime," in *Studies in Philippine Church History,* ed. Gerald H. Anderson (Ithaca: Cornell University Press, 1969), p. 69. The crown also provided each missionary with the costs of journeying between Spain and Mexico or the Philippines, an annual stipend amounting to 100 pesos and 250 bushels of rice, and all the wine and oil required for the administration of the sacraments (ibid., p. 45).

rule was a function of his obedience to God's rules, the exercise of his privileges, and his recognition of his obligations to the Father. To the extent that the king recognized and honored his debts to another realm, he could claim to be the transmitter of those debts to others in the world. The first law in the *Recopilación* puts forth this claim as it places colonization within the perspective of the Faith:

> God, our Lord, through His infinite Mercy and Goodness has deigned to give us, unworthy as we are, such a great portion of His Dominion in this world, and having joined in our Royal person the great kingdoms of our glorious progenitors . . . has obligated us further to . . . employ all the forces and power that He has given us to work so that He may be known and adored all over the world as the true God, as in fact He is, and Creator of all that is visible and invisible; and desiring the glory of the Holy Roman Catholic Church among the Heathen and Nations that inhabit the Indies, Islands and Other Lands of the Oceans as well as other parts subject to our dominion; and so that everyone universally shall enjoy the admirable beneficence of the Resurrection through the Blood of Christ our Lord, we pray and entreat the natives of our Indies who may not yet have received the Faith, since our end is to provide and to deliver to them Teachers and Preachers, for the purpose of their conversion and salvation, that they should receive and listen benignly to and believe totally in the doctrine of the Faith. And we command that all natives and Spaniards and other Christians of the various Provinces and Nations . . . firmly believe and simply confess the Mystery of the Blessed Trinity, Father, Son, and Holy Ghost, three distinct persons and one True God, the Articles of the Faith, and all that is taught and preached by the Holy Mother Roman Catholic Church. . . .

Here the law of the king comes close to miming the profession of faith set forth in catechisms. Grounded by what is beyond grounding, the law sets forth the king's authority as that of one who has a global reach. It conjures up dreams of imperial expansion and world domination with reference to an imagined source of limitless power. As the patron of both secular and ecclesiastical affairs, the Spanish monarch was at the apex of the colonial hierarchy. His position was seen to be sanctioned by an infinitely distant but omnipotent Authority whose laws were at the origin of colonial politics. We glimpse this sanction in the oath of office that the governors of the colonies had to take. It reads in part: "That you swear by God and by the Cross and by the words of the Holy Evangelists that you will faithfully use the office of Governor and Captain General which you have been granted, and you will guard it in the service of God and His Majesty the king" (1:117).

The overriding fable of Spanish authority was that all forms of political power stemmed from royal patronage, which in turn flowed from divine patronage. Every office, though it might have been paid for in cash,[10] was seen as a gift (*merced*) from above. The duties attached to such offices were carried out in the names of the king and the Father. For this reason the monarch took a personal interest in every exploratory voyage. All colonized areas were regarded as his personal property and all towns were chartered by the crown. In his name all offices and land grants were distributed as gifts to "deserving individuals" who had performed him a service. Colonial administration provided far more than material support for evangelization; the reality of Spanish colonial power was articulated in terms of a politics of conversion that converted politics itself into an instance of divine patronage manifested in the sovereign's selective distribution of land and offices to subjects of his realm.

By the sixteenth century, the Spanish Hapsburgs possessed an extensive transatlantic and transpacific empire along with sizable holdings in Europe and the Mediterranean. Control of these colonies required an elaborate administrative machinery. Among other things, J. H. Elliot has written, the administrators sought to maintain the "fiction central to the whole structure of the Spanish monarchy—the fiction that the king was personally present in each of the territories."[11] Councils were set up to formulate laws for the various territories. The Council of the Indies, established in Mexico City in 1524, functioned as late as 1834 as the main legislative and administrative body of the colonies in the Americas and the Philippines. It was charged with receiving information and petitions from all parts of these areas and forwarding them to the king. It also exercised the royal will by issuing licenses, land grants, offices, ordinances, and laws.

A complex bureaucratic structure attached to the Council of the Indies governed the colonies. Executive powers were exercised by two

10. See Onofre D. Corpuz, *The Bureaucracy in the Philippines* (Manila: University of the Philippines, 1957), pp. 27–28.

11. Elliot, *Imperial Spain*, p. 173.

viceroys, one in Peru, the other in Mexico. It was as a province of Mexico that the Philippine colony was administered. Following the Castilian model, regional *audiencias* assumed judicial functions in the colonies as early as 1511 and in Manila in the 1570s. The king's chief representative in the islands was the governor general, whose military and executive functions duplicated those of the monarch within the area of his jurisdiction. He also carried out the prerogatives of royal patronage vis-à-vis the church. By the end of Philip II's reign (1598), the bureaucratic network emanating from Castile to Mexico and thence to Manila had reached down to the village level of the conquered areas in the archipelago. "The empire," as one historian of Spain has noted, "was administered by the largest bureaucratic apparatus in the Western world" at that time. Philip II eschewed the activist role of his father, Charles V, and "spent his working day at his desk surrounded by piles of documents . . . symbolizing the transformation of the Spanish empire as it passed out of the age of the conquistador into the age of the civil servant."[12]

In the interest of preserving royal authority over such widely dispersed areas, an elaborate and confounding system of checks and balances was created to counter the relative autonomy of colonial officials. The *residencia,* for example, was a comprehensive accounting of an official's tenure of office before his successor and the *audiencia;* the *visita* was an annual inspection of a colony conducted by crown officials. Bureaucrats and priests were also obliged to write periodic reports (*relatos*) addressed directly to the king regarding the conduct of other officials, including their superiors. The infinite series of checks and balances often resulted in the mutual cancellation of colonial officials' authority. Records of seemingly endless conflicts between the governor general and the *audiencia* and between civil and ecclesiastical authorities abound in the archives of Manila and Seville.[13]

These bureaucratic conflicts, by neutralizing the authority of colonial officials, conserved the notion of the king as the supreme patron of his realm. Yet he was personally unknown and geographically remote from the overwhelming majority of his subjects. His authority as the paramount patron could be exercised only through an inter-

12. Payne, *History of Spain,* pp. 256, 167.
13. See Corpuz, *Bureaucracy,* pp. 22–91; David Steinberg et al., eds., *In Search of Southeast Asia* (London: Oxford University Press, 1971), pp. 87–91.

minable process of legislation acting on and reacting to veritable mountains of petitions, reports, and other documents. The growth of the bureaucratic apparatus was the occasion for and the result of this need to make the king's laws and demands known to his subjects. The bureaucracy, ideally, was meant to safeguard the transmission of royal authority. But the distance between Spain and its colonies made inevitable a gap between the proclamation of the king's will embodied in his laws and their enactment by his representatives overseas. When the gap became noticeable, more legislation was created to fill it.[14] The bureaucrats who were then appointed to implement the new laws more often than not abused them. Their transgressions in turn called forth new sanctions and regulatory devices, new checks and balances. Bureaucrats checked on bureaucrats as legislation multiplied to make up for lack of enforcement of previous legislation. Bureaucracy betrayed the law in two senses. Enforcement of laws created half a world away tended to deviate from the letters of those laws. More legislation was created to regulate the deviations. But more legislation multiplied the possibilities for bureaucratic abuse, and so on around the circle. The movement is familiar; we have seen its logic at work in conversion and confession. The notion of patronage made all social relationships subject to the letter of the law and the interested and interminable readings of the bureaucracy.

Given this situation, it is not surprising that the Spanish missionary should emerge as the most potent agent of colonial rule, particularly at the local level. Whether in the collection of tribute, the selection of natives for appointment to municipal and village posts, or the suppression of sporadic native revolts, the missionary priest was the acknowledged key to the actualization of Spanish power in everyday life.[15]

On the one hand, the priest was, by virtue of the *Patronato Real,* very much an integral part of the bureaucracy. His dependence on the crown for financial and military support made him in effect an employee of the government.[16] He was embroiled in the same bureau-

14. "The Government in Madrid . . . had an excessive . . . faith in the power of legislation per se. . . . Spain enacted a veritable plethora of laws for the governing of the colonies" (Corpuz, *Bureaucracy,* p. 143).

15. Ibid., pp. 118–122.

16. Horacio de la Costa, "The Development of the Native Clergy in the Philippines," in *Studies in Philippine Church History,* ed. Anderson, p. 70.

cratic processes, intrigues, and conflicts over areas of jurisdiction as any other civil authority. On the other hand, the regular clergy (that is, the members of the religious orders that dominated the Philippine parishes, as distinguished from crown-appointed secular priests) were also responsible to their provincial superiors. A priest's allegiance to his religious order tended to take precedence over his loyalty to the crown. The regular clergy's knowledge of the local language coupled with their long-term service in their areas (Spanish civil officials served for much shorter periods) were further sources of their political authority.

Most significant, however, was that unlike other bureaucrats, the Spanish missionary was seen to owe his position to something beyond royal patronage and legislation. He was a representative not merely of the royal will but of the divine will as well. As such, he could appeal to an authority beyond the endless spiral of legislation and bureaucracy—indeed, to the professed origin and destination of that spiral itself. Because he could move between the registers of divine and royal will, he could claim the ability to decipher native signs in terms of God's laws and natives' wishes in terms of the king's. In this way the priest could consolidate his position as an indispensable mediator between the sovereign patron and his disparate and anonymous mass of clients.

The power differential between civil authorities and Spanish missionaries had to do, then, with the priests' access not simply to the Spanish crown but to an external realm even more distant and more important in the context of conversion, one that was believed to constitute every single internal aspect of the king's realm. For by having recourse to God's will, the missionaries simultaneously had special access to human souls. On the threshold of divine and monarchical laws, they also stood poised between the sovereign will and native submission. The priests were invested with the capacity to traverse the terms of the colonial hierarchy. To this extent, they were presumed to be the site for the collection and reproduction of disparate voices: those of the subject natives and that of the benevolent monarch. For this reason the missionaries could address the other side of the royal will: the royal conscience.

The first Manila synod of 1582 was convoked precisely for the purpose of clearing up the collective conscience of Spain in connection with the conquest of the islands ten years after the establishment of the colonial capital in Manila. Led by the Dominican bishop Domingo de Salazar, the synod sought to set down the terms for the exercise of Spanish authority and the exaction of native submission within the framework of Christian justice. As the Jesuit historian John Schumacher has pointed out, the synod was concerned primarily with curtailing Spanish abuses and delineating native rights.[17] It mapped out the limits of colonial rule for the purpose of highlighting the raison d'être of the Spanish presence in the islands: the conversion of its native inhabitants. Hence its defense of native rights and denunciations of Spanish abuses were based on a universalistic and transcultural notion of justice which made everyone, *indio* and Spaniard alike, accountable to the same Law.

In their concern to establish the appropriate rules of conquest, however, the bishops by no means escaped the exigencies of colonial politics. They subscribed to the same economy of patronage: they sought to maximize the profit of native bodies and souls loyal to both crown and church and to minimize the military, financial, and moral costs of the venture. This aim is neatly summed up in a letter sent by Bishop Salazar to the king on the need to eradicate abuses suffered by the natives at the hands of both Spanish colonizers and native rulers: ". . . for His Majesty has appointed governors to this land for the correction of those . . . injuries, and thereby relieves his conscience through them. In regard to what is feared from any troubles, it is not credible that they will spring from a people so loyal and obedient to their king, because they are ordered to obey him in matters so just and reasonable."[18]

The "justness" and "reasonableness" of Spanish domination were recurrent themes of the synod, as the procedures for securing the natives' submission to the king's will had to be harmonized with God's laws. The missionaries wanted submission to be a matter not of

17. John Schumacher, S.J., "The Manila Synodal Tradition: A Brief History," *Philippine Studies* 27 (1979): 285–348. Schumacher defines a synod as the "meeting of the bishop with his advisors to make laws for the diocese" (p. 286). Other sources for the synod of 1582 include "Actas del primer sínodo de Manila (1582–1586)," *Philippiniana Sacra* 4 (September–December 1969): 425–537, which contains a facsimile copy of the *suma* of the meetings and a record of the bishops' recommendations. See also J. Gayo Aragón, O.P., "The Controversy over the Justification of Spanish Rule in the Philippines," in *Studies in Philippine Church History,* ed. Anderson, pp. 3–21.
18. In *Philippine Islands,* ed. Blair and Robertson, 34:329.

crude coercion but of true conversion. Conquest without conversion would nullify the king's claim to the islands and would burden the royal—and by extension the Spanish—conscience. Hence the validity and righteousness of Spanish authority hinged on the natives' willing submission: the natives had to wish to be embraced by the monarch. Their willing submission would attest to the imprint of the royal will on the native consciousness. Only then could the Spanish conscience be unburdened: royal patronage could be seen as the consistent reflection of divine benevolence, the king's law as the reflection of God's, and colonization as equivalent to evangelization.

The two most pressing matters that the synod undertook to clarify were the king's just title to the islands and the justification for the exaction of tribute from the conquered populace. The synod's recommendations with regard to these questions had far-reaching effects. They were eventually incorporated in the Laws of the Indies. More important, they were to transform Tagalog social relations in the coming centuries.

Conversion and the Ideology of Submission

The synod of 1582 posed the question of the legitimacy of the Spanish occupation of the Philippines as a way of grounding its other prescriptions regarding the "just" administration of the *indios*. The resolution of the question grew out of the writings of the mid-sixteenth-century Dominicans Francisco de Vitoria and Bartolomé de Las Casas and those of other Spanish jurists in Salamanca. These thinkers had sought to articulate the basis of the king's title to the newly colonized territories in America and to determine the scope of the natives' rights.[19]

When Ferdinand and Isabella drove the Moors from Spain in the fifteenth century, they could claim to have waged a just war against the enemies of the faith; their grandson Philip had no such claim in regard to the Philippines. Influenced largely by the polemics of the Dominicans, the synod settled the question by asserting the "supernatural sovereignty" of the king over the islands: the king derived his

19. J. H. Parry, *The Spanish Theory of Empire in the Sixteenth Century* (Cambridge: At the University Press, 1940), chaps. 1 and 2.

authority from his commission to preach the Gospel. Evangelization emerged as a distinct and prior consideration of Spanish sovereignty. The bishops were of the opinion that the *indios* were of such a "barbarous" disposition, so "blind and forgetful of God because of their sinfulness," and so "lacking even in natural law" that their laws, "if they had any, [were] from the Devil, the father of lies." It followed that the prevailing society in the islands was unsuited for the spread of the faith. To remedy this situation, the bishops recommended the establishment of a "quasi-imperial rule of supervision" over the conquered areas to maintain the work of conversion.[20]

The exercise of imperial authority was thus deemed secondary to the project of evangelization, as even the Laws of the Indies were to proclaim a century after the synod. As such, the monarch's rule had the status of an essential supplement to the spread of Christianity. In this sense, politics was analogous to language. Both were placed in the service of conversion, charged with providing the conditions for the natives' submission to God's laws. As we have seen, Castilian, the language of the Spanish *imperio,* functioned as a screen to reorder Tagalog in terms of Latin script and grammar, which would make it possible for the Gospel to be translated into the local language. Similarly, the entire colonial administrative apparatus functioned as a transparent grid to reposition the natives to receive God's Word as it enforced the royal will.

The totalizing impulse of a colonial rule harnessed to the project of conversion becomes equally apparent if we turn to the synod's other concern, the exacting of submission in the form of tribute. While the bishops issued no explicit statement about the nature of submission, they assumed that it always stood in relation to patronage. Simply put, Spain in the capacity of a benevolent protector had bestowed on the *indios* order, law, and, most important, the means to petition for God's mercy and grace. The natives were expected to express their gratitude for such gifts by signs of submission to the king and his representatives. Such signs took the form of tribute. Conversely, any Spanish official who failed to provide for the spiritual well-being of the indigent *indios* forfeited his position as the *indios'* patron. Because his behavior no longer conformed with the royal will, he could

---

20. Schumacher, "Manila Synodal Tradition," p. 294; "Actas del primer sínodo," pp. 435–438.

no longer demand the natives' submission and exact tribute from them. Any further such demands would constitute a perversion of the king's will and would weigh on his conscience, and theoretically on the consciences of all Spaniards.

Since a war against the natives would not be "just," the exaction of tribute was justifiable only in terms of evangelization. That is, tribute was to be collected only in exchange for the Christian doctrine. The bishops' condemnation of the rampant abuses in connection with the "unjust" collection of tribute in the late sixteenth century was due precisely to what they saw as the inversion of the hierarchical relationship between evangelization and colonial politics. Spanish bureaucrats and *encomenderos* (Spaniards and a few *maginoo* who had received a royal grant called an *encomienda,* the right to collect tribute from an area's populace) were accused of scandalously extorting tribute from the natives without supplying them with the conditions needed to become good Christians.[21] Native "rights" were thus violated. The *indios* were coerced into giving in without getting back the spiritual and moral "benefits" due them. This situation threatened to rupture the economy of royal benevolence as a reflection of divine will. The natives were being forced into subjugation rather than "persuaded" and "reduced by love," conquered by external force rather than converted through an internal acceptance of God's laws. The missionaries were particularly alarmed by the thought of submission that was short of all-inclusive, submission that implicated only the natives' bodies and omitted their souls.

Bishop Salazar had brought this problem to the attention of Philip II, and Salazar's successor, Miguel de Benavides, continued the bishop's efforts to resolve the problem. Claiming that the legitimacy of the Spanish presence in the Philippines was jeopardized by the unjust treatment of the natives, Bishop Benavides suggested that the *indios* be made to "freely elect" their subservience to the crown:

> If His Majesty sends sufficient religious and priests, and the bishops and the Governor and the *Audiencia* and the religious know how to handle matters, treating the *indios* well . . . it will be very easy to attract these infidels to the obedience of His Majesty, even before they become Christians.

21. Schumacher, "Manila Synodal Tradition," pp. 297–299; "Actas del primer sínodo," pp. 443–444, 450–451.

. . . All these [benefits brought by Spain] are excellent occasions, if we present them properly, to attract the infidel *indios* in such a way that lords and vassals will voluntarily and freely desire and have and choose and swear fidelity to His Majesty and to his successors as their legitimate king and lord and pay him tribute.[22]

In response to the bishop's urgings, Philip II issued in 1597 a decree that basically confirmed the synod's contentions regarding the collection of tribute. It was his will "not to contradict the preaching of the Gospel," that "tribute should be imposed and levied on them with the principal obligation of indoctrinating them," and "that those who have not yet received the faith" should not be expected to pay. Through the "scrupulous observance" of these conditions, the officials in the colony would be "satisfying my conscience by satisfying theirs."[23] The then governor general of the Philippine colony, Tello de Guzmán, wrote to the king later the same year: "From the hand of the bishop [Benavides] . . . I have received Your Majesty's royal writing in which you ordered me, by the best and most gentle methods possible, to attract the natives of these islands to give obedience to Your Majesty (this ceremony having been neglected at first) so that the tribute they pay may be collected with more justification."[24]

The "ceremony" that Guzmán mentions parenthetically refers to the ordering of the provincial judges to read out the king's decree to the native populace of their jurisdiction. By informing them of the king's will, the Spanish officials would be working toward the "greater peace of your royal conscience."[25] This practice was not unique to the Philippines. Similar "ceremonies" of soliciting native consent to Spanish rule in order to legitimize the collection of tribute had been carried out in the New World as early as 1510. There the practice was referred to as the *requerimiento,* or requisition. As a British historian describes it, it involved the rather bizarre process of reading aloud to the natives a "solemn legal document" that called on them "to submit peacefully and receive the Faith . . . [and] devote time and thought to the theological views propounded before making their

22. Cited in Schumacher, *Readings in Philippine Church History*, p. 36.
23. A copy of Philip II's decree is found in Jesús Gayo, O.P., ed., "Tratado segundo de la preparación evangélica y el modo de predicar el Santo Evangelio por Fr. Miguel de Benavides, O.P.," *Unitas* 21 (January 1948): 158.
24. In *Philippine Islands,* ed. Blair and Robertson, 10:253–254.
25. Ibid.

reply." The Spanish jurist, Juan López de Palacios Rubios, who had formulated this practice, conceded that although the natives might not understand the contents of the *requerimiento*, all that was necessary to assuage the Spanish conscience was the proper observance of the formal aspects of its reading. Those natives who persisted in their refusal to receive the faith and pay tribute to the crown after hearing the document read could then be justifiably subjected to a military assault.[26]

The Philippine version of the *requerimiento* was introduced three decades after the Spaniards had staked their claim to the islands. In order to ratify a fait accompli, the "ceremony" sought to satisfy the royal conscience by aligning the native's will with the king's. Thus would subjugation, evinced in the rendering of tribute, become a matter of desiring the will of the king, who desired the will of God, who desired that His will be desired.

Governor General Tello's letter goes on to report that upon hearing the king's decree read out to them, the overwhelming majority of the Tagalogs signaled their consent to Spanish rule. In all probability, this meant that they would continue to render tribute and receive the Gospel. The only response that has come down to us from the natives occurs at secondhand. In 1630 the Augustinian priest Juan de Medina cited with much satisfaction the reply of a "rustic *indio*" to the bishop's explanations of the "advantages of Spanish rule": "We answer that we wish the king of Spain to be our king and lord, for he has sent Castilians to us to free us from the tyranny and domination of our principals [headmen] and also the Fathers to aid us against the Castilians themselves and defend us from them."[27]

It is impossible to know whether a "rustic *indio*" really made this statement, or for that matter whether Father Medina, thirty years after the event, accurately rendered what he thought he heard. It is apparent, however, that this statement is permeated by the same sort of missionary wishfulness that we have encountered in the synod's statements, in Philip II's decrees, and in the Laws of the Indies; that is, the wish to see native submission as always and everywhere a matter of conversion, a response to royal and therefore divine patronage. The natives' need for "protection" grew out of the grandiose and enduring fiction that they needed to be converted. Similarly, the solicitation of their consent to Spanish sovereignty stemmed from the need

26. Parry, *Spanish Theory of Empire*, pp. 7–8.
27. Quoted in Schumacher, *Readings in Philippine Church History*, pp. 37–38.

to unburden the Spanish conscience. Endowing the natives with "rights" and applying to them the principles of "justice" meant binding them to what the Spaniards saw was the ineluctable pull of divine will embodied in the language and laws of its privileged representatives.

The remarks of the Spanish jurist Juan de Solórzano Pereira in 1647 regarding the theologico-juridical basis for the exaction of tribute may well sum up Spanish thinking on the subject:

> If the Spanish kings are the true and absolute rulers and lords of the Indies, as they are, or even if they are only protectors or administrators of the Indians who dwell there, one must affirm that the Indians themselves should contribute something as recognition of the effort of Christianization and to aid in the cost of maintaining Christianity, civil administration, and the protection given them during peace and war.[28]

Note the rhetorical skids here: "If . . . as they are . . . or even if they are only . . . one must affirm . . .": perhaps the traces of an ambivalent conscience. Confessing Spain's guilt, as it were, the Spaniard resolves the question of tribute by framing it as a token of the natives' recognition of Spanish patronage. Thus tribute becomes the sign that identifies the native's will as a derivative of the king's and ultimately of God's; and as a symbol it can be dissociated from its material effects. In paying tribute, one not only lends support to the colonial state apparatus but also signals one's recognition of and desired dependence on another realm whose laws order one's world. By inserting one into a definitive hierarchy of indebtedness, tribute could be regarded, at least from the Spanish point of view, as a way of expressing one's willed surrender to authority. It is important, however, to note the highly specific terms of this form of "speech"— terms that were formulated not by the tribute-paying subject but by the tribute-collecting patron.

As early as 1589, Philip II had set the annual rate of the basic tribute as ten reales payable in cash or kind. This rate was not to change until 1874, when it was increased to fourteen reales.[29] All non-*maginoo* men between the ages of 18 and 60 were expected to pay; *maginoo* who were or had been *datu* and their sons were ex-

---

28. Quoted in Cushner, *Spain in the Philippines,* p. 101.
29. *Recopilación de las leyes,* 2:241; Phelan, *Hispanization of the Philippines,* p. 95.

empted from payments of any sort. In 1783, unmarried women were also required to pay tribute from age 20 on. Payments were subject to deadlines: a third of the total amount was to be collected on June 30, August 31, and October 31 of each year.[30]

Throughout the sixteenth and seventeenth centuries, most of the tribute was paid in goods, such as rice or chickens. The *audiencia* in Manila had drawn up in 1589 a *tasación* or computation of payments, assigning monetary values to goods offered as payment. These values varied from year to year and from place to place, in accordance with supply and demand. In 1642, for example, one hen was valued at two reales, one cock at half a real.[31]

Aside from annual payments in specie and kind, all able-bodied men were required to spend forty days a year on government projects (building galleons, roads, bridges, etc.) or in Spanish-led militias organized to put down revolts in other regions or fight against the Muslims in the south. By law, natives could avoid this requirement, called *polo,* by paying three pesos. But this practice, like most others connected with *polo,* was often abused. Natives who paid the money ended up serving at least part of the forty days in labor gangs. *Polo* demands for shipyard labor were particularly harsh. Men were taken away from their villages to work in the shipyards of Cavite, where they were meagerly compensated with food. The chronic shortage of money in the colony throughout the early colonial period—attributable largely to dependence on the erratic Manila–Acapulco trade—made it impossible to institute wage labor in practice, despite repeated legislation to that effect.[32] *Polo* demands became even more oppressive during the Dutch–Hispanic wars between 1609 and 1648, when natives were corralled to haul logs, build ships, and fight the Spaniards' battles. One result of this practice was the drastic decline of the native population under Spanish jurisdiction. The conscriptees either died or fled to the hills, beyond the reach of the Spaniards.[33]

As in the case of tribute payments, native *maginoo*—or *principales,* as the Spaniards now called them—were exempted from labor services. Other natives, not surprisingly, sought to commute *polo* requirements by paying another native from six to ten pesos to substitute for them. In the late seventeenth and early eighteenth centuries,

30. Cushner, *Spain in the Philippines,* pp. 110–111.
31. Ibid., pp. 104, 243.
32. Ibid., pp. 112–126.
33. See Phelan, *Hispanization of the Philippines,* pp. 99–100.

still others acquired exemption status by attaching themselves to landed estates, most of which were owned by religious corporations. A man who performed services for an estate did not need to do so for the crown. Despite a flood of legislation from Madrid mandating an easing of these requirements, natives continued to be forcibly drafted for labor until the last decade of the nineteenth century.[34]

Finally, the Manila government instituted the forced "sale" of goods called *vandala*. Each province was assigned an annual quota of crops and poultry to be collected by local officials and delivered to the provincial *alcalde*. As the natives' goods, like their labor, were seldom paid for, the *vandala* became yet another tax.[35]

Whether in the form of annual payments, labor, or forced sale, tribute was at the nexus of Spanish authority and native submission. We have already seen how the conditions attendant upon the exaction of tribute impinged on the Spanish conscience and the legitimization of Spanish rule. What effects did they have on Tagalog society and on the dynamics of submission to Spain?

From their earliest years in the Philippines, the Spaniards had tried to locate native ruling elites and incorporate them in the colonial hierarchy. Sixteenth-century Spanish accounts purporting to describe the social and political structures of *indio* society were compiled precisely for this purpose. They seized upon the *datu* and his *maginoo* kin as the "natural rulers" of their villages. Through them the Spaniards sought to extend the bureaucratic reach of the state to the local level. As early as 1574, royal decrees sanctioned the *maginoo*'s privileges, and twenty years later they were permanently exempted from payment of tribute, like the caciques of the New World.[36] This was when they began to be called *principales*. In contrast to *maginoo*, which denoted less a class than a code of behavior based on dealings with other villagers, *principal* emerged as a juridical designation for a native whose position was largely an effect of legal sanctions originating outside the *barangay*. This much is evidenced in the formal pronouncement of the Laws of the Indies regarding the rights and privileges of this group:

It is not just that the principal *indios* of the Philippines should be in no worse condition after having converted [than before]; they should be

34. Cushner, *Spain in the Philippines*, pp. 124–125.
35. Phelan, *Hispanization of the Philippines*, p. 100.
36. Ibid., p. 122.

favored in such a way as to maintain their fidelity. To the spiritual goods that God has communicated to them shall be added temporal benefits so that they will live happily and agreeably. To this end, we command the governors of those islands to treat them well, and entrust to them in our name the governing of the *indios* of whom they were formerly lords, and in all else to procure their services justly, giving to these *indios* the recognition due to them ever since the time of their paganism so long as it does not prejudice the tribute that they have to pay us.   [2:248]

Framed by the rhetoric of patronage, the "recognition" of the *principales'* "rights" was always conditional on something else: that those privileges, granted and guaranteed by Spain, should redound to its benefit. This is why the crown also reserved the authority to pronounce on any excesses committed by *principales*. Having endowed them with rights and privileges, the Laws of the Indies could also castigate and punish their transgressions.[37] As *principales,* native *maginoo* came within the scope of the law of a realm unknown to the *barangay*. By bringing the gift of law to the natives, the royal patron interposed himself in the interstices of native social relations. Through his representatives, he took it upon himself to lay down the terms that determined the dealings between the *indios* and their headmen. The discourse of Spanish patronage thus images the calculated intrusion of an outside force that seeks to reinvent the internal patterns of *indio* life.

The "temporal benefits" to which the law referred consisted of, among other things, the right to hold public office and exemption from all forms of tribute and forced labor. By the seventeenth century, two salaried positions in the colonial bureaucracy had been made available only to the members of the native elite: the office of the *cabeza de barangay,* or headman in charge of affairs in a village; and that of the *gobernadorcillo,* literally "little governor," who oversaw the affairs of a *municipio,* analagous to a county. Both incumbents were in turn responsible to a chain of authority that led from the provincial *alcalde* and the parish priest to the governor general in Manila.[38]

The position of *cabeza* was initially hereditary, the office passing

---

37. *Recopilación de las leyes,* 2:246.
38. The basic information in regard to these offices is outlined in Corpuz, *Bureaucracy,* pp. 107–118; Phelan, *Hispanization of the Philippines,* pp. 121–129.

from father to son. In 1786 it was subject to selective rotation every three years. The post of *gobernadorcillo* was reserved for former *cabezas*. The *principales* nominated people of their own rank to this post. Their choices were subject to the approval of the priest and the ratification of the government in Manila. The *gobernadorcillo* enjoyed a tenure of one year.

The main duties of the *cabezas* and the *gobernadorcillos* were the collection of tribute payments, the drafting of labor, and the delivery of annual quotas for the *vandala*. They were paid a small salary and, along with their immediate families, were granted the tribute exemptions already mentioned.[39] They were also granted the Spanish honorific titles *Don* and *Doña* together with such emblems of authority as canes, hats, and a retinue of deputies. The *principales,* as one might expect, also enjoyed close association with the church. Former *gobernadorcillos* and *cabezas* often served as *fiscales* or sacristans, overseeing indoctrination in the faith and attendance at church rituals. They also assumed the leadership of missionary-organized sodalities and confraternities (of which more will be said in Chapter 6). Not until the eighteenth century, however, were they allowed to enter the ranks of the religious, and then mostly as secular rather than regular priests.[40]

The sight of the new *principales* in their distinctive dress, with their new titles bestowed by an outside power, must have impressed the nonelites of the *barangay*. They were soon speaking some Castilian, too, learned from the Spanish authorities with whom they associated. Though few of them were fluent in the language, they knew enough to use fragments of it in their exchanges with both Spaniards and other Tagalogs, and in the legal documents they drew up in Tagalog for the benefit of Spanish courts. A 1696 text put together by the *maginoo* of Maybonga, a town near Manila, concedes to four *principales* the right to supervise the care of certain lands in the area and to collect rents on them in the following terms:

. . . to Captain Don Agustin Hota, Captain Don Alonzo Bonolong, Don Felipe Malaquiqui, and Don Guillermo Casinsin, *maginoo* of May-

---

39. The *gobernadorcillo* was entitled to one-half of 1% of the total amount of tribute collected. Any shortfall from the official tax assessments, however, came out of the *gobernadorcillo*'s and *cabeza*'s pockets.
40. See Costa, "Development of the Native Clergy."

bonga . . . all four of them are given the power [*poder*] and complete authority [*ganap na capangyarihan*] to care for the entirety of adjoining lands . . . to collect rent [*magpabouis*] from them . . . and to issue receipts and certificates of payment [*recibos at cartas de pago*] . . . [and] to represent them in court [*macsasacdal*] and ask for justice [*justicia*] from any court [*tribunal*] of the king. . . .[41]

The four *principales* are cited with the full complement of their Castilian honorific titles, *Capitan Don,* followed by their Spanish baptismal names. Yet they are also designated by the more traditional title of *maginoo.* Their hold over the lands in question is signaled by the Spanish word *poder,* "power," which is then juxtaposed with the Tagalog phrase *ganap na capangyarihan,* "complete authority." This authority enables them to collect rent (Tagalog *magpabouis*) but requires them to issue receipts and certificates of payment (Castilian *recibos* and *cartas de pago*). And in the event of conflict over their lands, they are to voice the town's interest (Tagalog *macsasacdal,* from *sacdal,* to accuse someone of something) and ask for *justicia* from the crown-appointed *tribunal.*

We see here the considerable facility with which the native elite moved between two registers, recognized two frames of reference: they were linked to both Spain and the *barangay.* Other natives who heard them speak in this way must have recognized other possibilities for exchange, for appropriating things from the outside, as well as a different *sense* of an outside. The *principales-maginoo* thus evinced a capacity to submit to Spanish demands while at the same time claiming for themselves a privileged position within the native community.

The community itself was subjected to a series of transformations throughout the late sixteenth and seventeenth centuries. Evangelization and tribute altered the Tagalog social structure, particularly in regard to the highly variegated and localized system of slavery.

The issue of local slavery had been taken up by the synod of 1582. Following the 1530 decrees of Charles V, the bishops strongly urged the abolition of all forms of local slavery and the "liberation" of all *indio* slaves from their masters. Their liberation was essential, the bishops declared, for the sake of clearing the Spanish conscience. For

41. Adapted from Nicolas Cushner, *Landed Estates in the Colonial Philippines* (New Haven: Yale University Southeast Asia Studies, 1976), Appendix E, pp. 82–84.

to tolerate their enslavement was to condone a distorted image of Christian social relationships based on the general subordination of all to One. Where the Spanish missionaries were concerned, the modes of *indio* enslavement did not proceed from a willed and voluntary obedience to the Law, but resulted from external coercion. As part of the odious residue of precolonial *abusos*, local slavery had to be eradicated lest it impede the realization of royal benevolence. It was then incumbent on the king and his representatives to "declare and concede" the "liberty which the *Indios* possess inherently." To do otherwise would be to commit a "grave sin" and fail in one's duty as the protector and patron of the natives.[42]

The prohibition of local slavery was formalized into law from Philip II onward. The Laws of the Indies expressly forbade the buying and selling of *indio* slaves within the archipelago and ordered that the slaves be restored to their state of "natural liberty."[43] At least on the conceptual level, the attempts to abolish local variants of slavery was part of a larger process of enforcing the natives' submission to Spanish ideas about the "person" as primarily a subject of divine and royal laws. A myriad of highly localized and displaceable relations of indebtedness would have detracted from the insertion of the person into an all-inclusive hierarchy of obligations. The practical effect of this system would be that a slave, being a thing that belonged to someone else, would not be liable to tribute payments. By prohibiting slavery, the law alleviated the Spanish conscience while at the same time increasing the number of taxable heads.

The imposition of tribute worked to concretize these proscriptions of local slavery. Colonial rule, by extending Spanish authority to the local level, generated a new division between natives who paid tribute and natives who collected it. Tribute reoriented the circulation of indebtedness by locating the source and destination of circulation itself in another, thoroughly different realm. One gained access to this realm only by submitting to a mediating chain of authority figures in possession of the "gifts" of God and king.

42. Blair and Robertson, eds., *Philippine Islands,* 34:325–331, translates the proceedings of Bishop Salazar's Council on Slavery.

43. *Recopilación de las leyes,* 2:201. It should be noted, however, that well into the eighteenth century there was a lively commerce in black slaves brought by Portuguese traders to Manila. Some Muslim captives who refused to accept Christianity were also sold as slaves by the Spaniards themselves.

Despite the theological and legal proscriptions of slavery, the categories of *alipin namamahay/sagigilid* continued to appear in Spanish records until the 1690s. Ironically enough, the practice of tribute collection allowed for the perpetuation of local slavery. Many Tagalogs who could not come up with either the money or the goods or who were intent on converting *polo* obligations into cash payments often ended up borrowing from the *principales* and becoming their *alipin.*[44] Thus while the *principales* had access to the novel realm of Spain, they could continue to lay claim to traditional arrangements of indebtedness within the *barangay*. By converting to Christianity and latching onto the colonial bureaucracy, they could assume another position from which they could draw on the reserve of those beneath them in the hierarchy. The positions of *cabeza* and *gobernadorcillo* were eagerly sought by the native elite. As Phelan remarks, "their response [to Spanish political arrangements] was on the whole enthusiastic, rapid and in many cases penetrating."[45] A man who became a *cabeza* or *gobernadorcillo* might convert the shock of Spanish intrusion into a regular relationship of interested transactions with people at the two ends of the colonial hierarchy. These positions, that is, gave the native elites a way to consolidate the consequences of their submission. They allowed them to keep their positions within the *barangay* as the bearers of a surplus of signs taken from the outside—Christianity, honorifics, money, Castilian, and the rest—with which to initiate and maintain a network of reciprocal indebtedness with the villagers. They thus profited from two kinds of hierarchy. The interests of the *principales-maginoo* lay not in synthesizing these two registers, as most scholars have suggested, but in keeping them separate. Keeping them apart—submitting to Spain while continuing to invest in Tagalog life—was then a matter of seeing in one the possibility of appropriating something from the other.

The native elites' submission to Spanish rule thus appears to be a matter of sheer opportunism. Perhaps. But what then of the submission of all the people who were not *principales?* What might have made submission to both types of hierarchy desirable to them? Such questions may be posed only within the context of the intrusion of Spain into Tagalog life. We may begin to explore possible answers by turning to the manner in which Spain changed the course of Tagalog death.

44. Phelan, *Hispanization of the Philippines*, p. 115.
45. Ibid., p. 121.

CHAPTER 6

Paradise and the Reinvention of Death

Generalizing Servitude

The following fragment is from a late-sixteenth-century explication of the Ten Commandments in Tagalog by the Franciscan Juan de Oliver:

> . . . tayong lahat aliping totoo nang P. Dios paran pinapamahay tayo mona nang P. Dios dito sa Lupa, at balang arao, cun mabaet tayo, at magalang sa caniya, ypagsasangbahay niya tayo doon sa langit, paparahin tayong anac, na pagpapalain niya doon sa caniyang bayan.[1]

> . . . we are all really slaves of the Lord God and it is as if we were temporarily housed here on earth, and someday, if we are good and respectful to Him, He will house us all in heaven, and treat us like His children and grant us His blessings there in His land.

We see here the missionizing impulse to reorient Tagalog social relations in accordance with God's laws. "We," *tayo*—here Spanish missionary and Tagalog convert alike—are "really slaves" of God. Slavery is seen as determining the basis of a collective identity in relation to the divine Master. In this sense, to be is to be enslaved by God via a mediating chain of representations. Enslavement arises from indebt-

---

1. Juan de Oliver, O.F.M., "Declaración de los mandamientos de la ley de Dios," in Antonio Ma. Rosales, O.F.M., *A Study of a Sixteenth-Century Tagalog Manuscript on the Ten Commandments: Its Significance and Implication* (Quezon City: University of the Philippines Press, 1984), pp. 26–67. The quotation is on pp. 36–38.

edness. But in the Christian context, indebtedness as sin defines "our" natural condition as creatures in a state of perpetual lack and therefore in constant need of protection. This condition of general enslavement overrides social distinctions. Indebtedness thus becomes a determinant less of status, as in traditional Tagalog society, than of person; a matter not of arbitrary transactions but of faith in the existence of an absolutely outside realm from which all gifts and punishments come.

Being good—that is, submitting to the divine Master—assures "us" of a place in this realm. Yet our arrival there is also a matter of "someday" (*balang arao*). The innovation of Christianity consists in introducing a different kind of temporal determinateness into the relationship between master and slaves. Surrender to the all-inclusive hierarchy proposed by the Spanish missionary is thus articulated with reference to a future life that is totally removed from "our" present one, when submission will pay off.

This idea of another life in another time allows for the simultaneous superseding and conservation of existing social relations. As a matter of faith, we are all slaves of God. But as a matter of fact, we are also enmeshed in a social order; and that social order, consisting of Spanish patrons and native wards, of *maginoo*-cum-*principales* and *alipin,* apparently is to endure until we receive God's blessings "in His land."

Masters, nonetheless, are so only by virtue of their prior surrender to God. Having accepted His Law, they are bound to uphold it:

> . . . ang tauong may alipin, catongcolang aralan naman at gayon din ang casangbahay, nang tantong pagsangpalataya, at pagsonod sa otos nang P. Dios, papagdasalin ninyo arao, arao, at pasimbahin naman, yayang otos din nang P. Dios sa inyong lahat.

> . . . the person who has a slave has the duty to teach him as he would others in his household how to believe and obey all the laws of God, to make them pray every day and to attend mass, inasmuch as this is what the Lord God commands all of you to do.

Masters who fail to obey this command risk the wrath of the Master:

> Ang aba nga ninyo, cun ypahamac yaring bilin nang Dios, na ang manga casangbahay ninyo, di sauayin cun masama ang gaua nila, cun ytotol ninyo sa canila ang dilan loob na di magaling, cayo pala ang

sisihin nang P. Dios sa cun hunhang ang inyong anac, ang inyong
casangbahay, cayo rin ang hahanapan nang Dios sa canila, cun
mapacasama sila, ydaramay cayo naman.   [Pp. 42–45]

For woe to you indeed if you transgress this command of God, if you do
not regulate the wrongdoing of those in your household and forbid
them to have bad thoughts. It will be you that the Lord God will blame,
for the foolishness of your son or a member of your household, it will
be you that God will hold accountable for their transgressions and you
will be implicated along with them.

And the exercise of any form of authority that deviates from the
prescriptions laid down by the divine Law accrues to the benefit of yet
another master, the devil: "paquinabang nang Demonio ang canilang
caloloua, ynaalipan din niya ang caloloua nang taoung macasalanan"
("it is the Devil who will make use of their souls; he will enslave the
soul of the sinner"; p. 50).

It was thus a question less of abolishing slavery than of choosing
one form of servitude over another. Conversion in this sense meant
redrawing all social relations as derivative of the natural relationship
between God and His creatures. That relationship was at the same
time fully realizable only through a temporal progression that would
culminate in the future. While one was alive one could experience it
only in language. For indeed, the actualization of this future was
possible only after death.

"Real" conversion, and with it submission to colonial rule, required the Tagalogs to be made dependent on this notion of an absolutely other realm. That dependence was invoked through an idiom of
futurity: the past and present selves were defined in terms of a potential self that was to be realized in some other place at some other time.
As we shall see, the appeal of this idea has to do with the emergence
of a collective investment in a certain representation of death and
practice of dying which would reconcile the present with the future,
the Master with His slaves.

Visualizing the "Outside"

In his path-breaking study of nineteenth- and early-twentieth-century peasant movements, Reynaldo Ileto has persuasively demonstrated the persistence of an ideology of resistance based on Spanish-

Christian notions of suffering and paradise.[2] Peasant revolts that now coincided with, now deviated from the elite-led nationalist revolution of 1896 were comprehensible to their participants insofar as they were couched in terms taken largely from seventeenth- and early-eighteenth-century devotional texts, which included prayers, poems, and such songs as *dalit, auit,* and the *Pasyon.* The popularity of these devotional writings attests to the fact that by the nineteenth century conversion had become commonplace, its discourse of paradise a vital part of Tagalog tradition.[3] Paradise, the absolutely other realm brought by Spain, had come to be seen as the source of the language with which to express the unity of all people, regardless of social status.

Why should a vision of paradise become so attractive to the Tagalogs, the surrender to and appropriation of its language so compelling? What was it in seventeenth- and early-eighteenth-century texts

2. Ileto, *Pasyon and Revolution,* esp. chaps. 1 and 2.

3. Early Spanish accounts routinely report a notion of an "afterlife" among ancient Tagalogs. Such writers as Plasencia and Morga were, as one might expect, quick to read such a notion in terms of the Christian heaven and hell. In Plasencia, for example, we read that the Tagalogs "used to speak and know of a life after death, which they called *maca,* and which we would call paradise, or by another name, the city of the dead. They say that those who go to this place are the just, and the brave, and those who lived without doing harm to others and were possessed of moral virtues" ("Costumbres de los tagalos," in Santa Inés, *Crónica,* 2:602). *Maca* as a word approximating the Spanish *paraíso* does not seem to have survived into the seventeenth and eighteenth centuries. The dictionaries of those periods render *maca* as "maybe" or "perhaps." Other accounts mention the word *caloualhatian* as analogous to "paradise." Yet, shorn of its Christian gloss, *caloualhatian* simply means a state of profound rest, as when one is in deep sleep, or dead. *Caloualhatian* does not, therefore, call to mind an absolute outside—at least before the 1580s—or a realm populated by a host of gods and spirits. Nor does *langit,* which Spanish devotional texts often used for "heaven." Rescued from its Christian trappings, *langit* refers to the sky or an arched roof.

Such is similarly the case with "hell." According to Plasencia, the Tagalogs "also have said that there is in the other life a place of pain, sorrow, and affliction, which they used to call *casanaan,* which was the place of anguish" (ibid., pp. 602–603). *Casanaan* literally means "abundance," as in *Saan ang casanaan nang salapi di sa Castilla?* ("Where is there a lot of money but in Spain?") or *Casanaan nang hirap di sa infierno?* ("Where is there much suffering but in hell?"). There is something wishful if not outright spurious about equating *casanaan* with hell. It is yet another way of saying that nothing in Tagalog—past, present, or future—cannot be read and comprehended in Spanish-Christian terms.

In short, notions of paradise and hell, contrary to received assumptions, are Spanish innovations with no Tagalog precedents. Indeed, the absence of a Tagalog mythology of rewards and punishments after death underlines the novelty of the heaven and hell introduced by the Spaniards.

on heaven—and its underside, hell—that lent itself to extensive quotation by the natives as a way of conceptualizing social and political strife?[4]

As the fragments of Oliver's sermon indicate, one's submission to God is always pitched on the register of expectation. In return for acceding to His laws, one can expect to have a place in His land (*bayan*), in heaven (*langit*), no longer as a slave but as a child of the Father.

This wish for a place in God's *bayan* is a common topos of seventeenth-century missionary texts in Tagalog. Its most prosaic formulation can be found in the earliest catechisms:

Tanong: ano ang ygaganti nang Dios sa manga banal na tauo?
Sagot: ang calualhatian sa langit doon maquiquita nila ang Dios, at matotoua at malili gaia, at lualhati magparating man saan.[5]

Question: What will God give back to holy people?
Answer: The tranquillity of heaven where they will see God, and obtain happiness, and joy, and rest forever and ever.

More elaborate lyrical descriptions of heaven include the poems of the prolific Dominican Blancas de San José (of *Arte de la lengua tagala* fame) and the Augustinian Pedro de Herrera.[6] Both employ a strikingly similar repertoire of images in conveying the vision of heaven—images that continued to be in common use in Tagalog writings of later centuries. These poems picture paradise as a state that is to be attained in an indefinite future, on a day of great joy and permanent absence of tension:

Arao na capitapita
lalong caligaligaya
cun ang macaguiguinhaua

4. See, for example, Apolinario de la Cruz's use of Herrera's 1647 *Dalit sa caloualhatian* (discussed later in this chapter), analyzed in Ileto, *Pasyon and Revolution*, pp. 46–52.
5. *Doctrina cristiana en lengua española y tagala* (1593), ed. Carlos Quirino (Manila: National Historical Commission, 1973).
6. Blancas's poem is titled "En alabanza de la Gloria" and is attached to the preface of the 1610 edition of his *Arte de la lengua tagala*; Herrera's, called "Dalit sa caloualhatian," is found at the end of his translation of a Jesuit meditation manual, *Meditaciones, cun manga mahal na pagninilay na sadia sa Sanctong pag exercicios* (Manila, 1645).

matingnan nang ating mata.
[Herrera, stanza 1]

The most eagerly awaited day
is even more joyful
when that which relieves us
will be seen with our eyes.

Di sinong di matoua
magpuri doon sa bayan oouian
nang aming caloloua
bayang colualhatian,
aming pamamayanan paratihan?
[Blancas, stanza 2]

Who will not rejoice
and praise the land
to which our souls will return,
land of tranquillity
that will be our home forever?

Both poems speak of this land as beyond speech (*ang bayang di masabi,* "the land that is beyond words" [Blancas, stanza 1]) and beyond thought (*Dili ngani mayysip / ang galing na masasapit,* "The joy that will be attained [there] / is unthinkable" [Herrera, stanza 4]). It is therefore a place that can be comprehended negatively, as something that is not what earthly existence is. In Blancas (stanzas 3, 4, 10):

. . . uala nang camatayan
pauoang toua,t, ligaya,t, cabuhayan
                    ·   ·   ·
Uala din caualan doon
nang balang namang ycaguiguinhaua.
                    ·   ·   ·
Galing aya nang bayan,
na ualan panglaopanglao, at pighati,
uala din calumbayan,
at ualan dalamhati,
uala din halohalong di loualhati.

. . . without death,
only joy and happiness and life.

. . .

[there is] also nothing lacking there
every wish will be fulfilled.

. . .

How wonderful is this land,
without sorrow and lament,
no sadness,
no tribulation,
nothing that is not glorious.

and in Herrera (stanzas 16–17):

Ualang gaby,t, pisang arao
ualang init, ualang ginao,
ualang gotom, ualang ohao,
ualan lumbay, ualan panglao.

Ualan tacot, ualan sindac,
ualang tolog, ualang poyat,
ualan balisang, paghanap,
ang dila,y, sadya,t, sangcad.

The day will have no night,
No heat, no cold,
No hunger, no thirst,
No sadness, no loneliness.

No fear, no shock,
no sleep, no sleeplessness,
no anxiety in searching,
speech will be fit and appropriate.

paradise figures the definitive expulsion of any sense of loss. Death itself has been vanquished. This possibility of the total negation of loss is reflected in the fact that in heaven there will be no "anxiety in searching, / speech will be fit and appropriate." In heaven everything can be and has already been said. One is thus relieved of the tension that arises from the difference between words and things, speech and intention. Heaven is the place of pure language, where the differences between signs and referents have been completely accounted for.

The smoothing out of semiotic gaps coincides with the flattening out of temporal delay. In heaven, thinking is already doing, desire its own fulfillment:

Yndi na lalabanan
nang cataoan ang ating caloloua:
pacaliua,t, pacanan
magsasabay capoua,
casamahan din nila ang dilan toua.
[Blancas, stanza 22]

No longer will they clash,
the body with the soul:
to the right and to the left
they go harmoniously,
accompanied by great joy.

Cumbaga sila,y, lalacad
tolin ybong longmilipad
malayo may matatangbad
dili magaabut quisap.

   . . .

pababa ma,t, paytaas
yto,t, yao,i, cagyat cagyat.
[Herrera, stanzas 6, 7]

And if they were to travel
they would go as swift as birds,
distant places can be reached
in a flash.

   . . .

upward or downward,
it would all be the same.

A seamless continuum between body and soul implies no apprehensible difference between "here" and "there." One has merely to think of being somewhere else and in "a flash" is there. As the site of pure language, heaven is also where everything has been conceptualized. The total regulation of differences means the end of work—particularly the work of translation, which seeks to establish correspondences and rules of correspondence.[7] And the absence of any kind of sensed delay results in the tenseless opposition of terms. Life/death,

---

7. It is not fortuitous, then, that these poems should appear in books that deal with language (Blancas's *Arte*) and translation (Herrera's *Meditaciones*).

day/night, heat/cold, sleep/sleeplessness—all such oppositions slide freely from one to the other, their relationship determined by an unending sense of "now."

Paradise marks the end of translation. For this reason it also signals the end of conversion, inasmuch as everything is already what it is not. Emblematic in this regard is the perfect fusing of body and soul as timeless simulacra of the image of Christ (Herrera, stanza 11; Blancas, stanza 22).

This is why the discourse of paradise furnishes the means of imaging the potential unity of all members of society. By signifying the possibility of total signification and by figuring the inexorable trajectory of history toward an ahistorical realm of pure concept, it also envisions the definitive abolition of all social categories:

> Galing tingnan nang mata
> cun buhayin nang Dios ang tanang tauo
> ualan matanda,t, bata
> mabuti ang pagcatauo
> manga dalaga,y, bagungtauo.
>
> Pisang caralagahan,
> at cabagong tauhang di mapayi
> paua ding cagandahan . . .
> [Blancas, stanzas 18–19]
>
> The eye will delight in seeing
> the way God will revive all people
> there will be neither old men nor
>   children
> everyone will behave well
> young men and women alike.
>
> Everyone will be youthful
> and their youthfulness will never
>   diminish
> everyone will be so beautiful . . .
>
> Baguntauo ma,t, dalaga
> manga tauo mang naona
> magulang caya,t, batapa
> magcacasing para para

Ang mahal ma,t, mababa
ang mayaman ma,t, ang ducha
magsising musing mucha
ang Dios ang may panata
[Herrera, stanzas 14–15]

Young men and women
ancestors of long ago
parents and even children
all will look alike.

The high and the low
the rich and the poor
they will all appear the same
this is what God has promised.

Yet this all-encompassing unity of men and women, young and old, rich and poor envisioned in heaven is purchased at the expense of a generalized subordination to the Father. Social categories are extinguished insofar as they are also subsumed in the governing distinction: that between God and everyone else. Unity thus arises only to the extent that hierarchy is conserved. And hierarchy is conserved by the establishment of complete harmony between individual desires and the demands of the Law (Blancas, stanza 21; Herrera, stanza 45). In such a state of harmony one's thoughts and memories cease to reflect a distinguishable past populated by ancestors and events. Instead, one's mind remains fixed on one thought:

di maaring sumala
sa Dios nang sa Dios ang alaala.
[Blancas, stanza 11]

you cannot sin there
to God and God alone will your
    thoughts be directed.

Cun ang ama mo,t, ang ina
sa Infierno,y, maquita
di mabauasang ligaya
asal di mangongolila.

Dios ang canilang Ama
At catoto,t, cabihasa
siya,y, inaalala
iba,y, inaalintana.
[Herrera, stanzas 33–34]

If your father and mother
in hell you'll see
your joy will not be diminished
you will not feel orphaned.

For God is their Father
Their companion and friend
He alone is kept in mind
everyone else is forgotten.

In paradise, then, one still thinks, but only of one thing. Similarly, one still speaks, but only of God; still sees, but only the Lord.

hamang ang Panginoon
pono nang dilan aua
tinitingnan din nilang ualang saua.

Naquiquita ding tanto
ang Poong Dios sa pagca Dios niya . . .

ang ponong Panginoon
ang pinagaauitan,
na ualan tahan tahang pagolitan.
[Blancas, stanzas 5, 6, 8]

only the Lord
full of mercy
will be looked at, without tiring.

And what will be seen
will be the Lord God in His
    Godhood . . .

it is to the Lord
that all will repeatedly sing
without ever stopping.

Dios ang pagcarongsolan
titingnan pagcaraniuan
siyang mata,t, titigan
ualang hompay, ualang hoyang

Doon sila nabobosog
napopono ang loob
na niig napag calogod
ualang sauang panonood.
[Herrera, stanzas 22–23]

All attend to God
looking steadily
into His eye
without interruption, without end.

There they will all be satisfied
they will be filled
with unceasing joy
watching [Him] tirelessly.

These expressions of the beatific vision, or what has been referred to as the "natural desire to see God," have a long genealogy. They are derived from Christian conventions formulated by the scholastics and their sixteenth-century commentators as well as from a tradition of Spanish religious writing.[8] One who sees God in His Godhood can want nothing else. In His face is revealed everything. God fills the eye just as He fills the mind, thereby pushing aside all other thoughts and desires. Thus do the eyes function like the ears, sight like heard speech. Nothing stands between the gaze and its object. The object is precisely what makes possible the operation of seeing and hearing.

In heaven one does not, therefore, merge with the divinity. One sees it, just as one is seen by it. In the same vein, one does not melt into the object of praise. One is absorbed into the ceaseless praises directed to

8. As Aquinas put it: "Final and perfect happiness can consist only in the vision of the essence of God" (in *Summa theologica,* cited in *New Catholic Encyclopedia,* 4: 801). Pope Benedict XII wrote in 1336 that "we possess the beatific vision as soon as we are worthy to do so after death" (ibid., 6:972). Where Spanish literature is concerned, we have the outstanding example of the Spanish mystic Saint John of the Cross, especially in such poems as "Coplas del alma que pena por ver a Dios," in *Obras escogidas,* 9th ed. (Madrid: Austral, 1979), pp. 30–32.

the Father. Communication of and with Authority is so perfect that to intend is to express, to give is to get. Heaven is the site and sight of perfect hierarchy. Order continues to exist, but it is no longer challenged by the vagaries of language, history, and human wishes. Heaven denotes the unalterable freezing of power relationships. Absolute unity arises from one's unconditional surrender to the unimpeded exercise of divine authority. In the context of a colonial politics tied to evangelization, the image of paradise could thus lend itself to the construction of ideal notions of authority and submission. Paradise figured the possibility of surrendering to an outside power located in the future which would make past and present fears eminently reasonable.

Yet paradise as a phantasmatic projection of a future condition that lay beyond death could take on currency and appeal only insofar as it was signifiable. Knowing about paradise meant experiencing it rhetorically. Embedded in the materiality of language, it could be confronted only as an ensemble of signs. Thus, its coherence and value arose from the way it differed from other signs. Heaven was intelligible and translatable to the extent that it could be hierarchically opposed to something else: hell. The idiom of paradise determined the direction and tone of one's wishfulness in relation to a perceived threat to the content of one's wishes—indeed, to wishfulness itself. It was in the conjuring up of that threat that fear could be generated. And against these manufactured fears a notion of paradise could be posed as an attractive alternative. Hence paradise gave current fears a context. But before it could do so, the context of fear—the other possibility of hell—also had to be established.

"With what will God punish sinners?" (Ano ang yparurusa niya sa manga tauong tampalasan?) the interlocutor-priest was to ask the native convert in a 1593 Tagalog catechism. The expected reply was "He will throw them into hell and there they will suffer and ache forever" (Yhoholog niya sa ynfierno doon maghihirap sila at maccacasaquet magparating man saan).[9] Whereas paradise is the final negation of loss, hell is the impossibility of overcoming it. As the site of sheer anguish, hell represents the consequences of exclusion from divine patronage: the unrelieved subjection to the interminable assault of everything that one fears. The prospect of total exclusion

9. *Doctrina christiana.* n.d.

from the circulation of gifts gives rise to the dread of being without the means to withstand the full force of the demands of authority— here figured as the punishments of God. Thus, while in hell one is maintained within the economy of divine circulation, one nonetheless is cut off from the possibility of reciprocating what one receives.

This notion of hell is highlighted in the very title of another poem by Father Herrera which is found in the same book as his lyrical celebration of paradise: "Dalit sa ualang catapusang hirap at saquit sa Infierno," "Poem on the never-ending sufferings and pains in Hell." Marshaling a rhetoric of fear, an accusatory voice addresses the convert:

O Binyagang balaquiot
lili sa Ama mong Dios
uala caman sinta,t, logod
dili carin matacot?

Cun icao ypahintolot
sa calalima,t, yholog
ang hirap mo,y, ualan togot
saquit na dili magamot.

Cocohan damay sa iyo
malupit na Demonio
ang galit nila,t, pagtampo
sa iyo rin ybobonto.
[Herrera, stanzas 1–3]

O deceitful convert
unfaithful to the Father your God
you have no love nor affection
Are you not even afraid?

If you were to be cast down
and thrown to the depths
your suffering will have no end
your pain will have no cure.

You will have the companionship
of the cruel Devil[s]
their anger and their rage
On you they will vent.

Hell is the other aspect of the outside realm introduced by Spain, the other part of Christianity's mythical geography where God's pity gives way to His wrath. The devil (always rendered in Castilian as *Demonio*) is God's agent. One who falls into the untold depths of hell can expect only the "companionship / of the cruel Devil." This threat subjects one to an unrelenting barrage of anger and remorse. The fear of hell arises from the vision of the parts of one's body as the targets of a series of attacks without hope of respite:

Magcacasaquit ang mata
ang bibig at ang taynga
ang camay sampon nang paa
magdurusang parapara

Apuy matapang na lubha
ang hapdi di mahanduca
alinmang apuy sa lupa
di cauangis di camucha.
[Herrera, stanzas 5–6]

The pain will spread to the eyes
to the mouth and the ears
the hands as well as the feet
will suffer alike.

Raging flames
Unrelieved agony
no other fire on earth
can quite compare [to them].

The self in hell is irremediably parceled out. Its parts are consumed by pain and raging flames. The lurid detailing of suffering as it spreads to various parts of the body is a way of pointing to the impossibility of reconstituting a self that might be able to respond to the assaults that are thrown its way. Whereas paradise sustains the wish to see a self revivified beyond pain and loss, hell offers a scenario of unending loss. Thus the representation of hell is based on the imagined fear of being cut off from a source of protection that would enable one to carry out exchanges with the outside figure of authority. That in hell one "can no longer hope to see / the holy face of God" (Herrera, stanza 8) further underlines the impossibility of exchange in the absence of a recoverable self. And in contrast to paradise, where speech fully contains the self that addresses the Father, in hell language utterly fails to express the self because of its exclusion from divine patronage:

> Ang arao nang iyong buhay
> susumpain ualan hompay
> Dios pa,y, pangungusapan
> uicang catampalasan.
> [Herrera, stanza 9]

> The days of your life
> will be spent cursing
> even God will be addressed
> with insulting words.

It is important to bear in mind, however, that this fantasy of exclusion, like that of perfect reciprocity and hierarchy, is rhetorically provoked. The fear that it generates among the listeners arises as a linguistic effect. In Herrera's poem, an impersonal voice addresses a second party in both the singular and plural (*icao* and *cayo*, respectively). Whose voice is this? Herrera's, perhaps? But the Spanish priest writes in another language, not his own. He uses a stock of images derived from other sources, scriptural and literary. The tropes in the poem about hell are calculated to produce horror. This intention makes them formulaic, hence not Herrera's inventions. The fact that the poem is printed in Tagalog makes it available for the appropriation of other voices, those of missionary and native convert alike. To ask about this voice is then to ask about the nature of the rhetorical force that produces fear of and subsequent surrender to the notion of an absolute outside.

From the position and tone of this voice, we get the impression that it can speak about the horrors of hell because it is itself exempt from the dangers of falling into the infernal abyss:

> At ang icadaralamhati
> yaong saquit ay lalaqui
> di guiguitis di oonti
> ualan hangan ang pighati.
>   . . .

Magyngat magpaca ingat
maca sumama ang palad
maca masingit sa pitac
na di ca mapucnatpucnat.
[Herrera, stanzas 7, 13]

And what anguish
as the pain grows
without interruption, without
    relief,
sorrow will have no end.
            .   .   .

Be ever so careful
your fate might turn out bad
and you might fall into a hole
from which there is no escape.

And earlier this voice had recounted images of paradise as if it had
witnessed their reality. In a sense, then, this voice is disembodied. It
seems, that is, to originate in no one in particular. Presumably anyone
who had been sufficiently exposed to the discourse of Christianity
and was skilled enough to read phoneticized Tagalog could take on
this voice. It speaks to the living from what seems to be a perspective
beyond life. It brings news of an outside that is wholly different from
yet constitutive of the inside, and in a future tense that orders the
articulation of past and present experience.

This voice suggests the ability to speak of things hitherto unheard
of in Tagalog: the horrors of an *infierno*, for instance, which remains
untranslated in devotional texts; or of familiar things in drastically
unfamiliar terms, such as *langit* and *caloualhatian*. The possibility of
speaking in this voice brings up the possibility of moving across the
boundary of what is and is not translatable. In this sense, it involves
speaking as an "I" (*aco*) that seems to be able to traverse this world
and what is thought to lie beyond it. Hence Blancas de San José's
poem about paradise begins:

Bucsyn mo ang aquing labi
o Panginoon Dios na con sabihin
ang bayang di masabi

Open my [*aquing*] lips
O Lord God so that I can speak
of the land beyond words.

The poet asks God to provide him with the words with which to speak of heaven. The "I" can image paradise insofar as it has been given another language issued from above. Conversely, this "I" can turn down to its listeners, urging them to submit their bodies to the demands of God in order to be deserving of His reward:

Aba ca na Cristiano
at ang cataoan ay papaghirapin;
at cahimat maano,
yto din ang sicapin,
at pacapagpilitan hanapin.
[Blancas, stanza 31]

Woe to you, Christians,
discipline your body
and regardless of what may happen
strive to attain
and endeavor to find.

Similarly, the "I" that pictures hell ends by addressing the "you" that listens. It demands from it the work of repentance as a way of avoiding damnation:

Samantalahin ang arao
yayang may capangyarihan
casalana,y, pagsisihan
ang Ama,y, tauaran.
[Herrera, stanza 14]

Take advantage of the day
while you are still able to
repent for your sins
ask forgiveness from the Father.

In Chapter 3 I suggested that conversion, by virtue of translation, sought to generate other "I's" within the native convert. The discourse of confession, for instance, was designed to produce two selves. Ideally, one who confesses speaks in terms of a divided self: one in the present, another in the past; the former posing as an agent of the Law, the latter as the secret and inherently errant object of its search. But in the rhetoric of paradise/hell, another kind of "I" emerges. It appears as one that never tires of voicing images of an outside realm reachable only upon death. This "I" tends to subsume those produced by confession. Its authority is derived not from its capacity to account for its past but from its ability to envision possibilities in the future. Issuing from without, it claims to speak from beyond the grave. As such, it assumes a somewhat ghostly tenor capable of instilling fear in the singular and plural "yous" it addresses. This "I" entails a shift to a different rhetorical register where one can articulate new claims and demands on others. Within the context of conversion, such a shift is possible because the "I" is associated with an outside that becomes most insistent on the verge of death. It is the emergence of this other "I" as the harbinger of a certain way of conceiving death and dying in Tagalog society that will now concern us.

Spirits and the Appeal of Christianity

During the early colonial period, one of the factors that impinged on the spread of Christianity was the considerable numerical disparity between priests and converts. By 1700 only about 400 clerics were ministering to some 600,000 native converts, most of them in the Tagalog areas.[10] The parish priest had to travel regularly to far-flung areas in order to administer the sacraments. The development of a native clergy might have alleviated this situation, but royal legislation, Spanish racism, and the lack of institutions to train natives for the priesthood worked to prevent it.[11] Not until the middle of the eighteenth century were appreciable numbers of natives ordained into the priesthood—and then only as seculars, with limited parish re-

10. Phelan, *Hispanization of the Philippines,* p. 81.
11. Horacio de la Costa, S.J., "Development of the Native Clergy," in *Studies in Philippine Church History,* ed. Anderson, pp. 65–104.

sponsibilities.[12] During the period under consideration, the priest had to resort to other solutions to keep converts within the faith.

One common alternative was the establishment of native confraternities (*cofradías*). Such organizations emerged in the early seventeenth century, spurred particularly by the Jesuits. Styled after those in Catholic Europe, native confraternities flourished throughout the Spanish colonial period.

The members of the confraternities were often, though not always, *principales*. As one early-seventeenth-century Jesuit account puts it, the *principales* were considered to be the "most prominent, most Christian, and most trustworthy in those villages." The same account specifies the basic duties of the confraternity members. They were to perform "pious acts" and "works of devotion" that would serve as "preventives against the . . . great evil of idolatry." Originally confraternities were intended to counter the influence of native shamans (*babaylans*) over the sick and dying. In the absence of the parish priest, confraternity members were to "ascertain who in the villages may be sick or dying . . . and attend [to] both . . . by frequent visits." In so doing, they would be able to "prevent the abuses, superstitions, idolatries, intoxications, dirges, music and wailing that had been the custom when they were pagans for both the sick and the dead."[13]

More than a century later Father Tomás Ortiz reiterated the crucial importance of native auxiliaries in supplementing the priest's spiritual care of converts. Like other Spanish writers, he stressed their value in ensuring against relapse into pagan beliefs, especially among the ill and dying. Members of confraternities and other "trustworthy" *indios* were to provide such converts with "spiritual consolation" and "with the necessary remedies against temptations, and help them achieve a good death [*buen morir*], and so that there should be no lack in this regard, the Ministers will take measures to assign and instruct some people in each *visita* or barrio so that they may not fail to provide others with the consolation of a good death."[14]

The dying were to be brought to the church to receive the last rites

12. By 1750, 142 of 564 parishes were administered by native seculars. The overwhelming majority of wealthy and populated parishes in the Tagalog region continued to be under the control of Spanish regulars (ibid., p. 87).

13. Chirino, *Relación de las Islas Filipinas*, 2d ed. (Manila, 1890), pp. 131–132.

14. Ortiz, *Práctica del ministerio*, p. 21.

in the event that the priest could not visit their homes. But given the shortage of priests and the difficulties of travel, the dying often failed to receive these rites.[15] Hence native auxiliaries were commonly left with the task of presiding over deaths. For this reason, Ortiz recommended that "responsible persons" in the village be provided with "some guide or little book" containing the necessary formula to help the dying achieve a "good death."[16]

These repeated injunctions to guard against the converts' tendency to fall back on their *abusos* and *supersticiones* during moments of imminent loss implies that so-called pagan practices continued to persist. As I remarked in Chapter 3, their systematic characterization as "sins" and their identification as the works of the devil were essential to the project of evangelization. Insofar as conversion meant turning away from something, that something had to be given a name; hence the missionaries' categories of *abusos* and *supersticiones*. Spanish Catholicism's hegemonic claim over the Tagalogs was tenable to the extent that it could be seen as a superior alternative to pagan beliefs, particularly at the point of imminent loss.

It should not surprise us, then, that the Spanish missionaries were especially concerned with addressing the need to provide "spiritual consolation" to the sick and the dying. On the threshold of loss, tensions between Christian and pagan beliefs and practices tended to be played out most explicitly. The approach of death brought into sharp focus the difference between possible modes of conversion because it raised the issue of the appropriate means for conceptualizing and thereby containing loss. It was for this reason that missionaries were urged by their superiors to acquaint themselves with native superstitions pertaining to death and the spirit world. Thus prepared, the missionary would be better able to guard Christian rituals from the threat of pagan contamination.

We get a sense of this concern in Father Ortiz's remarks on the Tagalog belief in the return of the spirit of the dead:

... the *indios* usually believe that the souls of the dead return to their house on the third day after their death in order to visit the people there, and attend their feast, and for this reason they hold a ceremony called *tibao*, which they cover and hide by saying that they come together in

15. Phelan, *Hispanization of the Philippines*, p. 82.
16. Ortiz, *Práctica del ministerio*, pp. 21–22.

the house of the dead to pray the rosary for [the departed soul]; and if they are told to recite the rosary in church, they prefer not to because this is not what they really do. For this reason, the Minister shall impede their gathering in the house of the dead after the burial, and shall not permit them to go to the house under some pretext, particularly on the third day.   [P. 12]

Tibao consisted of a feast held on the third and ninth day of mourning at the house of the deceased. This period of mourning, referred to as *sipa,* lasts for nine days after the burial, during which the family and relatives of the dead recite prayers and novenas.[17] It is during the feast of the *tibao* that "they light candles waiting for the soul of the dead; they place a mat on the floor and spread ashes on it so that the soul of the dead will leave behind its footprints, and in this way they can know whether or not the soul has arrived. They also place a jar of water on the door so that when the spirit comes, it can wash its feet" (p. 12).

Traditionally, the Tagalogs demonstrated their respect for the dead by decorating its body. Fourteenth- and fifteenth-century burial sites indicate the widespread practice of ornamenting the teeth, particularly with gold. Early Spanish accounts also note that the corpse was perfumed and dressed in its best clothes. Depending on the person's status, the deceased was buried with an assortment of goods, ranging from Chinese porcelain to weapons and jewelry. And as slaves were often interred with their master, the corpse retained a retinue of sorts.[18] The goods buried with the dead maintained the position of the deceased within a circle of exchange with the living; that position seemed to be enhanced by the ritual offerings of surplus goods. What accounted for this elevation of status?

As early Spanish accounts indicate, the "soul" of the dead was assumed to have joined the ranks of *nono,* or *anito,* as they were also called.[19] A period of mourning was marked by anticipation of the

17. See Rizal's annotated edition of Morga's *Sucesos,* p. 315 n. 1; Mas, *Informe,* 1:21–22.

18. Scott, *Prehispanic Source Materials,* pp. 33–38; Chirino, *Relación de las Islas Filipinas,* ed. Echevarría, pp. 87–88; Plasencia, "Costumbres," in Santa Inés, *Crónica,* 2:602.

19. Marcelo de Ribadeneira, O.F.M., *Historia del archipélago y otros reynos* (Barcelona, 1601; Manila: Historical Conservation Society, 1970), 1:52; Morga, *Sucesos,* p. 314n; Santa Inés, *Crónica,* 2:52.

return of the spirit of the dead. In *tibao* feasts, a jar of water was placed at the entrance of the house so that the spirit could wash its feet. A special place at the table was also reserved for the spirit, and the best food was put there.[20] The returning spirit, or *nono*, was the privileged guest. As we saw earlier, spirits had the capacity to ward off danger and fulfill the desires of the living. In one sense, then, the mourning rituals described by Ortiz and other Spanish writers endowed the dead with a new status, but *not* by consigning the spirit to another realm infinitely distant from the living. Such ceremonies as *sipa* and *tibao* suggest rather that the living actively solicited the return of the dead in their benign form as *nono* or *anito*. Mourning in this case seems to have involved a recognition of the dead as dead precisely because they could be petitioned for favors and protection. Thus the dead lingered on as part of the society of the living. Their authority was occasionally acknowledged in times of distress and want. And their access to a realm unavailable to the living made them attractive sources of the means to ward off illness, hardship, and unexpected disasters.

The desire to form reciprocal ties with the benevolent spirit of the dead arose in relation to the persistent native belief in the existence of malevolent spirits in the world. These spirits included, among others, *asuang, patianac,* and *tigbalang*. Each was believed to possess horrifying attributes underneath a variety of disguises. The *asuang,* for example, was a vampire-like creature that lured its male victims by putting on the appearance of a beautiful woman. At other times it took on the shape of an unusually proportioned domestic animal, such as a dog, cat, or pig.[21] The *patianac* was said to resemble a large birdlike creature called a *tictic*. It was believed to hover about the house of pregnant women, using its elongated tongue to snatch their fetuses. Finally, the *tigbalang,* encountered on deserted roads, caused one to lose one's way and fall ill. They assumed the form of either an old black dwarf or a monstrous horse.[22]

---

20. Mas, *Informe*, 1:21–22; Joaquín Martínez de Zúñiga, *Historia de las Islas Filipinas* (Sampaloc, 1803), p. 37.

21. Ortiz, *Práctica del ministerio*, p. 13; Raul Pertierra, "Viscera-Suckers and Female Sociality: The Philippine *Asuang,*" *Philippine Studies* 31 (1983): 319–337.

22. Ortiz, *Práctica del ministerio*, p. 13; Martínez de Zúñiga, *Historia de las Islas Filipinas*, pp. 35–36.

Belief in both benign and evil spirits persisted into the twentieth century, as Spanish accounts and ethnographic studies attest.[23] Yet it would be misleading to see an apparent dichotomy between good and evil spirits as analogous to Spanish-Christian conceptions of angels and devils. Both angels and devils are traceable to a single source, God. Both work to further His authority. As we have seen, the practice of converting the *indio* spirits into aspects of Christianity's prehistory, as the missionaries were wont to do, was never definitive. Indeed, the distinctions between good and bad spirits tended to be arbitrary. *Nono* and *anito* were just as capable of causing harm to anyone who failed to defer to them (as in the case of the *buaya* or crocodile, considered a *nono* by the Tagalogs) as of offering protection in times of trouble. Similarly, certain evil spirits could also be induced into pacts of friendship by the native skilled enough to deal with them. Ortiz's account, for example, notes the Tagalog practice of neutralizing the threat of the *tigbalang* by "delivering to him a Rosary and receiving [in return] such superstitious things as bits of its hair, herbs, rocks, and other things with which to accomplish prodigious things."[24]

In this connection, it should be noted that a variety of prescriptions existed (and continue to exist today)[25] for warding off the threat of spirits. The wearing of amulets, for instance, has been a standard means of keeping oneself safe from the danger of spirits. According to eighteenth- and nineteenth-century accounts, a man countered the

23. Spanish accounts include Miguel de Loarca, "Relación de las yslas filipinas" (1582), in *Philippine Islands,* ed. Blair and Robertson, 5:129–133, 163, 171–173; Plasencia, "Costumbres," in Santa Ines, *Crónica,* 2:600–603; Chirino, *Relación de las Islas Filipinas,* ed. Echevarría, pp. 60–64; Martínez de Zúñiga, *Historia de las Islas Filipinas,* pp. 34–37; Wenceslao E. Retana, *El indio batangueño,* 3d ed. (Manila: Chofre, 1888), pp. 89–95; José Castaño, *Breve noticia acerca del origin, religión, creencias, y superstitiones de los antiguos indios del Bicol* (Madrid, 1895), sections of which appear as Appendix III in Frank Lynch, S.J., "An Mga Asuang: A Bicol Belief," *Philippine Social Sciences and Humanities Review* 14 (December 1949): 401–428. Ethnographic accounts include Lynch, "An Mga Asuang"; Máximo D. Ramos, *Creatures of Philippine Lower Mythology* (Quezon City: University of the Philippines Press, 1971) and *The Aswang Syncrasy in Philippine Folklore* (Manila: Philippine Folklore Society, 1971); F. Landa Jocano, *Growing Up in a Philippine Barrio* (New York: Holt, Rinehart & Winston, 1969), chap. 13; Pertierra, "Viscera-Suckers."
24. Ortiz, *Práctica del ministerio,* p. 12.
25. See Lynch, "An Mga Asuang," p. 415.

harmful *patianac* by exposing his genitals to the air. Armed with a bamboo lance, he then slashed the air in all directions.[26]

Thus the *indio* spirit world was highly decentralized. Despite the elaborate typologies of beneficent and malevolent spirits and the popular lore regarding their characteristic disguises, their preferred victims, and modes of detection and defense against them, spirits had no reference to a comprehensive narrative of ultimate rewards and eternal punishments. Neither were they attributed to the workings of a single source that was simultaneously distant and omnipotent. As the repositories of all things strange that impinged on everyday life, spirits offered a multiplicity of possibilities—whether for loss or gain—in the world. One was always potentially within the purview of spirits; hence one was always likely to be surprised by the sight of them—although one never actually saw them, but encountered only their uncanny envoys.[27] The apprehension felt in the imagined presence of spirits was thus related to the feeling of being reduced to the status of an object for someone/something else's incomprehensible designs:

> The very thought of the *Asuang* so tormented them that when it flashed across their minds, they would abandon what they were doing, and would at times be heard crying out piteously in their uncontrollable fear, uttering horrible maledictions and sighing aloud. . . . If they then heard a dull sound like the rumbling of a distant storm, at once they were filled with a terrible fear and unreasoning trembling; for they believed the *Asuang* had actually come and was carrying off the entrails of some child or of some sick person.[28]

Fear is triggered by an unfamiliar sound of something unseen or, as in the accounts cited earlier, the sight of something that seems to have no recognizable place in the world. Such signs connote the potential occurrence of a chain of unexpected events. Their authority stems from the sense that they emanate from a presence that looks at one but that one cannot see. Fear arises from the inability to match the gaze that falls on one, that is, to localize the source of what one

26. Ortiz, *Práctica del ministerio,* p. 13; Martínez de Zúñiga, *Historia de las Islas Filipinas,* p. 36.
27. See, for example, Castaño, *Breve noticia,* pp. 425–426; Ramos, *Aswang Syncrasy,* esp. pp. 16–27, 49–50.
28. Castaño, *Breve noticia,* pp. 425–426.

receives and thereby perform the necessary return with which to domesticate the authority of that source.

Herein lies one explanation for the natives' acceptance of the Christian notion of paradise and hell. In paradise God's gaze is seen, and being seen, it can be returned. In the translation of the concept of the beatific vision lay an appealing solution to the prospect of being helplessly surrounded by unseen spirits. In aspiring to "see God," one aims at realizing the full visibility of the source of all potentiality. One thus eliminates the other, more dreadful possibility—that of being shocked out of a known realm of exchange. This vision is supported by the imagined perfection of the hierarchical distinctions between God/self, inside/outside, and source/signs. In heaven, the faultless and unmediated circulation of glances, language, and thoughts between God and humans results in the smooth and unending operation of reciprocity.

The solution that paradise offered, however, could be had only by acceptance of the Christian notion of death. Heaven was reachable only at the end of life. Insofar as Tagalog beliefs were concerned, death was but one in a series of possibilities that could be visited upon the individual by a spirit. There existed no necessary link between spirits and death. Christianity, though, insisted on that link. One became party to the company of the spirits only upon death. Access to God's realm was predicated on a highly specific and theoretically incontestable set of prescriptions for living whose culmination was signaled by a certain way of dying. It was perhaps for this reason that by the seventeenth century, such Christian rituals as novenas and the recitation of the rosary found their way into Tagalog celebrations of *sipa* and *tibao*.

At first glance, it would seem that the appropriation of Christian prayers and rituals to carry out transactions with the spirits was analogous to the popularization of confession. In each case one took on something new while implicitly circumventing the authority of its source. When one made a novena or recited the rosary to deal with the Tagalog spirit world, one did not fully return these signs to their divine source but displaced them somewhere else. As far as the Spanish missionaries were concerned, this practice was scandalous and needed to be suppressed. From the native point of view, however, it was a means of confronting authority without courting conflict. In the case of confession, the terms of *utang na loob* and *hiya* made for a kind of submission that did not necessitate the full incorporation of the colonial-Christian hierarchy. This much was also suggested in our reading of Pinpin's appropriation of Castilian as well as the popular response to the discourse of confession.

But where death was concerned, submission tended to be more problematic. In a pre-Christian situation, the arrival or postponement of death was occasionally, though not necessarily, attributed to the workings of spirits. That is, death was not accorded a privileged authority in orienting one's dealings with an unknown and unseen realm of potentiality. Christianity, however, reworks death into the ultimate basis of conversion. Within the colonial context, real conversion could be made to appear most desirable to the extent that death could be translated into a special element in the divine circulation of signs. Christianity's conceit was that it provided one with the absolute means of transcending death by conceiving loss itself from the perspective of an afterlife. As we have seen, notions of paradise and hell endowed death with a different temporal and ontological significance. Elaborate scenarios of celestial reward and eternal damnation allowed for the articulation of an identity that persisted beyond the destruction of the body.

Such notions were particularly appealing to those natives who had a special stake in the preservation of relations of inequality: the *principales*. Their privileged position linked them not only with the colonial bureaucracy but with the church as well. As *fiscales* (sacristans) and leaders of confraternities, they were in a peculiar relation to the rest of native society. In the absence of the Spanish missionaries, they supervised the instruction of new converts in the doctrines of the faith, encouraged them to attend mass and go to confession, and the like.[29] It was to them that the missionaries, following Father Ortiz's advice, entrusted copies of *recomendaciones del alma,* or manuals containing prayers for the dying which would conduct the convert toward a "good death."

At this point we might pause to recall that in the early colonial period, a full-fledged market economy did not exist outside the walls of the colonial capital. And even there, it was overwhelmingly restricted to the vagaries of the Manila–Acapulco trade. Cash crops,

29. Horacio de la Costa, S.J., *Readings in Philippine History* (Manila: Bookmark, 1964), pp. 29–30.

which were to introduce capital as a major factor in shaping the contours of power relationships in areas outside of Manila, did not come to the fore until the 1760s. In that case, what might have constituted the basis of *principal-maginoo* prestige during the period under consideration? I have suggested that it had to do with the capacity to move between Spanish and Tagalog social and political hierarchies. Here I further postulate that their authority within native society can be attributed in part to their control—a control analogous to that of the missionary—over the dissemination of a discourse that claimed to offer a way of domesticating death.

This ideological component of the *principales'* authority can be seen in the writings of one of the most important yet least-studied figures of Tagalog literature, Don Gaspar Aquino de Belen. A native of Rosario, Batangas, a province south of Manila, Aquino worked as a printer in the Jesuit press from 1703 to 1716. But unlike Pinpin (who worked as a printer for the Dominicans a century earlier), Aquino was also a *principal,* as evidenced by the honorific title "Don" attached to his Christian name. He is best remembered as the author of the first Tagalog *pasyon,* a long narrative poem recounting the suffering, death, and resurrection of Christ, published in 1703. Aquino's poem was, as Bienvenido Lumbera says, "the first of its kind in the history of Tagalog literature and the first written narrative poem, which makes him the first great Tagalog poet."[30] The poem served as the basis for subsequent Tagalog *pasyones,* which were to be enormously vital in shaping popular perceptions in the nineteenth and twentieth centuries.[31]

Aquino's *Pasyon,* all 984 stanzas of it, first appeared as a kind of appendix to a shorter work, Aquino's Tagalog translation of a 1613 Spanish manual of prayers for the dying. Written by a Spanish Jesuit, Tomás de Villacastín, it was originally called *La recomendación del alma,* rendered by Aquino as *Manga panalangin pagtatagobilin sa caloloua nang tauong naghihingalo* (Prayers with which to commend the soul of the dying person).[32] The supplementary position given to

---

30. Bienvenido Lumbera, "Assimilation and Synthesis (1700–1800): Tagalog Poetry in the Eighteenth Century," *Philippine Studies* 16 (October 1968): 634. Little else is known about Aquino's life.

31. See Ileto, *Pasyon and Revolution;* Nicanor Tiongson, *Kasaysayan at estetika ng senakulo* (Quezon City: Ateneo de Manila University Press, 1975).

32. Unfortunately, I have been unable to locate a copy of the original Spanish work that Aquino translated. A fifth edition was published in Manila in 1760—ample testimony to its popularity among the Tagalogs.

This woodcut engraving of the four evangelists appears as the frontispiece of the fifth edition of Don Gaspar Aquino de Belen's *Manga panalanging pagtatagobilin sa caloloua nang tauong naghihingalo* (Prayers with which to commend the soul of the dying person), followed by the earliest *pasyon,* or narrative of Christ's death and resurrection, in the Tagalog language (Manila, 1760).

the longer *Pasyon* is indicated on the title page: beneath the main title, we read that this work, by Villacastín and translated (*ysinalin*) by Don Gaspar, is "followed by [*ysinonod*] the Holy Passion of our Lord Jesus Christ in verse." And the license granted by Melendez Llamas, the synodal examiner of the Manila bishopric, refers to the poem as having been "inserted" in the *Recomendación*. Indeed, Aquino himself, in the preface of the book, speaks initially and at greater length about the translated prayers than about his verse narration of Christ's passion—despite the fact that the *Pasyon* is, by all indications, an original work, not simply a Tagalog rendition of a Spanish poem.[33] Thus the *pasyon* idiom, which was to assume crucial significance in framing Tagalog experience in later centuries, was initially framed by something else: a discourse on death. Interestingly enough, that discourse was a translation done not by a Spanish missionary but by a Tagalog don.[34] It is this movement from one frame to another—from a process of translation to a discourse on death and dying which eventually called forth a narrative of suffering—that merits closer attention.

Desiring a Beautiful Death

Aquino's book opens with a prose dedication to the "most exalted image [*cataastaasang larauan*] of Jesus of Nazareth":

Con aco may di dapat P. co na magalay sa camahalan mo nitong monti cong pagala,y, hindi co liningon ang cababaan co, at ang tinongo co,y, ang cataasan mo na Dios na totoo, at Tauo namang totoo; na di pa sucat ang pagcaquinapal mo,t, nilalang ang boong calangitan, at ang calupaan, ay tinobos mo pa nang dogo mong mahal ang sang-catauohan . . . Ytong yniaalay cong ito sa cataasan, mo,y, hindi sa yba cundi sa iyo nga, caya sa iyo co rin naman ynihahayin, at siya namang yquinapangahas niring loob cong culang . . . yaring loob co, sa pagca ang nacababalot lamang, ay ang ualan hangang pagsoay, at ang di maysip na pagcacasala sa iyo gabit arao; gayon man daquila cong poon, ay sa camahalang gracia mo aco ongmaasa, na sa matoto, o dili, ytong

33. Lumbera, "Assimilation and Synthesis," pp. 634–648.

34. Other than Pinpin's 1610 *Librong,* Aquino's 1703 *Panalangin* was the only book by a Tagalog to be published during the early colonial period and the first sustained translation of a Spanish text into Tagalog by a Tagalog.

gaua cong yniaalay sa capangyarihan mo,y, aquing momolan, sa pagca
iyo yto,t, sa iyo rin yniaalay. . . . Ang bocod dito,y, camtan co naua,t,
at camtan din naman nang lahat na tauo, yaong catamistamisan mong
ualan pagcacaiba, doon sa caharian mong pono nang ligayang di
matatapos magparating man saan. Siyanaua.   [Folios 1–3]

Undeserving as I am, my Lord, to render to your highness this offering
of mine, I look not upon my lowliness but instead regard your exalted
position as the true God and true man. And having created and given
birth to all of heaven and earth, you also ransomed mankind with your
holy blood. . . . This offering of mine to your exalted person is meant
only for you, which is why I serve it to you; this is what I have dared to
do in my *loob* that is so wanting . . . this *loob* of mine that is enveloped
only in unceasing disobedience and unthinkable sinfulness, day and
night; despite this, my great Lord, I trust in your most holy grace, that
whether or not this work of mine which I offer to your power is accomplished, I may begin it, for this really belongs to you and to you alone is
it given. . . . Moreover, grant that I, along with everyone else, attain
your sweet unchangingness there in your kingdom full of joy, forever
and ever. Amen.

The most striking thing about this opening passage is its tone.
There is an earnestness and heaviness about it that differs considerably from the nimble evasiveness of Pinpin's *Librong*. This tone,
which permeates the *Panalangin,* calls to mind the writings of the
Spanish missionaries. So do the prominence of the "I" that directly
addresses Christ and the "lowliness" of its position (*cababaan*) in
relation to the "exalted" status (*cataasan*) of Christ.

The positioning of this "I" within the communicative circuit of
divine exchange appears as the consequence of the author's recognition of his debts to God. The dedicatory intent of this section is
appropriately couched in an explicitly confessional mode. The writer
can speak directly to God insofar as his speech is propelled by the
thought of his "unthinkable sinfulness." The "I" here is thus the
product of the author's recognition of his own inner lack (*loob cong
culang*) in relation to the fullness of God's Word.

What weighs down Aquino's words is the very history of conversion as translation; that is, the sense that one's language is one's own
by virtue of having been given to one from above, so that speaking
this language constrains one to return it to its Source. Such is ex-

plicitly brought out in Aquino's preface when he writes that "itong lahat nang aquing sinaysay, ay hindi galing sa sarili cong aco, cundi paquinabang co sa aquing quinapapalagyan" ("nothing of what I relate here comes from me but is something that I owe to my position"; folio 7). The "I" therefore signifies Aquino to the extent that he has himself been converted into a sign of the Sign. The dedication of his work to the image of Christ is borne by Aquino's desire to identify the "I" that speaks with the Word that has been spoken. In this case, speech and self are regarded as coextensive in that they are made to function as transparent passages for conducting God's language back to Him. For what the Tagalog writer writing in his own language submits to Christ is a text that is acknowledged to have always been His. For this reason Aquino can "dare" (*yquina-pangahas*) to offer his *loob* and to ask God for something in return: the "sweet unchangingness" of His Sign.

Submission to God's Word also results in a specific set of earthly gains. The author wins the approval of Spanish ecclesiastical and civil censors, whose licenses and laudatory remarks follow the dedication. Aquino's work is credited with "promoting the Christian zeal of the natives" by making available to them "the ultimate remedy that our Mother Church has provided to encourage the confidence of one approaching death." As the standard phrase of the day put it, his book "contains nothing contrary to our Faith and Good Customs and allows great profit for the Tagalogs" (folios 3–4). In exchange for his pronouncement of surrender to God, Aquino is vested with the authority to address his fellow Tagalogs regarding the nature of Authority itself. He does so in the preface to the *Panalangin:*

> Sa babasa Nitong Libro
> Catoto cong babasa nitong Libro naito,t, inihahayin co sa iyo itong munti cong quinapagalan, na bagaman sa ibang Librong iyong naqui-quita, ay ang pagtatagobilin sa caloloua nang naghihingalo,y, siya ring nahoholi, at na sa catapusan, ay houag cang manguilalas ngayon nitong gaua co, ang pagca siyang naoona, at caya gayo,y, ang quinoconan cong halimbaua ay yaong sabi sa mahal na Escritura (na ang uica) Ang mataos na pacacac, ay siyang pupucao sa pagcagopiling nang sangdaig-digang tauo, at siya ring mangongonang lalabas doon sa holing arao na casindacsindac, at caquilaquilabot na ating madarating, paghocom baga nang somacop sa lahat.   [Folio 5]

To the Reader of this Book

To my companions who will read this book: I serve to you this meager task of mine. In other books you will see that the prayers commending the soul of the dying are placed at the end; here, do not be surprised when you see in my work that these [prayers] are placed at the beginning. I have done it this way because I have taken as my example what is written in the Holy Scripture (which says): The sharp sound of the trumpet will awaken mankind from his slumber, and it will be the first sign of the Last Day, one that will be most amazing and most terrifying, that is, the Judgment of Him who rules us all.

It appears at first glance that Don Gaspar speaks to other Tagalogs as if they were his equals. He addresses them as *catoto co,* my companions. Yet the sermon-like quality of the preface quickly makes it apparent that he speaks from a special place that permits him to know and to articulate the unknown. The "unknown" in this case is the end of all things: the death of the self as well as that of the world. Aquino sees his task as that of "serving" this knowledge of death to his readers.

But the author also alerts his readers to the peculiar organization of his book. It is, he admits, unlike other devotional texts, where prayers for the dying are usually found at the end. By placing the end at the beginning, he seemingly crosses temporal barriers and speaks from a posthumous perspective. In this way he solicits readers' interest. The author's voice seems to be capable of setting up the possibility of surprising its listeners (*maguilalas*) and then allaying the fears that grow out of that surprise. In the space of that possibility of surprise and its anticipation the author's "I" establishes its authority over the "you." Readers will attend to the author because he promises the means to anticipate—in the double sense of expecting and forestalling—the sudden arrival of the "end." Indicative of this promise is the author's ability to paraphrase Scripture. Aquino cites the apocalyptic sound of the trumpet that will herald the last day. Hearing it, humans will arise from their slumber and face "the most amazing and most terrifying" spectacle of the last judgment.

In the same way that the sound of that trumpet warns of the approaching end, the utterance of the prayers translated by Aquino prepares the living for the inevitable arrival of death:

O catoto cong babasa, caya itong pagtatagobilin sa caloloua nang naghihingalo, ay siya cong yniona dito sa Libro, macahalimbaua na baga (anaquin) niyong mataos na pacacac, nang touina,y, nonocao sa ating madlang cahimbingang quinacamtan sa layao nang calupaan, at con siya nang siyang na diringig, at naquiquita, ay opan ang loob nating matologuin, at malimotin sa mabangis na camatayan, ay maguising din, na di maralitang di imulat ang boong loob, bait, at alaala, at ang ualan pagsalang tayong lahat, ay mamatay! [Folio 5]

O my companions who will read this, the reason I have placed these prayers for the dying at the beginning of the book is so that they may be like the sound of the trumpet that will rouse us up from our collective sleep born of our earthly indulgence; and in hearing and reciting these prayers often, our sleepy *loob,* which is often forgetful of the fierceness of death, will awaken too, and we will not fail to realize with all of our *loob,* our minds, and our thoughts, that without exception, we are all going to die!

Aquino compares the prayers in the book to the trumpet that will usher in the last day. Just as the sound of the trumpet will call forth the dead from their graves, the recitation of the prayers will rouse (*nonocao*) the living from the slumber of their earthly indulgence (*layao nang calupaan*) to the indisputable fact that "without exception we [*tayo*] are all going to die!" The certainty of Aquino's exclamation underlines the shock effect that is meant to be produced by the realization of the approach of death. And he directs his readers' attention to the fact that the living are bound to the dying by that which lies beyond death. Indeed, it is to the dying person that the living ought to turn if the shock of death is to be overcome:

Caya baga man di anong iyong libang, o cacaonin, ay tingnan mo mona itong asal nang naghihingalo, at con maquita mona,t, mapagmalas, ay nang ang iyong loob ay maglubag sa ano mang panimdim, at gauang ipagcasasala. . . . Caya, con maquita naman nang tauo ang larauan nang mamamatay, sa pagca siya,y, mamamatay din ualaapagsala, . . . ay pasucan ang caniyang loob nang sindac, at pighati na con ano,t, siya,y, nagcasala sa daquilang Dios. [Folios 5–6]

So whatever you do or wherever you go, look for a while at the dying person, and in seeing him, may your *loob* unveil the memory of all your sinful acts. . . . And in seeing the image of one who is about to die, realize that you yourself will surely die, . . . and your *loob* will be taken up by surprise and sorrow as well at the thought that you have sinned against Almighty God.

Mirrored in the dying are the accumulated losses of the living. The death of an other, by being converted into an image (*larauan*), becomes the means for instilling within the self the startling (*sindac*) fact of its sinfulness. But more, the initial awakening to one's state of loss should lead to sorrow (*pighati*) for what one owes to God. The aesthetization of death is thereby designed to hasten the living's surrender to the Father. This idea, of course, grows out of one of the cornerstones of Christian doctrine: that death is the culmination of a life that originates in sin. Saint Thomas's compact formulation is to the point: "Death and all consequent bodily defects are punishments of original sin. And although these defects are not intended by the sinner, nevertheless, they are ordered to the justice of God, who inflicts them as punishments."[35] As death is outside the compass of what can be humanly determined, it comes from God. Human mortality is comprehensible in Christian terms as the "necessary contingency" that allows the Divine Master to assert His authority over His creatures, in the same way that the primordial existence of sin makes possible the indefinite extension of grace. Attending to the dying as a way of imaging one's own death is thus the prelude to a confession of one's faith in the Source of both life and death. What the living ought to see in the dying is a sinful past that delivers the present to an Eternal Creditor. Death is thus reintroduced as the locus of the fear of and subsequent surrender to Authority. As such, it takes on a value as the threshold to another life untouched by loss: "ang camatayan nang banal ay dili tinuturang camatayan cundi cabuhayan" ("the death of the holy person is not considered death but the renewal of life"); whereas failure to read in death the power of its Source and the imperative to submit to It results in sheer loss:

35. From *Summa theologica*, questions 1–7, in *The Basic Writings of Saint Thomas Aquinas*, ed. Anton C. Pegis (New York: Random House, 1944), 2:701. In Western Europe, the idea of a *speculum mortis* had been part of popular devotional practices from the late twelfth century and became a standard feature of manuals of prayers for the dying in Catholic regions, particularly during the Counterreformation. See Philippe Ariès, *Western Attitudes toward Death: From the Middle Ages to the Present*, trans. Patricia M. Ranum (Baltimore: Johns Hopkins University Press, 1974), pp. 28–37.

"At ang camatayan nang macasalanan, ay siyang camatayan totoo" ("And the death of the sinner is real death"; folio 6).

The inevitability of death and the possibility of total loss are thus made over into the basis for the recollection of the past indelibly marked by indebtedness to God. Thoughts of indebtedness function to assure one that loss—real, physical loss—can be figured into a set of images that open up to an infinite order of perfect reciprocity. What is crucial, then, is the reconceptualization of loss and the fear attached to it. Fear may be managed—in the sense of being re-produced and contained—by the ritual language of prayer that comes down to the convert as a sort of gift from the church:

> . . . ang paquinabang dito sa boong cabilogan nang S. Iglesiang Yna natin, ay ang panalangin nang isa,t, isa, sa isa,t, isa rin, tayo,y, mag-panalanginan, aco,y, bigyan din nang daquilang Dios nang magandang camatayan, siya mong hingin, yaon, at hihingin quita naman di man aco dapat. Vale.   [Folio 7]

> . . . the profits to be derived from the Holy Church, mother of us all, are the prayers of one for the other and the others for one. Let us all pray. Ask God to give me a beautiful death, just as I ask Him to give you the same though I may be undeserving of it. Amen.

Death's indiscriminate claims make it necessary to anticipate its arrival. Anticipation in this case is triggered by the shock of recognizing in another's death the possibility of one's own. Fear arises as a way of localizing this shock and seeing in it the existence of another Source. Where conversion is concerned, fear is ordered toward submission to that other realm where death is thought to originate. Submission is mediated by a ritual discourse derived from the church, which acts as a broker in the transaction of divine beneficence. By driving one to accede to a language of anticipation, the fear of death thus promotes a hierarchy that coordinates the movement of conversion.

Submission premised on the fear of death gives rise to a new con-stellation of social relations, which is manifested and articulated in prayer. Prayer in this context becomes the privileged means of ex-change between the author and the reader, just as it binds the living to the dying. It brings both parties under the common patronage of God, within the ambit of His Law. But in taking on the language of prayer, one is also expected to surrender to a particular structure of wishfulness characterized by the active desire for a "beautiful death" (*magandang camatayan*). Prayer thus turns death around. For by conjuring up the image of a beautiful death, it invests death with a negative authority over the convert's past and present life; that is, the exchange of prayers is meant to reveal death not as sheer loss but as that which contains the potential for validating all that one has given up in submitting to the domination of an outside realm. Endowed with a language of anticipation, one ideally can banish one's fear of death's shocking intrusion and see death as the approach of another order whose reality is, at least initially, rhetorically constituted in prayer.

We get a sense of this idea in the prayers translated by Aquino. The person who commends the soul of the dying invokes the name of the Father (*Sa ngalan nang Dios Amang macapangyayari sa lahat, na congmapal sa iyo,* "In the name of God the Father, creator of all things, who has made you") and calls upon those who occupy a place in the celestial hierarchy: the Son, the Holy Ghost, the angels and archangels, the cherubim and seraphim, the apostles and evangelists, the martyrs and saints, the Virgin Mary, and on through a long list. Hence prayer signifies the operation of divine patronage directed through a chain of protectors in heaven and made manifest by the Father's earthly representatives. In the presence of death "sila nauang lahat ang magampon at magtangol sa iyo, na magmola sa arao na ito,y, tangapin ca nila,t, magcamit ca rin nang ligayang ualang hangan sa Bayan nang Dios na catatahanan mo" ("may all of them adopt and protect you, and from this day on, accept you in their company, that you may receive the endless joy of living in the land of God"; folio 8). Here, as in the rest of the *Panalangin,* the rhetoric of prayer posits the possibility of reading into death an indestructible identity amid the company of those already in "the land of God."

At this point, however, we would do well to return to the question of the agency that poses through prayer this notion of an afterlife.

The prayers translated by Aquino are divided into two sets of *panalangin* (literally, petitions). The first were to be recited by the person in charge of watching over the dying (folios 9–16). The second set of prayers, called "Bonton Hininga" ("Last Sighs") were to be recited by the dying person; they petitioned Christ for a beautiful death (folios 16–23). A litany of saints in heaven ("Litania sa manga Santos") follows (folios 23–24).

The first set of prayers rehearses a move we saw earlier in our discussion of paradise and hell. Peculiar to the *Panalangin* is a mobile voice that can be assumed by whoever takes charge of watching over the dying; that is, a voice that insistently shuttles between divine and human addressees. It appeals first to the Father on behalf of the dying: "Dios na maauain . . . Magdalita ca,t, tonghan mo nang mata mong maauain, ytong alipin mong si N. at patauarin mo nang manga casalanan niya, at paquingan mo din ang pagdaying niya sa iyo" ("Merciful God . . . May you deign to look with your merciful eyes upon your slave N. and forgive him his sins, and listen to his plaints"; folio 9). Then it turns to the dying person, commending him or her to divine mercy: "Ypinagtatagobilin quita sa ating Panginoong Dios . . . capatid co, yayamang siya ang gongmaua sa iyo, sa caniya rin quita ypinagcatitiuala, at nang con mabayaran mo na sa pag-camatay mo ang tanang naquin otang mong gaua sa yquinabuhay mo, ay maoui ca rin ualan bahala sa P. Dios" ("I commend you to our Lord God . . . my brother, since it was He who made you, it is to Him that I entrust you, and may you pay with your death all the debts you had incurred while you were still alive, and may you return without worry to the Lord God"; folio 9). This voice continues to address the dying in the second person singular, infusing him or her with a familiar set of wishes: that "your soul" may be met in heaven by the angels and saints, and there "you may look calmly on the radiant face of Christ"; "may you not have to know the pain of the everlasting darkness of hell, or hear the anguish of those burning there" in the company of Satan (folios 9–10).

Midway through the prayer, the voice abruptly turns from the dying person to God.

Tangapin mo P. naming Dios diyan sa Caloualhatian ytong alipin mo, na sa pagca maauain mo,y, ynaasahan din niya sa iyo. Siyanaua.

Yadya mo P. namin ang caloloua nitong alipin mo sa dilan panganib na ycapapacasama sa Infierno at ycagogolo nang loob dito sa dilan casaquitan niya. Siyanaua.

Yadya mo Panginoon namin ang caloloua nitong alipin mo, para nang pagaadya mo cay Enoch, at cay Elias sa camatayan dinaraanan nang sanglibotan. Siya naua. [Folio 10]

Accept, our Lord God, into your realm this slave of yours, who trusts in your mercifulness. Amen.

Protect, our Lord God, the soul of your slave from all the dangers of Hell and from the temptations that arise from his pain. Amen.

Protect, our Lord God, the soul of your slave, as you protected those of Enoch and Elias from the death that claims all people. Amen.

It goes on and on in this vein with a lengthy series of petitions stated in the fashion of a litany, all of which convey the same wish: that God protect His slave (*alipin*) from hell and grant him the joys of heaven (folios 10–15). Here the voice speaks for the dying person, soliciting the Father's patronage and surrendering to His authority.

In providing the formulaic expressions with which to anticipate death, this voice thus acts as a third term in the exchange between God and the dying person. On the one hand, it articulates the latter's wishes—which are assumed to be already informed by the fear of death and anticipation of what lies beyond it—and directs them to God. On the other hand, it exhibits the means by which to solicit the patronage not only of the Father but of a seemingly endless series of angels and saints as well. In addressing the dying and the living who attend to the prayers as "you," it implicitly assumes the position of an "I" capable of recalling the link between indebtedness and death. But in petitioning God, it can also adopt the position of a "we" (as in *Panginoon naming Dios,* "our Lord God") that never tires of invoking the generalized dependence of all on One. By switching rhetorical registers, this voice thus traverses the distance that separates heaven from earth, death from a state beyond death. Whoever appropriates this voice seems to be in control of a Tagalog discourse thoroughly permeated with untranslatable Spanish words. The petitioner thereby mimes the linguistic authority of the Spanish missionary. It is for this reason that the person who prays can preside over the death of the convert, translating, as it were, the dying body into a sign that can be traced from and returned to a divine referent. And by unleashing a potentially interminable litany of appeals directed to the celestial hierarchy, the petitioner appears to have access to an inexhaustible reserve of protectors in association with God. The highly formulaic petitioning for their aid fills the listeners' minds with a catalogue of names that block other chains of associations that death's approach otherwise might trigger. These prayers substitute for the threat of loss the monotonous comfort of names that numb the living to death just as they offer to the dying the prospect of assuming another identity that, because it exists only in language, is immune to death.

The deployment of this mobile voice through prayer raises the possibility of "real" conversion. Its appropriation allows for the imaging of an alternative standpoint from which to negate death's claim. Given a language of anticipation, death can then be seen as yet another sign from the Father. Thus its arrival need not be dreaded but can be actively desired. We see this possibility in the "Bonton Hininga" ("Last Sighs"), to be recited by the dying person:

> Jesus, bigyan mo aco nang magandang camatayan.
>
> Jesus na Panginoon co, caya mo aco guinaua,y, ang aco,y, iyo at sa iyo na man aco mamamatay.
>
> Panginoon co, sa iyon pagcamatay, ay bigyan mo aco nang camatayan, at aquing pasasalamatan.
>
> Aquing Panginoon, yayang di na aco mabubuhay na magsilvi aco sa iyo, ybig co na ang mamatay, ay ypagcaloob mo na sa aquin, at tina-tangap co,t, pinasasalamatan.   [Folio 16]

> Jesus, give me a beautiful death.
>
> Jesus, my Lord, you made me so that I can be with you, and so it is with you that I die.
>
> My Lord, through your death give me my own death, and for this I will be thankful.
>
> My Lord, inasmuch as I will no longer live to serve you, I want to die. Give me this death, and I will accept it and thank you for it.

Here the "I" is in some ways reminiscent of the one that appears in Aquino's dedication. Though it is meant to be a dying rather than a writing self, it is made to bear the similar burden of establishing a correspondence between the self that prays and the Figure that it addresses. The last gasps or sighs of the dying (*hininga* can mean either) are seen to mark the interval or *loob* between life and death. These prayers are designed to occupy that interval. By generating an "I" capable of issuing a series of ordered appeals for a "beautiful death," prayer endows the dying's sporadic expenditures of breath with the syntax of Christian wishfulness.

At the center of this wishfulness is the image of Christ. It is to

Christ that one appeals for a beautiful death. The model Sign furnishes one with the model for death. Christ is thought to figure the perfect fusion of appearance and essence, contingency and necessity, loss and gain. To die beautifully thus amounts to miming his death in that it entails the conversion of one's fear of loss into a sign of one's surrender to the Father. Having submitted, one can then replace the dread attached to death with an active desire for it. This wish is repeatedly expressed:

> Liuanag co, bigyan mo aco nang caliuanagan, at nang aco,y, may ycaquita. Aquing yniibig, bigyan mo aco nang pagca ibig sa iyo na tanggapin mo.
> Panginoon co, yaring saquit co,y, tinatangap co na parang Cruz na quinacamtan mo, at siya cong ycaaalaala sa iyo.   [Folio 17]

> My Light, give me light with which to see. My Love, give me love with which to love you so that you may accept me.
> My Lord, I accept this pain of mine like the cross that you bore and by which I remember you.

Christ is both "my Light" and the source of light with which to see, "my Love" and the source of love with which to recognize and reciprocate what one has received. He is at once the force behind the circulation of light and love and the cherished object of circulation. From this perspective, Christ can be seen as the ultimate cause and effect of loss. All forms of pain and deprivation derive their significance and value from the Image that has always already suffered and died. Hence to assume the "I" that speaks before Christ is simultaneously to convert the self into a fixed element in the history of salvation. When one submits the self to the Sign, one receives a language with which to conjecture the positive image of an immutable identity beyond the negativity of death: "Sa damdam co,y, naquiquita co na ang Langit na pinagcacapisanan nang lahat nang nagpupuri nang calachan mo, at doon mo din naman patatahanin ang boo cong loob" ("I think that I already see heaven, which is populated by all those who praise your glory, and it is there that you will place my entire *loob* at rest"; folio 18). And by placing the image of Christ at the locus of human wishes, prayer reframes death in terms of a scenario of perfect reciprocity that recalls the thematics of paradise. Suffering and death now take on the aspect of payments of what one owes the Father: "Ybig co nang mamatay sa pagaalaala co nang aquing manga casalanan. . . . Ama nang aua, tangapin mo yaring anac na matitiualag yayang ynaalaala ca, at nagsasaoli sa iyo" ("I want to die while remembering my sins. . . . Father of mercy, accept this errant child of yours while he remembers you, and wants to return to you"; folio 18).

The memory of one's indebtedness is meant to subsume the thoughts of approaching loss. Within this context, longing for death can be substituted for the fear of it. Again and again the "I" petitions for a death that will complete the payment of its debts. Such is the prospect held forth by the notion of a beautiful death: definitive relief from the pressures of demands for repayment and accountability. Thus is death remythologized. It is not simply the threat of the self's dissolution into insignificance; it also becomes a highly charged "gift" that one receives and is compelled to return to an outside Source.

Death is reinvented by the same process that converts the "I" into an element of God's Word: translation. Translation, the exchange of one language for another, alongside the notion of untranslatability— the juxtaposition of two languages—generated, as we have seen, a linguistic hierarchy within colonial society. The successful consolidation of this hierarchy depended on the acceptance, whether implicit or explicit, of the primacy of a second, alien language over one's first language. Castilian had become invested over time with the sense of signaling possibilities beyond what could be said in Tagalog. Appropriating Castilian, particularly as it was used in Christian discourse, was a way of establishing a relationship with the unseen and unknown realm of colonial authority, thereby anticipating even to the extent of miming its presence in Tagalog life. Submission to the hierarchy of languages presented such natives as Tomas Pinpin and Don Gaspar Aquino de Belen with the chance to contract colonialism; that is, translation enabled them to negotiate with Spanish authority and hence to contain its demands, including the demands implicit in the Christian notion of death.

Translation instituted just as it allowed for the circumvention of Spanish signifying conventions and the power relations that accompanied them. Thus a plurality of conversions emerged among the Tagalogs, as we see in the differences between the writings of a *ladino* such as Pinpin and a *maginoo-principal* such as Aquino. Pinpin's submission to a linguistic hierarchy was predicated on the evasion of its signifying force, the parrying of the shock of Castilian with the sounding of an *auit*. Aquino submitted to that force in order to produce a translation of death, a prescription for dying, and consequently a new grammar and vocabulary of desire. It may be argued that this new language of desire set the ideological basis for a wish that was to emerge among another group of *indios* a century and a half later, who in their turn sought to translate a history of colonial rule into an idiom of patriotism and national duty. About 1892 Jose Rizal, the national hero of the Philippines, wrote to a friend in Macao: "I prefer to risk death and willingly give my life to free so many innocent people from such unjust persecution. . . . I also want to show those who deny our patriotism that we know how to die for our duty and our convictions."[36]

36. Cited in León Ma. Guerrero's introduction to the English-language edition of Rizal's novel *Noli me tangere* (Hong Kong: Longman, 1961), p. xiii. That the letter, like the writings of most university-educated nineteenth-century nationalists, was written in Spanish is not surprising, given the historical situation I have described.

Translation and the Colonial Legacy

The anthropologist James T. Siegel has written about the pervasive connection between translation and the formation, breakdown, and subsequent reformulation of social order.[1] Although his assertions pertain specifically to the present-day Indonesian city of Solo in central Java, much of what he says is relevant to my discussion of Tagalog conversion. Siegel claims that translation arises from the need to relate one's interest to that of others and so to encode it appropriately. Translation in this case involves not simply the ability to speak in a language other than one's own but the capacity to reshape one's thoughts and actions in accordance with accepted forms. It thus coincides with the need to submit to the conventions of a given social order. Deferring to conventions of speech and behavior (which, precisely because they are conventions, antedate one's intentions), one in effect acknowledges what appears to be beyond oneself. Translation is then a matter of first discerning the differences between and within social codes and then of seeing the possibility of getting across those differences. To do so is to succeed in communicating, that is, in recognizing and being recognized within the intelligible limits of a linguistic and social order. Hence, if translation is to take place at all, it must do so within a context of expectation: that in return for one's submission, one gets back the other's acknowledgment of the value of one's words and behavior. In this way, one finds for oneself a place on the social map.

1. Siegel, *Solo in the New Order,* pp. 3–12, 294–307, 332–333. Readers familiar with this book will recognize my indebtedness to Siegel.

Social expectations, however, are historically determined, so that the context within which translation can be said to occur is itself always shifting. This is especially true during moments of instability, as at the onset of colonial rule. In such instances, conventions of intelligibility are far from settled, as social discourse is informed by a plurality of interests that have yet to be reordered into a stable hierarchy. Conversion in early Tagalog colonial society was predicated on translation; yet Spaniards' and the Tagalogs' notions and practices of translation differed to the degree that the relative position of one to the other remained ambiguously defined. Christian conversion and colonial rule emerged through what appeared to be a series of mistranslations. But in fact, as I have tried to demonstrate, such mistranslations were ways to render the other understandable. Each group read into the other's language and behavior possibilities that the original speakers had not intended or foreseen. For the Spaniards, translation was always a matter of reducing the native language and culture to accessible objects for and subjects of divine and imperial intervention. For the Tagalogs, translation was a process less of internalizing colonial-Christian conventions than of evading their totalizing grip by repeatedly marking the differences between their language and interests and those of the Spaniards. Indeed, it is not until the early eighteenth century that we have sustained evidence of Tagalog conversion that coincided with rather than simply circumvented Spanish intentions. The consolidation of the colonial hierarchy over time made this sort of conversion conceivable. Appropriating the style and substance of missionary rhetoric, native *principales* such as Aquino de Belen found ways to reorient native fears of the spirits and the unknown toward Christian notions of paradise and hell and the longing for a beautiful death.

The fact that translation lends itself to either affirmation or evasion of social order is what gives it its political dimension. It draws boundaries between what can and cannot be admitted into social discourse even as it misdirects the construction of its conventions. Translation, in whatever mode, leads to the emergence of hierarchy, however conceived. This tendency raises another possibility that haunts every communicative act: that at some point translation may fail and the social order then may crumble. As Siegel points out, a risk is involved in any attempt to traverse the gap that separates one from others. Instead of proffering intentions in their expected forms, one may find oneself unable to convert them into something that has significance and thus can be taken as a form of language. Conversely, one may fail to appropriate the signs that come from others and thereby fail to make an appropriate return. In either case, one is unable to account for the other in one's thoughts or to be accounted for in the other's mind. One who fails to translate blurts out only undecipherable signs devoid of referent and context, and so appears thoroughly alien to others. Removed from language, one is also outside of hierarchy, unavailable as either a source or a recipient of social recognition.

In the Tagalog context we've been examining, we can readily recognize the risk that translation entails in relation to the notion of *walang hiya* and its synonym, *walang utang na loob* (the loss of shame and the absence of gratitude/respect). As we have seen, native converts who failed to anticipate and so to appropriate the terms of Spanish Christianity were unable to convert their desires into a code that could be sent back to the missionary, and thus were filled with a sense of *walang hiya*. They found themselves with no position from which to bargain with colonial authority. Deprived of linguistic reserve, they could neither respond to the missionary's demands nor expect a return. One who has no speech has no status as a convert and hence as a potential recipient of gifts and patronage. Instead, one faces the prospect of being assailed by words and things beyond one's control, totally subsumed by outside forces that obliterate one's inside or *loob*. In place of mutual indebtedness, fear arises, fear that can neither be converted to the respect inherent in *utang na loob* ties nor translated into the longing for a beautiful death. It is the fear associated with the threat that language may lead not to the emergence of order but to its dissolution.

The danger inherent in translation affected the missionaries as well as their converts. We have already seen how the Spanish notion of translation tended to be subverted by *baybayin*, the precolonial native syllabary, and exceeded by Tagalog idioms of reciprocity, particularly in the context of confession. Such cases tended to arouse concern about the adequacy of the natives' conversion and thus pointed up the tenuousness of the missionaries' authority. If translation could work in ways that could not be fully accounted for, at some point it might cease to function altogether.

To get a sense of what this possibility might have been like, let us return to the sermon scene in Rizal's novel with which we began. The

Castilian part of the sermon, as we saw, elicited from the natives a response that was at odds with Father Damaso's message. Hearing the barely comprehensible words of the priest, the people were nonetheless stirred to read other narratives and other images into the bits of Castilian that they managed to fish out. Their interest, like that of the early-seventeenth-century *ladino* Tomas Pinpin, was aroused not by the actual referents of Spanish discourse but by what fragments of them evoked in their minds. In this sense, they were translating in their own way what the priest was saying. Attending to the untranslated fragments in Castilian, they discovered the points of intersection between their thoughts and the signs of clerical authority. It was for this reason that they could return to the priest's sermon with "redoubled attention."

When we view the sermon scene in Rizal's novel in conjunction with the work of Pinpin in the early seventeenth century and the writings of Aquino de Belen in the early eighteenth, we see it as a striking condensation of the crucial importance of translation in the emergence of a colonial-Christian order. Missionary discourse produces in the native devotees a series of mild shocks that they attend to in a state of distraction. They give in to colonial authority, but they do not give up. Yet they are able to dodge the priest's message only to the extent that they are able to acknowledge words and things Spanish at the horizon of their own thoughts.

To defer to a second language in this context is to reorder what one had in mind. Whether one fished, composed an *auit,* or recited prayers for a beautiful death, one recast one's thoughts in a different register. One could do so in Tagalog as well as in Castilian, for evangelization systematically located Latin and Castilian at the boundary of Tagalog. Christian conversion was inseparable from a hierarchy of languages, for as we have seen, when Christian discourse was translated into the vernacular, its key terms retained their original forms. Tagalog, thus permeated by words that had no equivalents in the vernacular, was made to appear to have a source other than its native speakers. Conversion thereby translated Tagalog into a new language. For this reason, interest in conversion was conjoined with an interest in hearing in one's first language the recurrence of a second with which to formulate one's claims on authority and manage one's fears of the unknown.

Yet the alternative possibility always loomed: if translation failed, even if only momentarily, social order might collapse. Such a scenario occurs in the second half of Father Damaso's sermon. Switching from Castilian to Tagalog, he "improvised in this language, not because he knew it better but because he took the Filipinos in the provinces to be ignorant of rhetoric so that he did not fear committing blunders before them. . . . It is well known that none of those present understood the whole sermon in Tagalog. . . . Nevertheless, this part had more consequences than the first" (p. 174).

For Father Damaso, one could ignore the rules of rhetoric when one spoke Tagalog, so he did not have to fear committing blunders (*disparates*). He felt that speaking Tagalog entailed no risk. The result, however, was a kind of untranslatable discourse that produced not interest but an interminable oscillation between boredom and random violence:

> He started with a *"Mana capatir con cristiano"* [badly pronounced Tagalog that his English translator renders as "My diar bradders in Hesoos Christ"] which was then followed by an avalanche of untranslatable phrases. He spoke of the soul, of hell, of *mahal na santo pintacasi* ["belobbed pahtron saint"] of the *indio* sinner and the virtuous Franciscan fathers.[2]
>
> "Damn!" said one of those irreverent Manilans to his companion. "This is all Greek to me. I'm leaving."
>
> And seeing that all the doors were locked, he left through the sacristy to the great scandal of the people and of the preacher, who turned pale and was stopped in midsentence; some expected a violent reaction, but Padre Damaso contented himself with following the man with his eyes and continuing with his sermon.
>
> He unleashed maledictions against the age, against the lack of respect, the nascent irreligiosity. This theme was apparently his forte, for he seemed inspired, expressing himself with force and clarity. He spoke of sinners who did not confess, who died in prison without receiving the sacraments, of bad families, of arrogant and vain "little mestizos" [*mesticillos*], of pseudo-intellectual youths [*jóvenes sabihondos*]. [P. 174]

The breakdown of translation results in something scandalous: the sight of someone leaving in the middle of the priest's sermon. Father

2. León Ma. Guerrero's translation is widely regarded as the standard one in English. The chapter on the sermon appears on pp. 191–200. The translation here is my own, from the 1958 facsimile edition.

Damaso tries to recover from this shock by resorting to a different kind of rhetoric. Rizal doesn't tell us at this point whether Damaso speaks in Castilian or Tagalog, only that he thunders, unleashing an "avalanche" of tirades against all those he imagines as opposing his authority. Indeed, the breakdown of translation unleashes in Damaso's mind an extravagant paranoid fantasy about the failure of conversion, the futility of his and his predecessors' labors among the natives, and thus the impotence of their authority. When Damaso "improvises" in Tagalog, ignoring proper forms, he gets back not the respect and submission of his flock but a shocking sense of the gap that separates his words from his intentions and consequently from the thoughts of others. What comes across with "force and clarity" is no longer the message of the sermon but the intensity of Damaso's wrath, the din of his frustration at the loss of comprehensibility. "His enthusiasm . . . rising by degrees" (p. 175), the priest compulsively continues his attack, returning again and again to the *indio*'s lack of respect for the priest, the unmitigated stupidity and barbarity of natives, the presumptuousness of youth, and so forth. Yet, far from restoring order, the priest's assaults only induce more boredom and further scandalous outbreaks:

> But in spite of the shouts and gesticulations of the preacher, many had fallen asleep or were distracted, for sermons like these were always the same; in vain did some devoted women try to sigh and cry over the sins of the impious, but they had to give up their enterprise for lack of partners. Sister Pute [a member of one of the local confraternities], on the contrary, thought otherwise. A man seated beside her had gone to sleep in such a manner that he had fallen against her, crumpling her dress. The good woman took her slipper and woke him up with blows, screaming:
>
> "Ay! Get off me, you savage, you animal, you devil, you carabao, you dog, you damned fool!"
>
> A commotion ensued. The preacher stopped, raised his eyebrows, surprised by this great scandal. Indignation choked down the words in his throat and he could only bellow, hitting the pulpit with his fists. This had its effect: the old woman let go of her slippers with many a grumble, and crossing herself repeatedly fell on her knees.
>
> "Aaah! Aaah!" the indignant priest finally exclaimed, crossing his arms and shaking his head. "For this I spend the whole morning preaching to you, you barbarians! . . . Aaah! You have no

shame . . . no respect. . . ! This is the fruit of the lust and incontinence of the age! It's just as I said! Aaah!

And on this theme he continued to preach for half an hour. The Governor was snoring, María Clara was nodding, having no more paintings or images to study or to amuse herself with. Neither word nor allusion had an effect any longer on Ibarra. . . .

Father Salvi had had the altar bell rung twice, but this was merely adding fuel to the fire. Father Damaso was stubborn and made his sermon even longer. Father Sibyla was biting his lips and fingering his gold-rimmed rock-crystal glasses. . . .

Finally, God said enough; the orator was exhausted and came down from the pulpit.

All knelt and gave thanks to God. The Governor rubbed his eyes, stretched out an arm, sighed profoundly, and yawned.

The Mass continued.   [Pp. 175–176]

We see in this passage the remarkable contagiousness of boredom and violence. Assailed on all sides by Damaso's anger, people hear only a kind of dismissable noise, a "sermon that was like all others." Yet the compulsive monotony of the priest's voice makes it impossible for them to fish out words with which to fend off the verbal barrage. They are confronted by language out of control. Unable to appropriate anything from the priest, the people grow bored. Boredom leads to random explosions of violence, followed by automatic responses. A man slumps in sleep against his neighbor, crushing her dress; she explodes in words that seem to repeat those of the priest. Blows follow: she hits the man with her slipper; the priest pounds the pulpit with his fist; the woman responds by repeatedly kneeling. These events register in a series of exclamations: "Aaah! Aaah!"

Such exclamations signal the disintegration of signification. Rather than fish out the priest's words and turn them into other narratives, the listeners either fall asleep or merely repeat his words and gestures. As their mimicry is not willed but compelled, it does not lead to a recognition of authority and the restoration of order. The mechanical repetition of gestures and words drains language of its sense, exhausting it of any communicative possibility. A kind of general paralysis sets in: the Governor snores, the *principales* nod off, the rest of the clergy are rendered powerless to halt the chaotic stream of words from the pulpit. To see translation fail is thus to see the confounding of social order as well.

Rizal comments that the second part of the sermon, when Father Damaso was unable to make himself understood, "had more consequences than the first part." Whereas the measured delivery of Latin and Castilian in the first half of the sermon enabled the priest to command his listeners' attention, however sporadically, the unrelieved opacity of the second part resulted in the momentary collapse of linguistic and social hierarchy. By pointing to this other moment, Rizal seems to suggest the possibility of language wrenching itself free from social order. Just as the vernacular could be used to shore up colonial authority, it could also nullify the discursive limits prescribed by evangelization and translation. That such a possibility was of great consequence to Rizal had to do with the particular historical conditions of his life and work.

Rizal was not writing a book on how to learn Castilian, like Pinpin, or a translation of a conversion text, like Aquino de Belen. Writing during the last two decades of Spanish rule, he wished, as he says in the preface of his novel, to "lay bare" (*exponer*) the "social cancer" afflicting the country. I understand him to mean that his concern was to chart the anatomy of power and its breakdown in Philippine society during the late nineteenth century. In doing so, he took a risk (for this is the other sense of *exponer*, "to put in danger, to hazard, to expose to chance"): he so antagonized both church and state that he was arrested, exiled, and, in 1896, executed before a firing squad. As he wrote, Rizal knew he might die, as indeed he did. But he was also aware, as Reynaldo Ileto has persuasively pointed out, that other Filipinos would recognize in his death a kind of counterdiscourse with which to oppose colonial rule.[3] In this sense, his death was translatable into revolutionary action, for even before his execution, his name and deeds had inspired a nationwide uprising against Spain.

Yet we can construe the risk of which Rizal spoke in another way. The danger existed that rather than comprehend social ills and thus prescribe their cure, he could contract them. Like the Spanish priests and the native devotees of whom he was so critical, he might fail to translate his message, to find the appropriate code with which to register his distress. He could just as well have been caught in the kind of semiotic confusion that he so scrupulously describes and fallen into

---

3. Ileto, "Rizal and the Underside of Philippine History," in *Moral Order and the Question of Change,* ed. Wyatt and Woodside, and "The Past in the Present Crisis," in *The Philippines after Marcos,* ed. R. J. May and Francisco Nemenzo (Sydney: Croom Helm, 1985), pp. 7–16.

the inarticulate defiance that is the substance of boredom or into random fits of rage that would never coalesce into conscious opposition or submission. In such a case, any other risks he took would remain unrecognized and unvalued by history.

Perhaps it was this possibility that led Rizal to put this scene of conversion and translation in a novel, a form of writing that was new at this time in the Philippines.[4] By writing it as fiction, Rizal could present the scene in the church as something that had been heard of and seen someplace else. The town of San Diego, though similar to many lowland Tagalog towns, is not an actual place; and the book's characters, though based on types familiar in colonial society, are framed at a remove from real people. Events in the novel are thus abstracted from the lived world, transposed into a fictive realm that parallels but never fully coincides with actual conditions. In this regard, it helps to recall that Rizal wrote *Noli me tangere* while traveling in Europe. Thus while the particular scene Rizal describes may not actually have occurred, it nonetheless posits a time and a place where it could have happened and might happen in fact. It is in this sense like a rumor that one hears and is compelled to pass on. Citing this rumor, Rizal transcribes not an empirically verifiable instance but the manner in which such instances could be produced. That language could be ordered toward conversion but could also run amuck, rendering translation impossible, exploding the contract between ruler and ruled, and thereby obscuring politics and history altogether—these were the possibilities Rizal imagined.

By writing his novel, Rizal established a space in which to juxtapose these two sides of language. In doing so, he found another position from which to conceptualize colonial society. He began, that is, to translate, to reformulate into a different code the possibilities that he saw. In this way he was able to maintain an interest in colonialism apart from those in colonial society who—Spaniards and natives alike—came before and would come after him. It was this capacity not only to move between languages but to distinguish be-

4. On the importance of the link between literary form, especially the novel, and the emergence of nationalist consciousness, see Benedict Anderson, *Imagined Communities,* pp. 17–49, 129–140. On the history of the Philippine novel, see Resil B. Mojares, *The Origins and Rise of the Filipino Novel: A Generic Study of the Novel until 1940* (Quezon City: University of the Philippines Press, 1983); and Soledad Reyes, *Nobelang Tagalog, 1905–1975: Tradisyon at Modernismo* (Quezon City: Ateneo de Manila University Press, 1982).

tween translation and its failure that enabled Rizal to posit a future alternative to Spanish domination: the Filipino nation. That is why he could say, toward the end of Father Damaso's sermon, that "finally, God said enough." For he, too, could assume a place analogous to that from which God spoke, but one that was wholly within the space and time of the novel and hence apart from those of the church, the state, and society. Miming the voice of a fictional God, the author puts an end to the sermon. The exhausted priest descends from the pulpit and the mass continues. But so does the novel.[5]

5. For a discussion of other instances in the novel when translation breaks down and then recovers, see Vicente L. Rafael, "Language, Identity, and Gender in Rizal's *Noli*," *Review of Indonesian and Malaysian Affairs* 18 (Winter 1984): 110–140.

Bibliography

"Actas del primer sínodo de Manila (1582–1586)." *Philippiniana Sacra* 4 (September–December 1969): 425–537.

Anderson, Benedict. "The Idea of Power in Javanese Culture." In *Culture and Politics in Indonesia,* ed. Claire Holt, Benedict Anderson, and James T. Siegel, pp. 1–69. Ithaca: Cornell University Press, 1972.

——. *Imagined Communities: Reflections on the Origin and Spread of Nationalism.* London: New Left Books, 1983.

Anderson, Gerald, H., ed. *Studies in Philippine Church History.* Ithaca: Cornell University Press, 1969.

Aquinas, Thomas. *The Basic Writings of Saint Thomas Aquinas.* Ed. Anton C. Pegis. 2 vols. New York: Random House, 1944.

Aquino de Belen, Don Gaspar. *Manga panalangin pagtatagobilin sa caloloua nang tauong naghihingalo.* 5th ed. Manila: Compañía de Jesús por Nicolas Cruz Bagay, 1760. First published Manila, 1703.

Archipélago Filipino, El: Colección de datos. Por algunos padres de la Misión de la Compañía de Jesús en estas islas. 3 vols. Washington, D.C.: U.S. Government Printing Office, 1910.

Ariès, Philippe. *Western Attitudes toward Death: From the Middle Ages to the Present.* Trans. Patricia M. Ranum. Baltimore: Johns Hopkins University Press, 1974.

Armas Medina, Fernando de. *Cristianización del Perú, 1532–1600.* Seville: Escuela de Estudios Hispano-Americanos, 1953.

Astete, Gaspar de. *Doctrina Cristiana.* Manila, 1777.

Augustine. *Saint Augustine's Confessions.* 1631. Ed. and trans. William Watts. Cambridge: Harvard University Press, 1950.

Barthes, Roland. *Sade/Fourier/Loyola.* Trans. Richard Miller. New York: Hill & Wang, 1976.

Benjamin, Walter. *Illuminations.* Ed. Hannah Arendt. Trans. Harry Zohn. New York: Schocken, 1969.

Blair, Emma, and James Robertson, eds. *The Philippine Islands, 1493–1898.* 55 vols. Cleveland: Arthur H. Clark, 1903–1909.

Blancas de San José, P. Francisco. *Arte y reglas de la lengua tagala.* Bataan: por Tomas Pinpin, 1610; 2d ed. Manila, 1752; 3d ed. Manila: D. Jose Ma. Dayot por Tomas Olivas, 1832.

——. *Librong Pinagpapalamnan yto nang aasalin nang tauong Cristiano sa pagcoconfesar at sa pagcocomulgar; nang capoua mapacagaling at capoua paguinabangan niya ang aua nang P. Dios.* 6th ed. Manila, 1792. First published probably before 1614; 3d ed. Manila, 1662.

——. *Memorial de la vida cristiana, en la lengua tagala.* 2d ed. Manila: D. Jose Ma. Dayot, 1835. First published Manila, 1605.

Castaño, P. José. *Breve noticia acerca del origen, religión, creencias, y supersticiones de los antiguos indios del Bicol.* Madrid, 1895.

Chirino, Pedro, S.J. *Relación de las Islas Filipinas.* Rome, 1604. Ed. with English trans. Ramón Echevarría. Manila: Historical Conservation Society, 1969.

Collier, George A., Renato I. Rosaldo, and John D. Wirth, eds. *The Inca and Aztec States, 1400–1800: Anthropology and History.* New York: Academic Press, 1982.

Corominas, Joan. *Diccionario crítico etimológico de la lengua castellana.* 2 vols. Madrid: Gredos, 1976.

Corpuz, Onofre D. *The Bureaucracy in the Philippines.* Quezon City: University of the Philippines Press, 1957.

Costa, Horacio de la, S.J. *The Jesuits in the Philippines, 1581–1768.* Cambridge: Harvard University Press, 1961.

——. *Readings in Philippine History.* Manila: Bookmark, 1964.

Covarrubias, Sebastián de. *Tesoro de la lengua castellana o español.* Ed. Martín de Riquer. Barcelona: S. A. Horta, 1943.

Cushner, Nicolas. *The Isles of the West: Early Spanish Voyages to the Philippines, 1521–1564.* Quezon City: Ateneo de Manila University Press, 1966.

——. *Landed Estates in the Colonial Philippines.* New Haven: Yale University Southeast Asia Studies, 1976.

——. *Spain in the Philippines: From Conquest to Revolution.* Quezon City: Ateneo de Manila University Press, 1971.

Derrida, Jacques. "Des Tours de Babel." In *Difference in Translation,* ed. Joseph F. Graham, pp. 167–185. Ithaca: Cornell University Press, 1985.

——. *Dissemination.* Trans. Barbara Johnson. Chicago: University of Chicago Press, 1981.

——. *Margins of Philosophy.* Trans. Alan Bass. Chicago: University of Chicago Press, 1982.

——. *Of Grammatology.* Trans. Gayatri Chakravorty Spivak. Baltimore: Johns Hopkins University Press, 1976.

——. *Writing and Difference.* Trans. Alan Bass. Chicago: University of Chicago Press, 1978.

Diaz-Trechuelo Spinola, María Lourdes. *Arquitectura española en Filipinas, 1565–1800.* Seville: Escuela de Estudios Hispano-Americanos de Sevilla, 1959.

Doctrina christiana en lengua española y tagala. Ed. Carlos Quirino. Manila: National Historical Commission, 1973. First published Manila, 1593.

Elliot, J. H. *Imperial Spain, 1469–1716.* New York: New American Library, 1963.

Febvre, Lucien, and Henri-Jean Martin. *The Coming of the Book: The Impact of Printing, 1450–1800.* Trans. David Gerard. Ed. Geoffrey Nowell-Smith and David Wooton. London: New Left Books, 1976.

Foucault, Michel. *The History of Sexuality.* Vol. 1, *An Introduction.* Trans. Robert Hurley. New York: Vintage Books, 1980.

Franch, Juan Alcina, and José Manuel Blecua. *Gramática española.* Barcelona: Ariel, 1975.

Gayo, Jesus, O.P., ed. "Tratado segundo de la preparación evangélica y el modo de predicar el Santo Evangelio por Fr. Miguel de Benavides, O.P." *Unitas* 21 (January 1948): 145–180.

Herrera, P. Pedro de. *Meditaciones cun manga mahal na pagninilay na sadia sa Sanctong pag exercicios.* Manila: Compañía de Jesús por Don Nicolás Cruz Bagay, 1762. First published Manila, 1645.

Hollnsteiner, Mary R. "Reciprocity in the Lowland Philippines." In *Four Readings on Philippine Values,* ed. Frank Lynch and Alfonso de Guzmán III, pp. 69–92. Quezon City: Ateneo de Manila University Press, 1973.

Hutterer, Karl. "Prehistoric Trade and Evolution of Philippine Societies: A Reconsideration." In *Economic Exchange and Social Interaction in Southeast Asia: Perspectives from Prehistory, History, and Ethnography,* ed. Karl Hutterer, pp. 177–196. Ann Arbor: Michigan Papers on South and Southeast Asia, 1977.

Ileto, Reynaldo C. "Orators and the Crowd: Philippine Independence Politics, 1910–1940." In *Reappraissing an Empire: New Perspectives on Philippine-American History,* ed. Peter W. Stanley, pp. 85–114. Cambridge: Harvard University Press, 1984.

——. "The Past in the Present Crisis." In *The Philippines after Marcos,* ed. R. J. May and Francisco Nemenzo, pp. 7–16. Sydney: Croom Helm, 1985.

——. *Pasyon and Revolution: Popular Movements in the Philippines, 1840–1910*. Quezon City: Ateneo de Manila University Press, 1979.

——. "Rizal and the Underside of Philippine History." In *Moral Order and the Question of Change: Essays on Southeast Asia*, ed. David K. Wyatt and Alexander Woodside, pp. 274–337. New Haven: Yale University Southeast Asia Studies, 1982.

——. "Tagalog Poetry and the Image of the Past during the War against Spain." In *Perceptions of the Past in Southeast Asia*, ed. Anthony Reid and David Marr, pp. 379–400. Singapore: Heinemann, 1979.

Jocano, F. Landa. *Growing Up in a Philippine Barrio*. New York: Holt, Rinehart & Winston, 1969.

Kamen, Henry. *Spain, 1469–1714: A Society in Conflict*. London: Longman, 1983.

Kaut, Charles. "*Utang na Loob:* A System of Contractual Obligation among Tagalogs." *Southwestern Journal of Anthropology* 17, no. 3 (1961): 256–272.

Lewis, Charlton, and Charles Short. *A Latin Dictionary*. Oxford: Clarendon, 1969.

Lisboa, P. Marcos de. *Vocabulario de la lengua bicol*. Sampaloc: Convento de Nuestra Señora de Loreto, 1754.

Lumbera, Bienvenido. "Assimilation and Synthesis (1700–1800): Tagalog Poetry in the Eighteenth Century." *Philippine Studies* 16 (October 1968): 622–662.

——. "Poetry of the Early Tagalogs." *Philippine Studies* 16 (April 1968): 223–230.

——. "Tagalog Poetry during the Seventeenth Century." *Philippine Studies* 16 (June 1968): 99–130.

Lynch, Frank, S.J. "An Mga Asuang: A Bicol Belief." *Philippine Social Sciences and Humanities Review* 14 (December 1949): 401–428.

——. "Social Acceptance Reconsidered." In *Four Readings in Philippine Values*, ed. Frank Lynch and Alfonso de Guzmán III, pp. 1–68. Quezon City: Ateneo de Manila University Press, 1973.

MacCormack, Sabine. "From the Sun of the Incas to the Virgin of Copacabana." *Representations* 8 (Fall 1984): 30–60.

——. "'The Heart Has Its Reasons': Predicaments of Missionary Christianity in Early Colonial Peru." *Hispanic American Historical Review* 65 (1985): 443–466.

Magdalena, P. Agustín de. *Arte de la lengua tagala sacado de diversos artes*. Manila, 1679.

Marcilla, P. Cipriano. *Estudio de los antiguos alfabetos filipinos*. Malabon: Asilo de Huérfanos, 1895.

Martínez de Zúñiga, P. Joaquín. *Historia de las Islas Filipinas.* Sampaloc, 1803.

Mas, Sinibaldo de. *Informe sobre el estado de las Islas Filipinas.* 2 vols. Madrid: I. Sancha, 1843.

Minguella, P. Toribio. *Ensayo de gramático hispano-tagalo.* Manila: Plana, 1878.

Mojares, Resil B. *The Origins and Rise of the Filipino Novel: A Generic Study of the Novel until 1940.* Quezon City: University of the Philippines Press, 1983.

Morga, Antonio de. *Sucesos de las Islas Filipinas.* Ed. Jose Rizal. Paris: Garnier, 1890. First published Mexico City, 1609.

Nebrija, Antonio de. *Gramática de la lengua castellana.* Ed. Ig. González-Llubera. London: Oxford University Press, 1926. First published Salamanca, 1492.

New Catholic Encyclopedia. 17 vols. New York: McGraw-Hill, 1967.

Nietzsche, Friedrich. *On the Genealogy of Morals.* Trans. Walter Kaufmann and R. J. Hollingdale. New York: Vintage Books, 1969.

Noceda, P. Juan de, and P. Pedro Sanlucar. *Vocabulario de la lengua tagala.* 3d ed. Manila: Ramírez y Giraudier, 1860. First published Manila, 1754.

Noreña, Carlos. *Studies in Spanish Renaissance Thought.* The Hague: Martinus Nijhoff, 1975.

Nuttall, Zelia. "Royal Ordinances Concerning the Laying Out of New Towns." *Hispanic American Historical Review* 5 (May 1922): 249–254.

Oliver, P. Juan de. "Declaración de los mandamientos de la ley de Dios." Balayan, 1583–91. In Antonio Maria Rosales, O.F.M., *A Study of a Sixteenth-Century Tagalog Manuscript on the Ten Commandments: Its Significance and Implications,* pp. 26–67. Quezon City: University of the Philippines Press, 1984.

Ortiz, P. Tomás. *Práctica del ministerio que siguen los religiosos del orden de N.S. Agustín en Filipinas.* Manila: Convento de Nuestra Señora de los Ángeles, 1731.

Parry, J. H. *The Spanish Theory of Empire in the Sixteenth Century.* Cambridge: At the University Press, 1940.

Payne, Stanley G. *A History of Spain and Portugal.* 2 vols. Madison: University of Wisconsin Press, 1973.

Pertierra, Raul. "Viscera-Suckers and Female Sociality: The Philippine Asuang." *Philippine Studies* 31 (1983): 319–337.

Phelan, John Leddy. *The Hispanization of the Philippines: Spanish Aims and Filipino Responses, 1565–1700.* Madison: University of Wisconsin Press, 1959.

Pinpin, Tomas. *Librong Pagaaralan nang manga Tagalog nang uicang Castilla.* In *La primera imprenta en Filipinas,* ed. Manuel Artigas y Cuerva, pp. 235–359. Manila: Germania, 1910. First published Bataan, 1610.

Plasencia, P. Juan de. "Costumbres de los Tagalos." In *Crónica de la Provincia de San Gregorio Magno de Religiosos Descalzos de N. S. San Francisco en las Islas Filipinas, China, Japon, etc.*, ed. P. Francisco de Santa Inés, 2d ed., pp. 592–603. Manila: Chofre, 1892. First published Manila, 1676.

Rafael, Vicente L. "Language, Identity, and Gender in Rizal's *Noli*." *Review of Indonesian and Malaysian Affairs* 18 (Winter 1984): 110–140.

Ramos, Máximo D. *The Aswang Syncrasy in Philippine Folklore*. Manila: Philippine Folklore Society, 1971.

———. *Creatures of Philippine Lower Mythology*. Quezon City: University of the Philippines Press, 1971.

Real Academia Española. *Diccionario de la lengua española*. 20th ed. Madrid, 1984.

Recopilación de leyes de los reynos de las Indias. 3 vols. Madrid: Consejo de la Hispanidad, 1943. Facsimile of 4th ed., Madrid, 1791.

Reps, John. *Town Planning in Frontier America*. Columbia: University of Missouri Press, 1980.

Retana, Wenceslao E. *El indio batangueño*. 3d ed. Manila: Chofre, 1888.

Reyes, Soledad. *Nobelang Tagalog, 1905–1975: Tradisyon at Modernismo*. Quezon City: Ateneo de Manila University Press, 1982.

Ribadeneira, P. Marcelo. *Historia del archipelago y otros reynos*. Ed. with English trans. Pacita Guevarra Fernández. 2 vols. Manila: Historical Conservation Society, 1970. First published Barcelona, 1601.

Ricard, Robert. *The Spiritual Conquest of Mexico*. Trans. Lesley Byrd Simpson. Berkeley: University of California Press, 1966.

Rizal, Jose. *Noli me tangere*. Quezon City: R. Martinez, 1958. Facsimile of 1st ed., Berlin, 1886. English trans. León Ma. Guerrero, Hong Kong: Longman, 1961.

San Agustín, P. Gaspar de. *Compendio del arte de la lengua tagala*. Manila: Colegio del Señor Santo Tomás de Aquino, 1703, 2d. ed. Sampaloc: Convento de Nuestra Señora de Loreto, 1787.

———. *Confesionario copioso en lengua tagala para dirección de los confesores, y instrucción de los penitentes*. 2d. ed. Sampaloc: Convento de Nuestra Señora de Loreto, 1787. First published Manila, 1713.

San Buenaventura, P. Pedro de. *Vocabulario de la lengua tagala*. Pila: Tomas Pinpin y Domingo Loag, 1613.

San Juan de la Cruz. *Obras escogidas*. 9th ed. Madrid: Austral, 1979.

Santa Ana, P. Alonso de. *Explicación de la doctrina cristiana en la lengua tagala*. Manila: Amigos del País, 1853. First published Manila, 1672.

Santa Inés, P. Francisco de. *Crónica de la Provincia de San Gregorio Magno de Religiosos Descalzados de N.S.P. San Francisco en las Islas Filipinas, China, Japón, etc.* Manila: Chofre, 1892. First published Manila, 1676.

Santamaría, P. Alberto. "El 'Baybayin' en el archivo de Santo Tomás." *Unitas* 16 (February 1938): 441–480.

Schachter, Paul, and Fe T. Otañes. *Tagalog Reference Grammar.* Berkeley: University of California Press, 1972.

Schumacher, John S.J. "The Manila Synodal Tradition: A Brief History." *Philippine Studies* 27 (1979): 285–348.

———. *Readings in Philippine Church History.* Quezon City: Loyola School of Theology, 1979.

Scott, William Henry. *Cracks in the Parchment Curtain.* Quezon City: New Day, 1982.

———. *The Discovery of the Igorots.* Quezon City: New Day, 1974.

———. *Prehispanic Source Materials for the Study of Philippine History.* Manila: University of Santo Tomás Press, 1968; rev. ed. Quezon City: New Day, 1984.

Serrano-Laktaw, Pedro, ed. *Diccionario tagalog-hispano.* Manila: Santos y Bernal, 1914.

Siegel, James T. *Rope of God.* Berkeley: University of California Press, 1968.

———. *Shadow and Sound: The Historical Thought of a Sumatran People.* Chicago: University of Chicago Press, 1979.

———. *Solo in the New Order: Language and Hierarchy in an Indonesian City.* Princeton: Princeton University Press, 1986.

Steinberg, David, et al., eds. *In Search of Southeast Asia.* London: Oxford University Press, 1971.

Sturtevant, David R. *Popular Uprisings in the Philippines, 1840–1940.* Ithaca: Cornell University Press, 1976.

Tiongson, Nicanor. *Kasaysayan at estetika ng senakulo.* Quezon City: Ateneo de Manila University Press, 1975.

Todorov, Tzvetan. *The Conquest of America: The Question of the Other.* Trans. Richard Howard. New York: Harper Colophon, 1984.

Totanes, P. Sebastian. *Arte de la lengua tagala y manual para la administración de los Santos Sacramentos.* Manila: Convento de Nuestra Señora de Loreto, 1745.

———. *Manual tagalog para auxilio a los religiosos de esta provincia de S. Gregorio Magno de Descalzos de N.S. Padre S. Francisco de Filipinas.* Sampaloc: Convento de Nuestra Señora de Loreto, 1745.

Vacant, Alfred, and Eugène Mangemot, eds. *Dictionnaire de théologie catholique.* 30 vols. Paris: Letouzey & Ane, 1911.

Wolters, O. W. *History, Culture, and Region in Southeast Asian Perspective.* Singapore: Institute of Southeast Asian Studies, 1982.

Wyatt, David K., and Alexander Woodside. *Moral Order and the Question of Change: Essays on Southeast Asia.* New Haven: Yale University Southeast Asia Studies, 1982.

Index

Vicente L. Rafael is Associate Professor in the
Department of Communication at the
University of California, San Diego.

Library of Congress Cataloging-in-Publication Data

Rafael, Vicente L.
Contracting colonialism : translation and Christian conversion in Tagalog society under
early Spanish rule / Vicente L. Rafael. — 1st pbk. ed.
p.   cm.
Originally published: Ithaca : Cornell University Press, 1988.
Includes bibliographical references (p.   ) and index.
ISBN 0-8223-1341-3 (acid-free paper)
1. Tagalog (Philippine people)—History.   2. Converts—Philippines.   3. Christianity—
Philippines.   4. Spanish language—Translating into Tagalog.   5. Philippines—
Colonization.   I. Title.
[DS666.T3R34   1993]
95.9.9'02—dc20   92-32739
                                                                                                            CIP